to: DAD ♡

Love

CN00919866

ker

June, 1991

AMERICAN COMBAT AIRCRAFT OF WORLD WAR II

Edited by David Donald

This edition first published in 1997 by Motorbooks International Publishers & Wholesalers, 729 Prospect Avenue, PO Box 1, Osceola, WI 54020 USA

This material was previously published in 1990 as part of the reference set *Airplane*

Library in Congress Cataloging-in-Publication Data available

ISBN 0-7603-0463-7

Conceived and produced by
Brown Packaging Books Ltd
Bradley's Close
74–77 White Lion Street
London N1 9PF

Printed and bound in the Czech Republic

CONTENTS

F6F Hellcat

The Hellcat was the aircraft which dispelled the shadow of the Mitsubishi Zero from over the American forces in the Pacific. In the hands of Navy and Marine Corps pilots, flying from tiny carrier decks and island airstrips, it was the aircraft which founded the reputation of Grumman's 'Iron Works'.

The Grumman F6F Hellcat was certainly not the fastest fighter of World War II, or the most agile, or the most heavily armed; and its massive size was diametrically opposed to the beliefs of many (such as A. S. Yakovlev) who, even ignoring the question of cost, were convinced that success in air combat had to be the prerogative of the small and lightweight fighter. Yet in the war against Japan the F6F was by far the most important single aircraft, because it very quickly indeed turned the tables on what had previously been an unbroken run of almost too-easy success and struck fear into the heart of every Japanese pilot. Of the total score of 6,477 confirmed victories by US Navy carrier-based pilots, the F6F (which only entered the fray on 31 August 1943) gained 4,947.

Most of the other victories were gained with great skill and courage by pilots flying the Grumman F4F Wildcat. Though this had begun life as a biplane it eventually matured in 1940 as a tough and agile mid-wing monoplane, which did all that could be expected of an engine in the 746-kW (1,000-hp) class. Used by the UK's Fleet Air Arm as the Martlet, this type shot down a Ju 88 as early as Christmas Day 1940, but the Grumman Aircraft Engineering Corporation soon had no doubt of the fighter's shortcomings. Toughness, good turn radius, reliability and the powerful armament of six 12.7-mm (0.5-in) guns added to a great deal, but the F4F was deficient in level speed and climb, and could not fight the Messerschmitt Bf 109E on level terms. Against the Mitsubishi A6M Zero-Sen it was the same story, but long before that happened Grumman and the US Navy had decided to build an improved fighter with much more power.

There was no direct attempt to rival the Vought F4U, which was in a different class; merely to build an improved F4F, and that was the way the new fighter was described in the prototype contract of 30 June 1941. The obvious engine was the Wright R-2600, or two-row Cyclone 14, already in production for bombers and indeed for Grumman's own TBF Avenger. The contract was for two aircraft, an XF6F-1 (BuAer No. 02981) with the 1194-kW (1,600-hp) R-2600-10 and an XF6F-2 (02982) with the new turbocharged R-2600-16. Speed of development led to an understanding that the F6F would be a minimum-change improvement of the F4F, but all the reports from the Royal and US Navies cried out for much higher flight performance, to the point that Grumman increasingly looked at a more powerful engine, the great Pratt & Whitney R-2800 Double Wasp. Also used in the F4U, this was starting life in the 1492-kW (2,000-hp) class, but it could never fit an F4F.

Grumman's management comprised mainly engineers, notable examples being president Leroy R. Grumman, executive vice-president Leon A. Swirbul and vice-president engineering W. T. 'Bill' Schwendler. Before Pearl Harbor on 7 December 1941 these men had roughed out a scheme for a completely new F6F, larger and much stronger than the F4F and not only offering higher performance but also much greater fuel and ammunition capacity. The wing was made larger than on any other major single-engined fighter of World War II, at 31.03 m^2 (334 sq ft) compared with 29.17 m^2 (314 sq ft) for the F4U, 27.87 m^2 (300 sq ft) for the P-47 and below 23.23 m^2 (250 sq ft) for most other fighters. This immense squarish

This is a genuine wartime colour photograph showing an F6F-3 on test over Long Island. The aircraft is finished in sea blue, blue and white, and wears the red-bordered insignia used only in July/August 1943.

wing had three spars, fabric-skinned ailerons and split flaps, and was pivoted on skewed axes at the front spar at each end of the horizontal centre section to fold back beside the fuselage with upper surface outward. Each folding outer panel contained three 12.7-mm (0.5-in) machine-guns each with 400 rounds. The wing was moved down from the F4F's mid-position to the mid-low position, which improved accommodation of fuel under the floor of the cockpit and shortened the landing gears, despite a great and welcomed increase in track. Each main gear, stressed for 4.27 m (14 ft) per second vertical descent, pivoted to the rear with the wheel rotating 90° to lie flat in the wing ahead of the flap. The fuselage was much larger than that of the F4F, the pilot being perched in the top of a cross-section changed from a circle to a pear shape, giving great width in the lower part but leaving a narrow dorsal region similar to early 'razorback' P-47s. (Unlike the US Army fighter the F6F never received a moulded bubble canopy, and its rearward view was always a weak point.)

Design of an R-2800 installation went ahead in early 1942, but the Wright machine was installed in the first aircraft, the XF6F-1, which was flown by Selden Converse on 26 June 1942, less than a year after the go-ahead. Results were good, though longitudinal stability was excessive for a fighter, and trim changes on varying engine power or cycling gear or flaps were unacceptably large. Fortunately there was nothing calling for substantial redesign, because in May 1942 the US Navy had begun placing massive production contracts for the chosen R-2800 aircraft as the F6F-3. Only a month after the first, the second prototype flew on 30 July with the 1492-kW (2,000-hp) R-2800-10 driving a Curtiss Electric propeller with spinner, with the designation XF6F-3. This was a superior aircraft, and it is remarkable that Grumman was able to fit the larger and heavier engine into an aircraft of basically unchanged dimensions or fuel capacity while still preserving centre of gravity position.

New premises for Grumman

Grumman was a hive of activity in early 1942, with constant feedback from combat units, a colossal load of production on high priority and the need to build a complete new plant at Bethpage alongside the original works to build the F6F. A plan to build under licence at Canadian Vickers never bore fruit. In spring 1942 the company bought up thousands of steel girders from the old 2nd Avenue elevated railroad and a World's Fair pavilion, and thus speeded the new factory. Assembly jigging often preceded the roof, and F6F-3s were on the line long before the plant was finished. Little redesign was needed, though the main-gear fairings were simplified (the lower part of the wheel being left exposed in the wing), the engine attitude was slightly altered (though it was still 3° nose-down) and the propeller was changed to a Hamilton Hydromatic with no spinner. The tilt of the engine was matched with a zero-incidence wing setting, which meant that at take-off or in cruising flight the engine was horizontal while the rest of the aircraft was tail-down. At full power the fuselage became horizontal for minimum drag.

One of the few photographs of the very first Hellcat, the XF6F-1 with the Wright R-2600-10 Cyclone 14 installed. The rest of the aircraft, apart from the landing-gear fairings, was almost identical with that of the 12,275 F6Fs that followed in the subsequent three years – all off one assembly line.

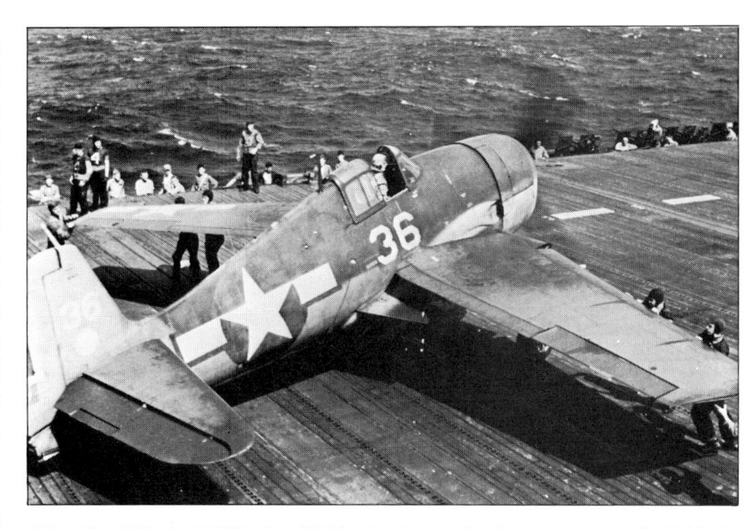

Like the F4F and TBF, the F6F had wings which were manually folded about skewed hinges to the rear, coming to rest with upper surfaces outwards. The photographer aboard USS Hornet *in June 1944 caught this F6F in a seemingly swept-wing state. It had returned after a raid on the Marianas.*

Grumman F6F-5 Hellcat cutaway drawing key

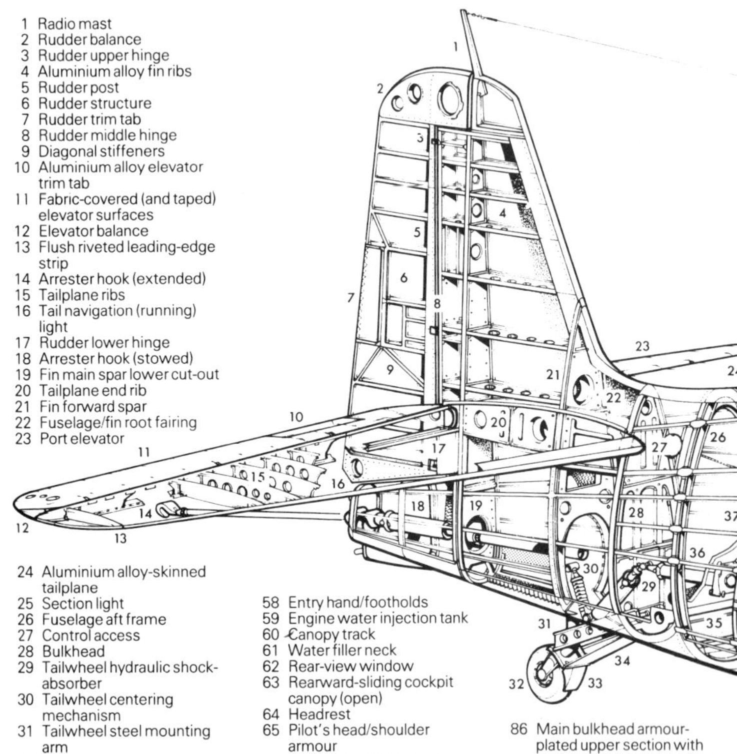

1 Radio mast
2 Rudder balance
3 Rudder upper hinge
4 Aluminium alloy fin ribs
5 Rudder post
6 Rudder structure
7 Rudder trim tab
8 Rudder middle hinge
9 Diagonal stiffeners
10 Aluminium alloy elevator trim tab
11 Fabric-covered (and taped) elevator surfaces
12 Elevator balance
13 Flush riveted leading-edge strip
14 Arrester hook (extended)
15 Tailplane ribs
16 Tail navigation (running) light
17 Rudder lower hinge
18 Arrester hook (stowed)
19 Fin main spar lower cut-out
20 Tailplane end rib
21 Fin forward spar
22 Fuselage/fin root fairing
23 Port elevator
24 Aluminium alloy-skinned tailplane
25 Section light
26 Fuselage aft frame
27 Control access
28 Bulkhead
29 Tailwheel hydraulic shock-absorber
30 Tailwheel centering mechanism
31 Tailwheel steel mounting arm
32 Rearward-retracting tailwheel (hard rubber tyre)
33 Fairing
34 Steel plate door fairing
35 Tricing sling support tube
36 Hydraulic actuating cylinder
37 Flanged ring fuselage frames
38 Control cable runs
39 Fuselage longerons
40 Relay box
41 Dorsal rod antenna
42 Dorsal recognition light
43 Radio aerial
44 Radio mast
45 Aerial lead-in
46 Dorsal frame stiffeners
47 Junction box
48 Radio equipment (upper rack)
49 Radio shelf
50 Control cable runs
51 Transverse brace
52 Remote radio compass
53 Ventral recognition lights (3)
54 Ventral rod antenna
55 Destructor device
56 Accumulator
57 Radio equipment (lower rack)
58 Entry hand/footholds
59 Engine water injection tank
60 Canopy track
61 Water filler neck
62 Rear-view window
63 Rearward-sliding cockpit canopy (open)
64 Headrest
65 Pilot's head/shoulder armour
66 Canopy sill (reinforced)
67 Fire-extinguisher
68 Oxygen bottle (port fuselage wall)
69 Water tank mounting
70 Underfloor self-sealing fuel tank (60 US gal/227 litres)
71 Armoured bulkhead
72 Starboard console
73 Pilot's seat
74 Hydraulic handpump
75 Fuel filler cap and neck
76 Rudder pedals
77 Central console
78 Control column
79 Chart board (horizontal stowage)
80 Instrument panel
81 Panel coaming
82 Reflector gunsight
83 Rear-view mirror
84 Armoured glass windshield
85 Deflection plate (pilot forward protection)
86 Main bulkhead armour-plated upper section with hoisting sling attachments port and starboard)
87 Aluminium alloy aileron trim tab
88 Fabric covered (and taped) aileron surfaces

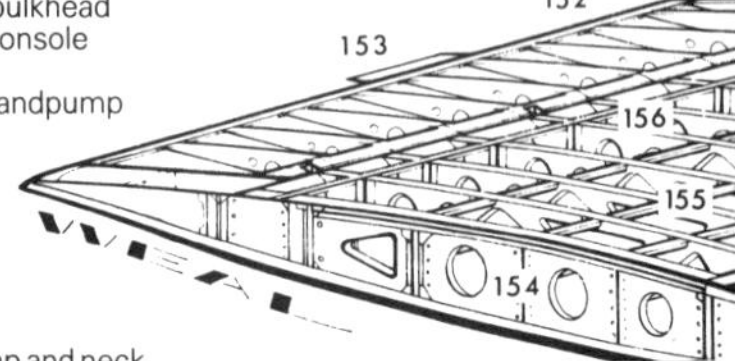

89 Flush riveted outer wing skin
90 Aluminium alloy sheet wing tip (riveted to wing outer rib)
91 Port navigation (running) light
92 Formed leading-edge (approach/landing light and camera gun inboard)
93 Fixed cowling panel
94 Armour plate (oil tank forward protection)

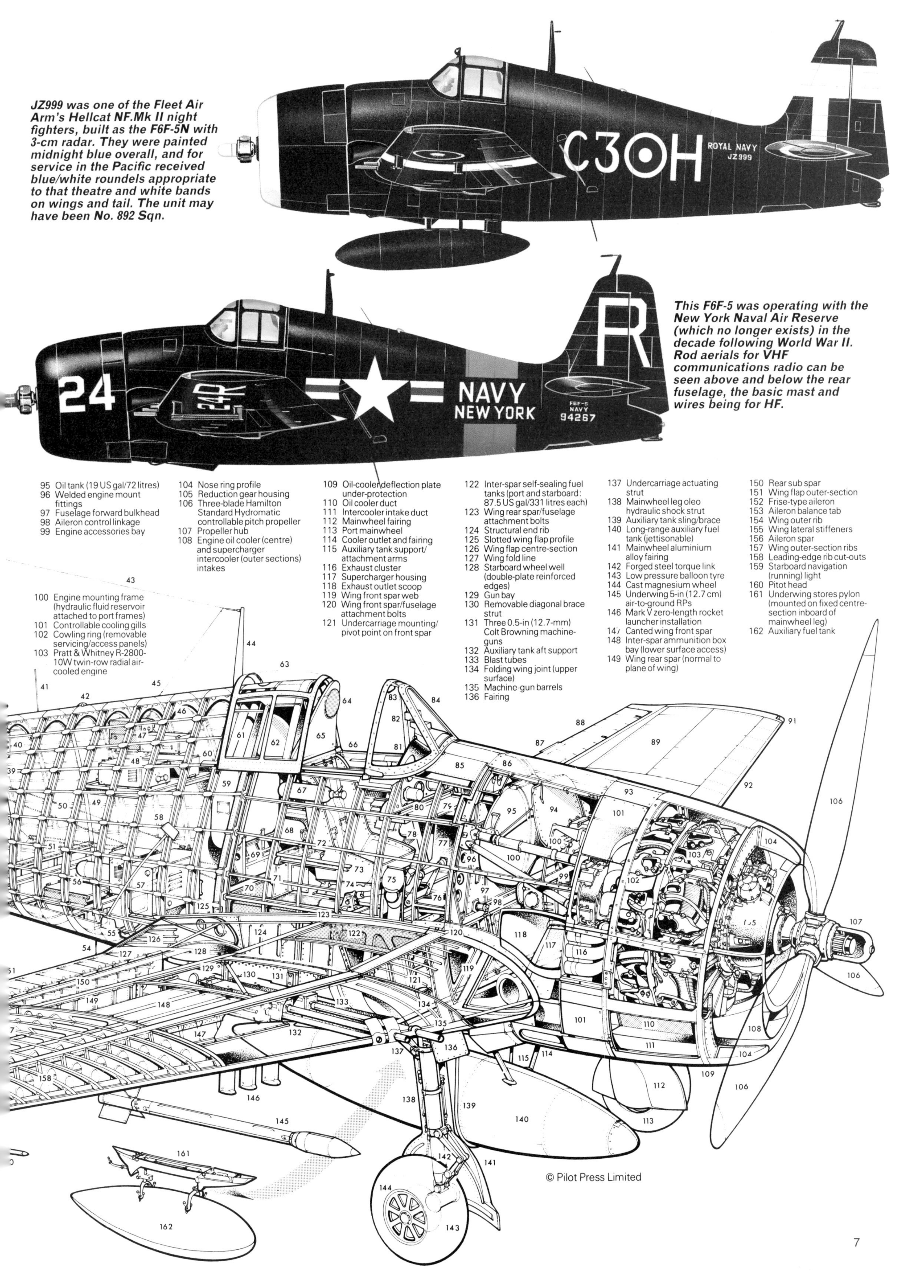

JZ999 was one of the Fleet Air Arm's Hellcat NF.Mk II night fighters, built as the F6F-5N with 3-cm radar. They were painted midnight blue overall, and for service in the Pacific received blue/white roundels appropriate to that theatre and white bands on wings and tail. The unit may have been No. 892 Sqn.

This F6F-5 was operating with the New York Naval Air Reserve (which no longer exists) in the decade following World War II. Rod aerials for VHF communications radio can be seen above and below the rear fuselage, the basic mast and wires being for HF.

US Navy BuAer No. 79603 was one of a vast block of 3,000 F6F-5 Hellcats whose precise subdivision into variants is not known (but it included F6F-5N, -5P and -5K models). Clearly with a post-war Reserve unit, it appears to be over the western tip of Long Island, and thus close to the former NAS New York.

On 2 October 1942 the first prototype flew as the XF6F-4 with a two-speed R-2800-27, but this engine was not adopted. The second aircraft was brought up to production F6F-3 standard, except for the landing-gear fairings, and among other things was used for trials with drop tanks and other stores under the fuselage. From the start both prototypes had bulletproof windscreens and 96 kg (212 lb) of cockpit armour, and very few changes were needed to the Hellcat for the rest of its career except in armament and equipment. One of the puzzles is that, though both prototypes had structural provision for the six guns, they were not installed and the wing leading edges had no apertures! Armament was certainly present on the first production F6F-3, from the block 04775-04958, which flew on 4 October 1942. The finish was graduated shades of blue, ranging from greenish blue (called medium sea blue) above, through a paler blue to an underside that was pale blue in the first block and later gull grey or insignia white. These were low-contrast colours strongly resembling some in use today. In July 1943 the national insignia grew the side rectangles with red border, changed to dark blue a month later, and the usual finish became overall midnight blue.

Double Wasp power

Features standardised in production included a self-sealing tank for 227 litres (60 US gal) under the cockpit and one of 331 litres (87.5 US gal) in each inner wing for a total of 889 litres (235 US gal), armour around the oil tank and cooler under the engine, retractable tailwheel with solid rubber tyre, sting-type hook extended to the rear from the extreme tail (this area required strengthening because of failures), fabric-skinned control surfaces with pilot-operated metal trim tabs, and a regular B-series R-2800-10 Double Wasp with a 3.99 m (13 ft 1 in) propeller. Most fighting in the Pacific was at medium or low altitudes, and though turbochargers continued to be studied they were never adopted. In late 1943 an F6F-3 (66244) was diverted as a test aircraft with a turbocharged R-2800-21. The installation required a deepened lower duct for the turbocharger and cooling air, with waste gates on the underside of the fuselage just aft of the leading edge, and a special four-bladed propeller with root cuffs was fitted. The work had low priority and eventually this aircraft, which was given the defunct earlier designation of XF6F-2, was given the BuAer number 43137 as a standard F6F-3 (and in fact the last of this model) in April 1944. Despite the enormous numbers of Hellcats built, no attempt was ever made to fit any engine other than the R-2800 into any subsequent F6F.

Former fighter No. 78594 was photographed at one of the Naval Air Rework Facilities in the late 1950s after being converted into an F6F-5K. The wingtip pods each contained six ciné cameras giving all-round coverage to record arrival of AAMs and SAMs fired at the aircraft while the latter was radio controlled.

Into service with the Navy

Deliveries began on 16 January 1943 to US Navy fighter squadron VF-9, embarked aboard USS *Essex*. At this time the F4U had been flying almost three years yet was still not qualified for carrier operation. Indeed, competition from the rapidly produced F6F is held to have acted as a major spur to the Vought team which had had to effect major changes to their basically superior aircraft. By January 1943 prolonged trials had been held with various kinds of external ordnance under F6Fs, but so far as is known none of the 4,402 (not 4,403 for, as noted, nos 66244 and 43137 were the same aircraft) F6F-3s built had provision for any external load except the 568-litre (150-US gal) drop tank, though some were given bomb or rocket attachments after delivery.

Reception to the Hellcat was very positive and, despite the rather poor forward view, tendency to weathercock on the ground unless the tailwheel was locked, and long-stroke legs which could allow the big propeller to hit the ground, pilots soon converted and found few problems in operating even from light escort carriers. By August 1943 many Hellcats were at readiness aboard the fleet carriers USS *Essex, Yorktown* and *Independence*, and aboard the light carriers USS *Belleau Wood* and *Princeton*. The first combat mission was flown by VF-5 in the second attack on Marcus Island on 31 August, operating from USS *Yorktown*, followed on the same day by VF-9 from USS *Essex*. Many good results were obtained, including improved cruise control for greater mileage per gallon, procedures for

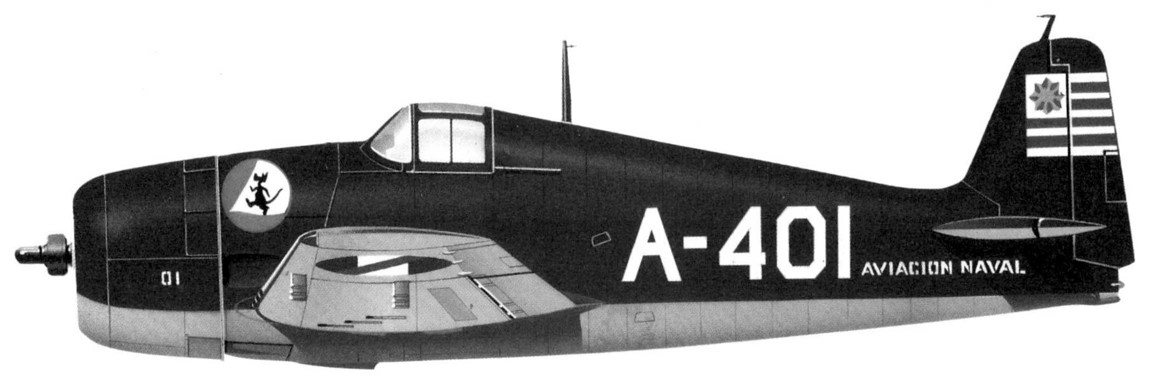

This F6F-5 was one of 12 supplied under US aid to Uruguay, where they were used to form a squadron in the Aviación Naval. This unit was operational from 1945 until 1961 and was certainly the last in the world to use the F6F in its fighter role. Operations were from two bases on the Plate estuary.

rapid strike-down on deck and high reliability in intensive operations involving two missions per aircraft per day. In the first big air battle, in the Kwajalein/Roi area on 4 December 1943, 91 Hellcats met 50 A6Ms and destroyed 28 for the loss of two.

By the end of 1943 deliveries had reached 2,555, with only minor deficiencies becoming apparent. None of the aircraft in action in that year had bomb racks, but an extremely important new development, following a few months later than the same development on the F4U, was the installation of radar for night interceptions. The story of the US Navy radars working on the short wavelength of 3 cm is a long one, and of course began with the British gift of the magnetron in 1940. There were eventually nine different sets, four of which went into production. That for the F6F was derived from the AI Mk III (SCR-537) by Sperry with designation AIA (it was the progenitor of the ASH set used in British naval aircraft). The production sets derived from it were the APS-4 and APS-6 families, both of which had the main power units, timebase and other items in the fuselage but the scanner in a pod far out on the right wing, where it rotated at 1,200 rpm whilst sweeping through a 60° spiral scan. No tremors were felt in the cockpit and aircraft handling was little affected, though the pod reduced maximum speed by some 32 km/h (20 mph) and in a sideslip gave a falsely high airspeed reading.

The first night-fighter version was the field-converted F6F-3E, 18 of which were converted at MCAS Quonset Point, which had hand-built the first night-fighter Corsairs three months earlier in June 1943. The F6F-3Es had the AIA with a Philco RF head originally tailored for ASV (air-to-surface vessel) use with a wide but shallow scan. Other changes included red cockpit lighting and removal of the curved Plexiglas firing ahead of the bulletproof windscreen, which experience had shown easily became scratched and progressively less transparent. Then followed a factory-built XF6F-3N and 205 production F6F-3N night-fighters with the APS-6 radar, radio altimeter and IFF. These were fine aircraft, and at one time it was planned to fit APS-6 to half of all future Hellcat production (limiting factors were insufficient radars and insufficient qualified night-fighter pilots). The 3-cm story is a great one, but 1943 was full of Japanese activity at night and while waiting for the proper night-fighters both the US Navy and US Marines tried alternative schemes.

The San Francisco Bay Bridge gives away the location of these Hellcats from the Reserve Unit at NAS Oakland soon after World War II. Nearest is F6F-5N no. 79270. Furthest are radarless F6F-5s from the same block but aircraft '23' is a later F6F-5, no. 94439. All have rail type rocket launchers.

F6F Hellcat

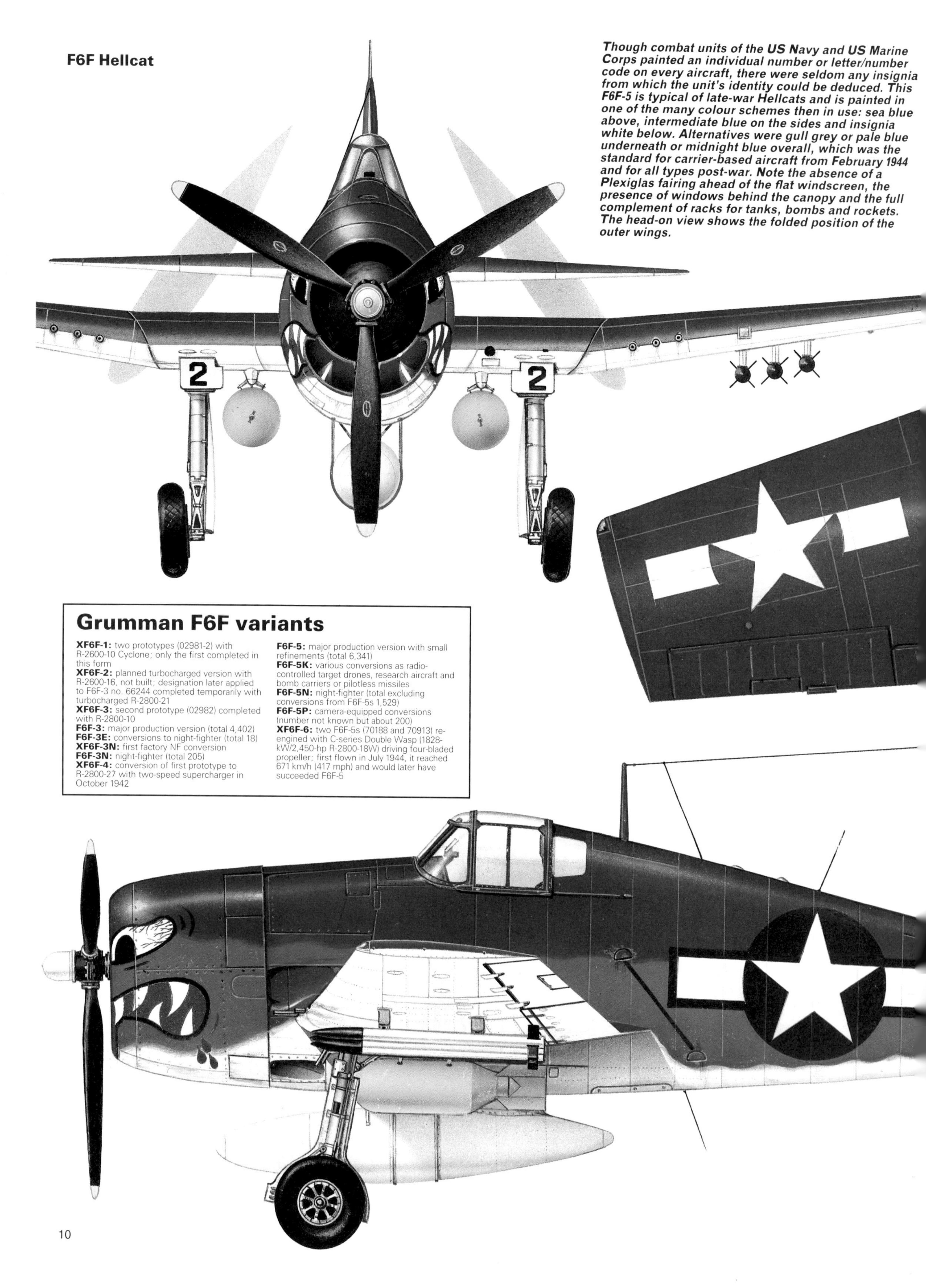

*Though combat units of the **US Navy** and **US Marine Corps** painted an individual number or letter/number code on every aircraft, there were seldom any insignia from which the unit's identity could be deduced. This F6F-5 is typical of late-war Hellcats and is painted in one of the many colour schemes then in use: sea blue above, intermediate blue on the sides and insignia white below. Alternatives were gull grey or pale blue underneath or midnight blue overall, which was the standard for carrier-based aircraft from February 1944 and for all types post-war. Note the absence of a Plexiglas fairing ahead of the flat windscreen, the presence of windows behind the canopy and the full complement of racks for tanks, bombs and rockets. The head-on view shows the folded position of the outer wings.*

Grumman F6F variants

XF6F-1: two prototypes (02981-2) with R-2600-10 Cyclone; only the first completed in this form
XF6F-2: planned turbocharged version with R-2600-16, not built; designation later applied to F6F-3 no. 66244 completed temporarily with turbocharged R-2800-21
XF6F-3: second prototype (02982) completed with R-2800-10
F6F-3: major production version (total 4,402)
F6F-3E: conversions to night-fighter (total 18)
XF6F-3N: first factory NF conversion
F6F-3N: night-fighter (total 205)
XF6F-4: conversion of first prototype to R-2800-27 with two-speed supercharger in October 1942
F6F-5: major production version with small refinements (total 6,341)
F6F-5K: various conversions as radio-controlled target drones, research aircraft and bomb carriers or pilotless missiles
F6F-5N: night-fighter (total excluding conversions from F6F-5s 1,529)
F6F-5P: camera-equipped conversions (number not known but about 200)
XF6F-6: two F6F-5s (70188 and 70913) re-engined with C-series Double Wasp (1828-kW/2,450-hp R-2800-18W) driving four-bladed propeller; first flown in July 1944, it reached 671 km/h (417 mph) and would later have succeeded F6F-5

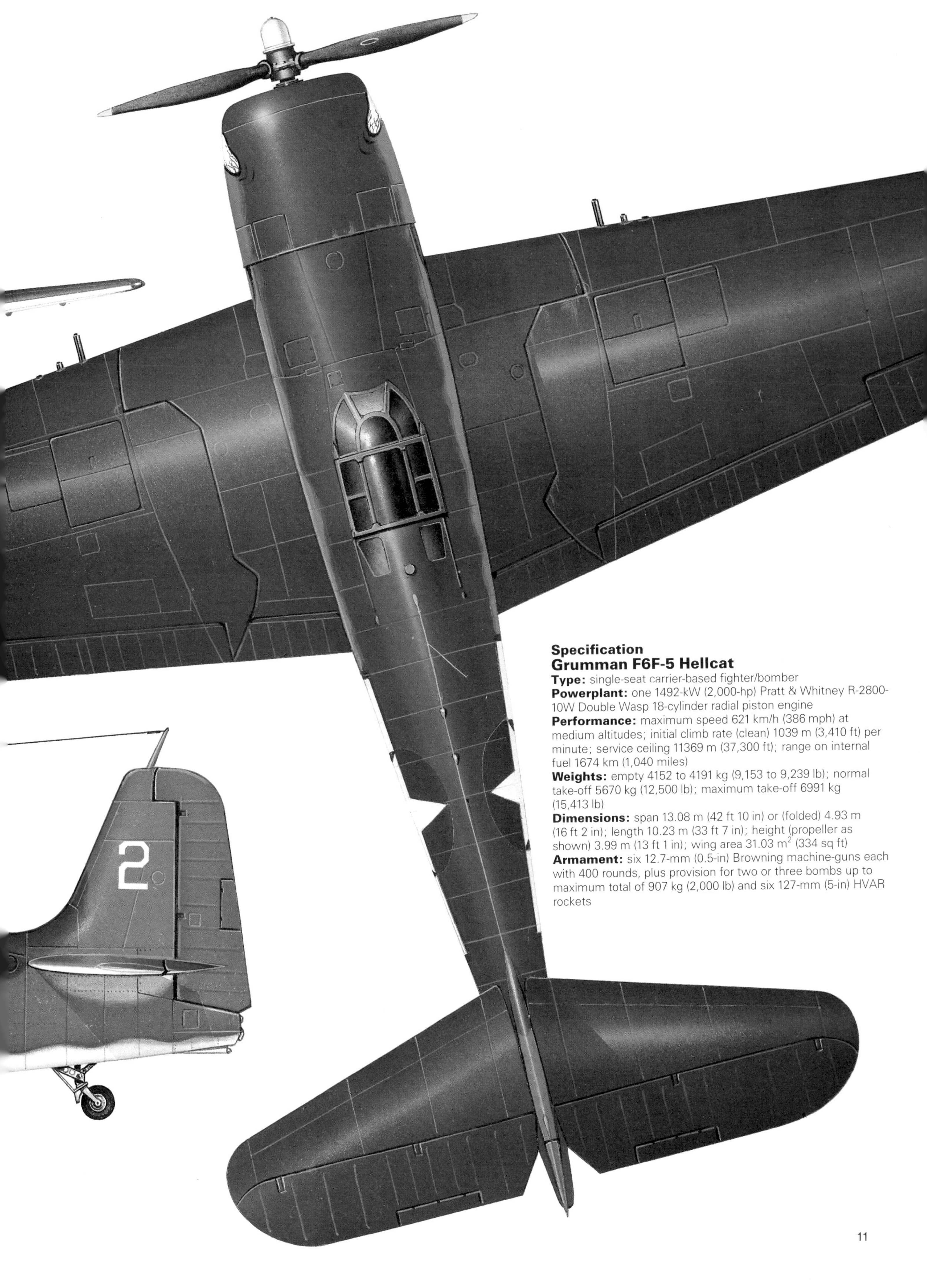

Specification
Grumman F6F-5 Hellcat

Type: single-seat carrier-based fighter/bomber
Powerplant: one 1492-kW (2,000-hp) Pratt & Whitney R-2800-10W Double Wasp 18-cylinder radial piston engine
Performance: maximum speed 621 km/h (386 mph) at medium altitudes; initial climb rate (clean) 1039 m (3,410 ft) per minute; service ceiling 11369 m (37,300 ft); range on internal fuel 1674 km (1,040 miles)
Weights: empty 4152 to 4191 kg (9,153 to 9,239 lb); normal take-off 5670 kg (12,500 lb); maximum take-off 6991 kg (15,413 lb)
Dimensions: span 13.08 m (42 ft 10 in) or (folded) 4.93 m (16 ft 2 in); length 10.23 m (33 ft 7 in); height (propeller as shown) 3.99 m (13 ft 1 in); wing area 31.03 m^2 (334 sq ft)
Armament: six 12.7-mm (0.5-in) Browning machine-guns each with 400 rounds, plus provision for two or three bombs up to maximum total of 907 kg (2,000 lb) and six 127-mm (5-in) HVAR rockets

F6F Hellcat

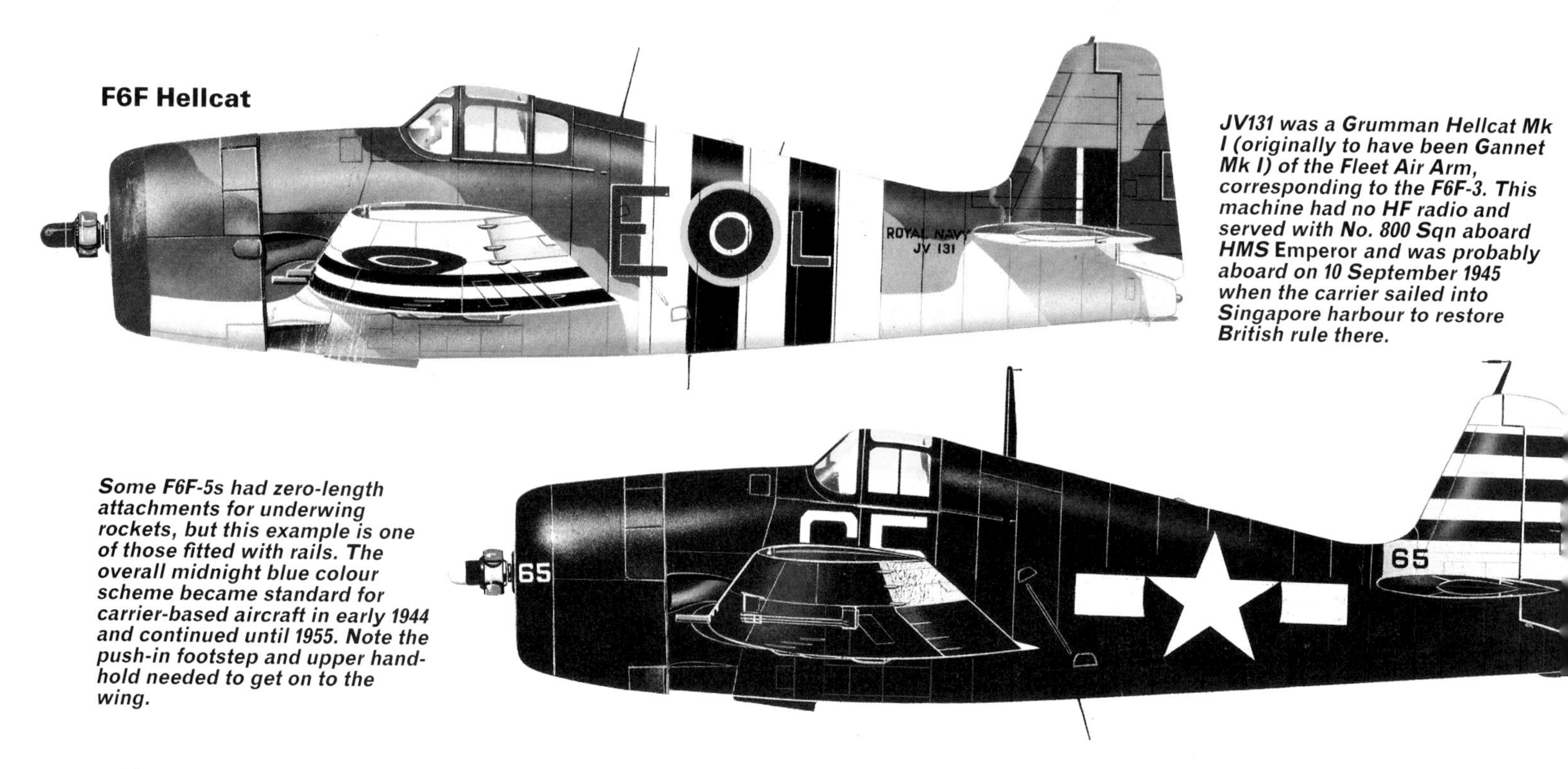

JV131 was a Grumman Hellcat Mk I (originally to have been Gannet Mk I) of the Fleet Air Arm, corresponding to the F6F-3. This machine had no HF radio and served with No. 800 Sqn aboard HMS Emperor and was probably aboard on 10 September 1945 when the carrier sailed into Singapore harbour to restore British rule there.

Some F6F-5s had zero-length attachments for underwing rockets, but this example is one of those fitted with rails. The overall midnight blue colour scheme became standard for carrier-based aircraft in early 1944 and continued until 1955. Note the push-in footstep and upper handhold needed to get on to the wing.

The one best-remembered was the hunter/killer team of from one to three single-seat fighters in formation with a TBF Avenger with ASV radar or a Dauntless with ASB. Teams had to work as a unit and practise together, and the first major night action took place on 26 November 1943. The team commander was Lieutenant Commander 'Butch' O'Hare, and he himself destroyed a Mitsubishi G4M but his TBF was shot down by Japanese fighters while the F6F-3s were making mincemeat of the main Japanese force; the world's busiest airport (at Chicago) is named in his memory.

Improvements right down the line

Like all 1944 F6F-3s, the F6F-3Ns had several improvements, the most important being the R-2800-10W engine rated at 1641 kW (2,200 hp) with water injection. The water tank was behind the cockpit, with a long duct from a filler in the top of the rear spine. This engine arrived at Bethpage right at the end of F6F-3 production, and is regarded mainly as one of the key features of the F6F-5 which from 21 April 1944 followed on the production line. Another standard modification was removal of the curved windshield fairing, which as noted earlier spoilt forward view for no significant gain in speed. Other changes included spring-tab ailerons, a changed design of main gear leg, a smaller upright radio mast and omission of the gun fairings, cockpit rear window and lower cowl flaps.

Thus the F6F-5, which poured from the Bethpage line at the rate of roughly 20 per day, was almost identical to the F6F-3. It is difficult to find any other aircraft made only in one factory to the tune of 12,274 examples, all substantially identical, in 2½ years. For cost-effectiveness and impact on a world war the F6F is right in the very front rank. Almost all the major air combats of the Pacific theatre from August 1943 onwards were dominated by it, and it was flown by all the US Navy aces of that period. From February 1945 it was flown by four US Marine carrier squadrons. Its superiority over the Japanese had by late 1944 become so absolute it maintained a continuous presence by day and night over the combat zones and Japanese airfields in what was called 'The Big Blue Blanket'. On the basis of contemporary unit records the ratio of F6F kills to losses exceeded 19:1.

Variants are listed separately, those produced in quantity being the F6F-5N night-fighter and F6F-5P photo aircraft. All had armament, and a substantial proportion of F6F-5 production, apparently including all F6F-5Ns and F6F-5Ps, had the innermost 12.7-mm (0.5-in) guns replaced by 20-mm cannon, each with 200 rounds. All F6F-5s had provision for an external load of ordnance, though as this was also a feature of many F6F-3s it cannot be regarded as a distinguishing feature. The centreline attachments could carry a 454-kg (1,000-lb) bomb or a 682-litre (150-US gal) tank. A similar rack was provided under each wing root for a 454-kg (1,000-lb) bomb or Tiny Tim rocket. The outer wings could each carry three HVARs (high-velocity aircraft rockets).

Painted midnight blue overall, JX822 was a Fleet Air Arm Hellcat Mk II used at the Aeroplane & Armament Experimental Establishment, Boscombe Down, for many weapon trials. Here it is carrying two British bombs of 454-kg (1,000-lb) size. Anti-ship attacks by the FAA began in April 1944 off Norway.

Hellcats overseas

Many other armament fits were investigated, and in the UK the trials programme included eight rails for 27-kg (60-lb) rocket projectiles. The Fleet Air Arm received 252 F6F-3s under Lend-Lease from late April 1943, the service at first calling the type Grumman Gannet Mk I until the name Hellcat was standardised. All had British camouflage and saw much action, initially with Nos 800 and 804 Squadrons, off Norway and in the Mediterranean. They were followed by 930 Hellcat Mk II (F6F-5) and 80 Hellcat NF.Mk II (F6F-5N), delivered midnight blue and almost all used in the Pacific with blue/white theatre roundels and often with white bands round nose, wings and tail. Some were camera-equipped Hellcat FR.Mk IIs and a few had guns removed to become Hellcat PR.Mk IIs. They operated throughout the East Indies, Malaya, Burma and in the final assault on Japan. By late 1945 all but two of 12 active squadrons had re-equipped, but one aircraft, KE209, was used by the commander of RNAS Lossiemouth as his personal mount until well into 1953.

At least 120 ex-USN Hellcats were supplied to France's Aéronavale for use in Indo-China, and survivors later served in North Africa. Other operators included the navies of Argentina and Uruguay (to 1961). Over 300 were converted as F6F-5K remotely-piloted targets and explosive-packed missiles, six of the latter being guided to North Korean targets in August 1952.

Boeing B-17 Flying Fortress

When viewing this earlier generation of Boeing classics, even the most sceptical observer cannot divorce the B-17 from the wartime fields of East Anglia, the strains of Glenn Miller and the monumental air battles fought over German cities from late 1942 onwards. However, there was a lot more to the B-17 than just its 8th Air Force service.

The vast armadas of the US 8th Air Force, equipped mainly with the Boeing B-17, ranged far and wide over Germany and occupied Europe in 1942-5, bombing individual factories and other precision targets and also whittling away at the fighter strength of the Luftwaffe in some of the largest and bloodiest air battles in all history. But in 1934 such battles could not be foreseen. The only targets within range of US bombers were in such unlikely places as Canada, Mexico and small British islands. In the Depression, money was tight; and the new monoplane Martin Bomber appeared to be all that was needed.

But when the US Army Air Corps put out a request for a new multi-engined bomber, a few far-sighted engineers at the Boeing Airplane Company decided to interpret 'multi-engined' as meaning not two engines (as had generally been done before) but four. Admittedly they did this mainly in order to get more height over the target, but it had the effect of making the Boeing Model 299 significantly larger than its rivals. Design began on 18 June 1934, and the prototype made a very successful first flight in the hands of Les Tower at Boeing Field on 28 July 1935. The main purpose of the new bomber was to defend the United States by bombing an invasion fleet (the only plausible kind of target) and it was the nature of this mission, rather than heavy defensive armament, that resulted in Boeing eventually registering the name Flying Fortress.

Triumph and disaster

On 20 August 1935 the impressive aircraft, unpainted except for US Army Air Corps rudder stripes and civil registration NX13372, flew nonstop to Wright Field at an average faster than the maximum possible speed of its twin-engined rivals. But on the first officially observed flight before the USAAC evaluation officers, on 30 October 1935, the great bomber took off, climbed far too steeply, stalled and dived into the ground, bursting into a ball of fire. The accident was caused entirely by someone having omitted to remove the external locks on the elevators, and though the immediate winner of the official trials had to be the Douglas B-18, the much greater potential of the great Boeing bomber resulted in a service-test order for 13, designated Y1B-17, placed on 17 January 1936.

These had many changes, especially to the landing gear, armament and in having 694-kW (930-hp) Wright Cyclone engines instead of 560-kW (750-hp) Pratt & Whitney Hornets. In 1937 the machines were delivered to the 2nd Bombardment Group at Langley Field, which subsequently flew almost 10,000 hours with no serious trouble and did more than any other unit in history to solve the problems of long-distance bombing, especially at high altitude. A 14th aircraft was built as the Y1B-17A with engines fitted with General Electric turbosuperchargers, which increased the speed from 412 km/h (256 mph) to 500 km/h (311 mph) and raised the operating height to well over 9145 m (30,000 ft).

Results with the B-17 (as the Y1B was called after its test period was complete) were so good the USAAC not only fought for massive production numbers, in the teeth of opposition from the US Navy, but also with Boeing collaboration even planned a next-generation bomber which became the B-29. US Navy anger was so intense that production numbers had to be scaled down, and the production batch of the first series model, the B-17B, numbered only 39. These had numerous minor changes as well as a redesigned nose and large rudder. They were the first aircraft in the world to enter service with turbocharged engines. The B-17B entered service in 1939 and was the fastest, as well as the highest-flying, bomber in the world. The US Army Air Corps had by this time embarked on a major programme of perfecting long-range strategic bombing by day, using the massed firepower of a large formation to render interception hazardous. It was expected that, because of the B-17's speed and height, opposing fighters would be hard-pressed to keep up and would present an almost stationary (relative to the bombers) target that could be blasted by the fire from hundreds of machine-guns.

Further power and speed

Boeing and Wright Field continued to improve the B-17 and in 1939 a further 39 were ordered under the designation B-17C. These were much heavier, weighing 22520 kg (49,650 lb) compared with about 19505 kg (43,000 lb) for a B-17, because of increased armour, self-sealing tanks, heavier defensive armament (with twin 12.7-mm/0.5-in guns above and in a new ventral 'bathtub', twin 7.62-

The short-lived Model 299 prototype had Hornet S1EG engines, and twin-strut main landing gears. On the fin is the Boeing Airplane emblem and model number, and the rudder carries US Army stripes and serial. Gross weight of 16 US tons (32,000 lb) was just half that of a laden B-17G. Making the Model 299 was a gigantic financial risk.

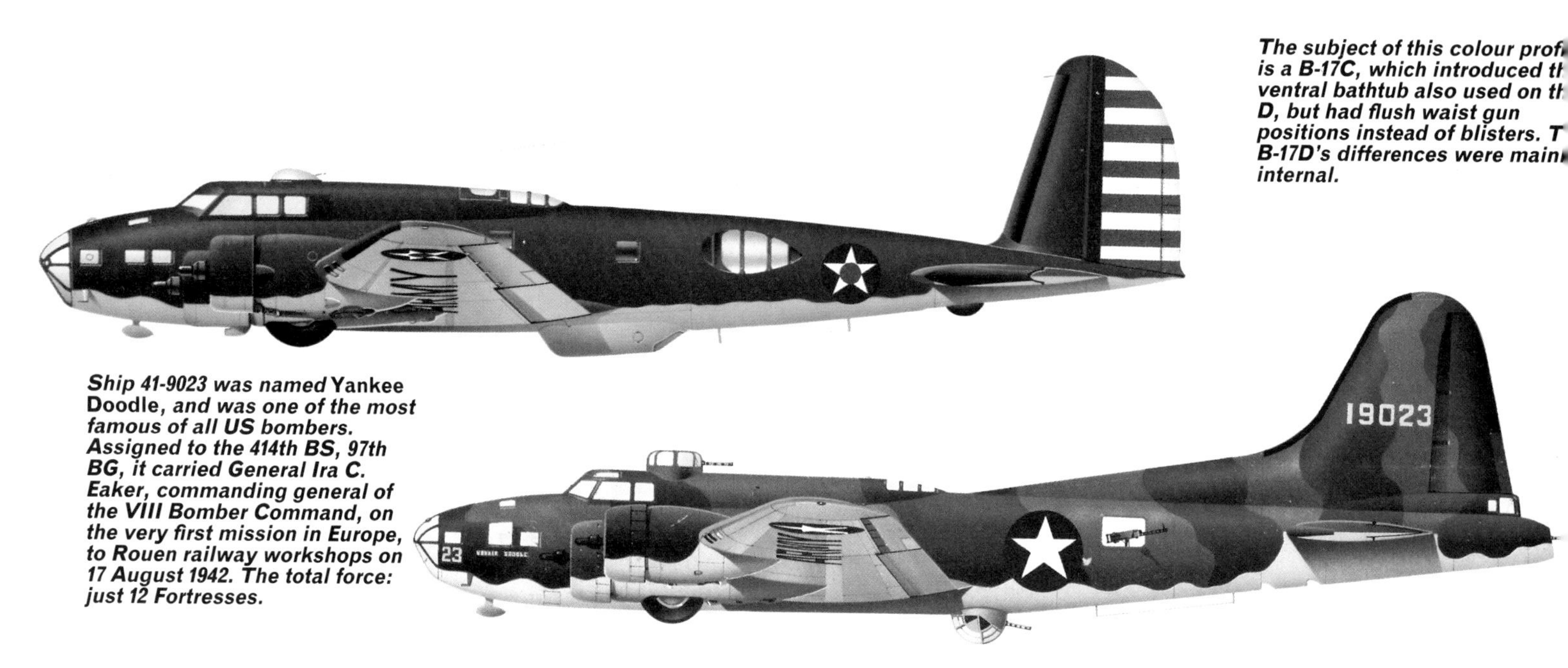

The subject of this colour profi is a B-17C, which introduced th ventral bathtub also used on th D, but had flush waist gun positions instead of blisters. T B-17D's differences were main internal.

Ship 41-9023 was named* Yankee Doodle*, and was one of the most famous of all US bombers. Assigned to the 414th BS, 97th BG, it carried General Ira C. Eaker, commanding general of the VIII Bomber Command, on the very first mission in Europe, to Rouen railway workshops on 17 August 1942. The total force: just 12 Fortresses.

mm/0.3-in guns in the nose and new flush side gun positions) and extra equipment. Despite the greater weight, the fitting of 895-kW (1,200-hp) engines made this the fastest of all versions, with a maximum speed of 515 km/h (320 mph). In Spring 1941 a batch of 20 was assigned to the RAF, following 15 months of negotiations which finally resulted in the aircraft being supplied in exchange for complete information on their combat performance (this was prior to the 1940 Lend-Lease Act). As RAF Fortress Is they had a disastrous and mismanaged career which dramatically reduced their numbers to a handful (about nine) which were transferred to Coastal Command and the Middle East.

Further extensive internal improvements, a new electrical system and engine-cowl cooling gills, led to the B-17D, of which 42 were ordered in 1940. This was the latest model in service at the time of Pearl Harbor (7 December 1941) when 30 were destroyed on the ground at Hickam Field and at Clark Field, Philippines, the following day. But by this time Boeing had developed a visually different model which incorporated all the lessons learned in World War II in Europe. Called Boeing 299O, it entered US Army Air Force service in December 1941 as the B-17E. Its most striking change was the much larger tail, with a giant dorsal fin and long-span tailplane giving better control and stability at high altitude. Armament was completely revised, with paired 12.7-mm (0.5-in) guns in a powered turret behind the cockpit, in a ventral turret at the trailing edge, and in a new manual turret in the tail. Another pair of guns could be fired by hand from the roof of the radio compartment, and with a single hand-aimed gun at each waist position this made a total of 10 heavy

Prior to January 1944, when camouflage paint was generally discontinued in the USAAF, various olive drab and green paint schemes were in use. This 1942 picture of B-17Fs of the 8th Air Force's 91st Bomb Group (322nd Bomb Squadron) shows on a few B-17s the irregular blotching of medium green (officially styled Shade 42).

machine-guns, plus two 7.62-mm (0.3-in) guns aimed from the nose. Further improvements in armour and equipment all helped to increase gross weight to 24494kg (54,000lb), so cruising speed inevitably fell from 231 to only 210mph (372 to 338km/h). This was the first B-17 in large-scale production, and deliveries totalled 512 including 45 sent to the RAF as Fortress IIAs.

Massive production

On 30 May 1942 Boeing flew the first B-17F with many further changes, allowing the gross weight to soar to 29,484 kg (65,000lb) with a potential bomb load for short ranges of 9,435kg (20,800lb), though on normal combat missions the load seldom exceeded 2268kg (5,000lb). The only obvious external change on the F-model was the more pointed nose moulded in one piece of Plexiglas. This type went into production not only at Boeing but also in a great nationwide pool with assembly lines at Douglas (Long Beach) and Vega (a Lockheed subsidiary at Burbank). Boeing built 2,300 of this model, and Douglas and Vega added 605 and 500 respectively.

With the B-17E and B-17F the US 8th Air Force built up its early strength in England. The first combat mission was flown on 17 August 1942 by 12 B-17Es of the 97th Bomb Group against a marshalling yard near Rouen. This was the small beginning to the greatest strategic striking force ever created, which was to lead to a three-year campaign in the course of which 640,036 US tons of bombs were dropped on German targets and, at the cost of grievous losses, supremacy was eventually obtained even over the heart of Germany in daylight.

By far the most numerous model of B-17 was the last. The B-17G was the final result of bitterly won combat experience and among other changes it introduced a chin turret firing ahead with twin accurately aimed 12.7-mm (0.5-in) guns. Previously German fighters had brought down many B-17s with head-on attacks, but the B-17G, with the chin turret plus two more 12.7-mm (0.5-in) cheek guns (and possibly the dorsal turret) firing ahead was a tougher proposition. The B-17G had enclosed waist positions, much greater ammunition capacity and, like most B-17Fs, paddle-blade propellers to handle the greater weight and prevent too much deterioration in performance. Most B-17Gs had improved turbochargers which actually increased service ceiling to 10,670m (35,0000ft), but these bombers were so heavy the cruising speed fell to 293km/h (182mph). This increased the time the gigantic formations were exposed to rocket and cannon attack by the German fighters; conversely, of course, it lengthened the time the B-17 guns could destroy those fighters.

Some idea of how deadly the German heavy radar-predicted flak could be is afforded by this picture taken during the bomb run of the 486th Bomb Group on the hated Merseburg oil plants on 2 November 1944. One of the 100-plus heavy guns scored a direct hit through solid cloud on a B-17G of the 834th Bomb Squadron.

Electronic versions

Boeing built 4,035 B-17Gs, Douglas 2,395 and Vega 2,250, a total of 8,680. The total of all versions was 12,731, of which 12,677 were formally accepted by the USAAF. The B-17F was used by the RAF as the Fortress II and the B-17G as the Fortress III, the main user being Coastal Command. Some were modified with a radar in place of the chin or ball turret, and for use against surfaced U-boats a 40-mm Vickers S gun was fitted in a nose mount. The B-17G was also the chief heavy carrier of special electronics for the RAF's No. 100 Group, Nos 214 and 233 Sqns being the pioneers of spoofing, decoy, jamming and intelligence missions with 19 types of electronic or related device, including the super-power emitters coded 'Jostle' and 'Piperack'. The only electronic device often carried by the USAAF B-17s was the early H_2X or Mickey Mouse radar used for bombing through cloud. This set's scanner was normally housed in a retractable radome under the nose or in place of the ball turret.

The ball turret, a retractable installation on the B-24 Liberator, was fixed on the B-17. Originally the B-17E had been fitted with a drum-type ventral turret aimed by a gunner in the fuselage, sighting via a periscope. This was soon replaced by the aptly-named spherical ball-turret made by the Sperry company. The gunner had to climb

Elimination of paint from the B-17 gave a measurable gain in speed or reduced fuel consumption (because cruising speed was preset at a figure all aircraft could easily maintain at full load). These B-17Gs, built by Douglas, were photographed with the 381st Bomb Group (VE code, 532nd BS; VP, the 533rd). Home base was Ridgewell.

Boeing B-17 Flying Fortress

This famed B-17G, A Bit o'Lace the 711th BS, 447th BG, based a Rattlesden, actually had nose a painted and signed by Milton Caniff (nose art, often featuring the female form, was invariably well executed). The 447th did n use squadron code letters but ended the war with this colourf yellow livery.

KJ109 was a B-17G-55 assigned to the RAF and completely re-equipped with chin and ball turrets replaced by a vast assortment of powerful electronics. It operated from Oulton with No. 223 Squadron on highly secret – and extremely effective – 'Jostle', 'Piperack' and 'Mandrel' missions, part of No. 100 Group's new art of electronic war.

into this and squat with his knees fully bent for perhaps five or six hours. A belly landing could flatten the ball-turret and its occupant, and there were many occasions when because of combat damage the turret doors jammed and a belly landing would have killed the ball-turret gunner. Normal procedure for a belly landing was to get the gunner out and then, using special tools, disconnect the whole turret from the aircraft and let it fall free. On one occasion a B-17 returned with severe combat damage and jammed landing gears, and near its home airfield it was found that the special tools were not on board. The executive officer of the station was notified by radio; within minutes he had grabbed a set of tools and taken off. For more than two hours he circled in close formation with the stricken B-17 trying to pass the tools on the end of a cable. He succeeded.

In 1942 various special versions of B-17 were produced by Vega to serve as escort fighters. The first was the second Vega-built B-17F, which was rebuilt as an XB-40 with many armament changes including a second dorsal turret and a bomb bay full of ammunition. It was followed by 20 YB-40s with even heavier armament including quadruple gun mounts at nose and tail and a total of as many as 30 guns of up to 37- or 40-mm calibre! So heavy were these 'fighters' that they could not even keep formation with the B-17 bombers, and though they flew nine combat missions in 1943 they were judged unsuccessful.

In 1943 Boeing converted the ninth production B-17E to have

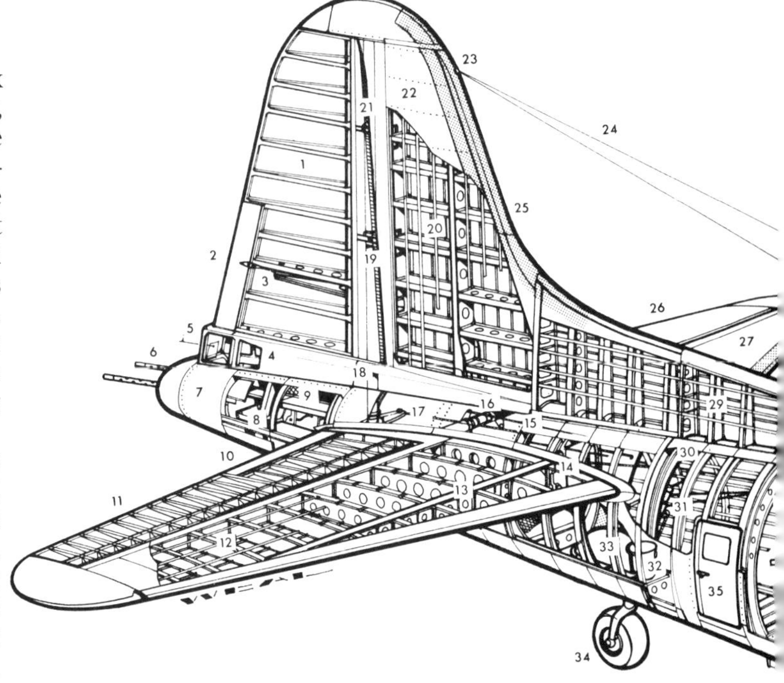

Boeing B-17F Flying Fortress cutaway drawing key

1 Rudder construction
2 Rudder tab
3 Rudder tab actuation
4 Tail gunner's station
5 Gunsight
6 Twin 0.5-in (12.7-mm) machine-guns
7 Tail cone
8 Tail gunner's seat
9 Ammunition troughs
10 Elevator trim tab
11 Starboard elevator
12 Tailplane structure
13 Tailplane front spar
14 Tailplane/fuselage attachment
15 Control cables
16 Elevator control mechanism
17 Rudder control linkage
18 Rudder post
19 Rudder centre hinge
20 Fin structure

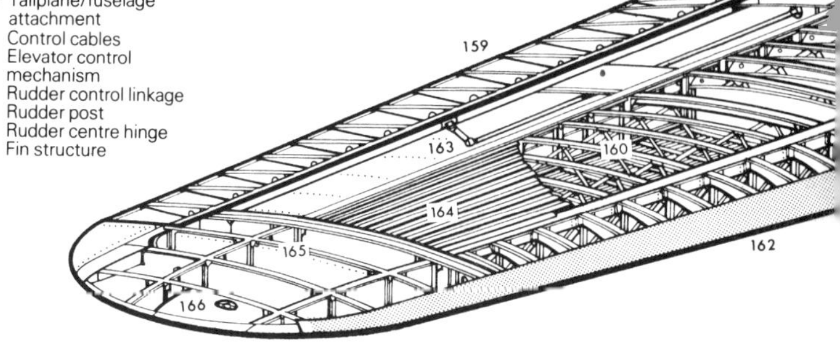

21 Rudder upper hinge
22 Fin skinning
23 Aerial attachment
24 Aerials
25 Fin leading-edge de-icing boot
26 Port elevator
27 Port tailplane

Provision of adequate forward-firing defensive armament was always a problem with the B-17, but culminated in the B-17G series with four 12.7-mm (0.5-in) guns in two turrets (dorsal and chin, each with two guns) supplemented by a pair of manually operated cheek guns, one on each side of the nose.

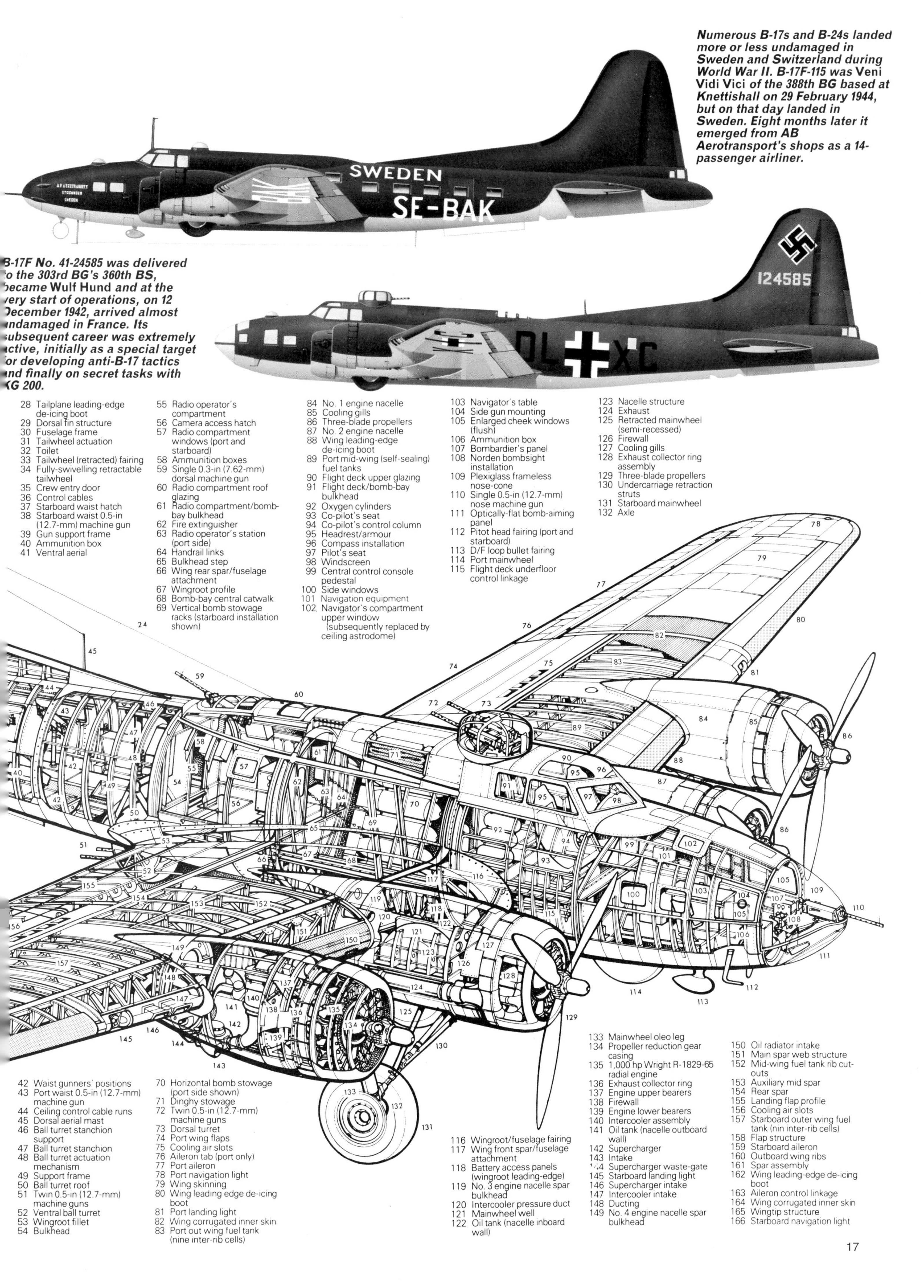

Numerous B-17s and B-24s landed more or less undamaged in Sweden and Switzerland during World War II. B-17F-115 was* Veni Vidi Vici *of the 388th BG based at Knettishall on 29 February 1944, but on that day landed in Sweden. Eight months later it emerged from AB Aerotransport's shops as a 14-passenger airliner.

B-17F No. 41-24585 was delivered to the 303rd BG's 360th BS, became* Wulf Hund *and at the very start of operations, on 12 December 1942, arrived almost undamaged in France. Its subsequent career was extremely active, initially as a special target for developing anti-B-17 tactics and finally on secret tasks with KG 200.

In a typical story of amazing nerve and skulduggery, the infant Israeli air force, the Heyl Ha'Avir, managed to get hold of three B-17Gs in 1948. Devoid of guns, and with turret holes gaping open or with wood/plaster sealing (for the chin hole), and devoid of navigation gear, they bombed Cairo on their way to Israel!

liquid-cooled Allison engines of 1063kW (1,425hp) each; these naturally resulted in improved performance but it remained a one-off prototype (designated XB-38). Another unique machine was the plush XC-108 VIP transport which began life as a B-17E (41-2593) but was converted for General Douglas MacArthur, Supreme Commander in the Pacific, with a comfortable interior for 38 passengers. The XC-108A was a similar conversion but for cargo, with a large door on the left side. The YC-108 was a VIP conversion of a B-17F, and the XC-108B was a B-17F tanker which ferried fuel 'over the hump' from India to China.

Oddities and other developments

The F-9s were a batch of 16 B-17Fs rebuilt by United Airlines at Cheyenne as strategic reconnaissance machines with from six to 10 cameras in fuselage installations. Another 45 B-17Fs were converted as F-9As or F-9Bs, while 10 B-17Gs were turned into F-9Cs, the post-war designation for survivors being FB-17 up to 1947 and RB-17 thereafter. One B-17F served with the US Navy, and late in the war 40 B-17Gs were transferred to the US Navy to pioneer the technique of AEW (airborne early warning) with the newly developed APS-120 radar in a vast chin blister; this variant was designated PB-1W.

A strange wartime rebuild was the Aphrodite cruise-missile conversion in which war-weary B-17Fs and B-17Gs were stripped of everything that could be removed and packed with 10 tons of Torpex, a British explosive with 50 per cent greater blasting power than Amatol. Under the project names 'Perilous' and 'Castor' many tests were made, the take-off being made by two pilots in an open cockpit who then baled out to leave the Fortress (official designation BQ-17) under radio control from an accompanying aircraft such as a B-17 or PV-1. Though 11 combat launches were made on German targets the idea was judged rather too perilous after one BQ-17 had made a crater over 30 m (100 ft) in diameter in England and another had broken radio link and orbited a British city before heading out to sea.

In 1944 British experience was used in converting B-17Gs into B-17H air/sea rescue aircraft with an airborne lifeboat and search radar; post-war these were designated SB-17G. Other post-war variants included the CB-17 and VB-17 transports, TB-17 trainers, radio-guided QB-17 versions and DB-17 radio director aircraft. These soldiered on with the USAF after its formation in 1947, and also with various minor air forces. Many others became civil airliners. Seven of the 68 which landed in Sweden during the war entered service as airliners with AB Aerotransport, and another was used as an executive transport by TWA. One firefighting conversion was powered by Rolls-Royce Dart turboprops, and the B-17 was a popular testbed for experimental jet and turboprop engines in the late 1940s.

No history of the B-17 would be complete, however, without reference to its exciting cloak-and-dagger operations with I/KG 200, the clandestine Gruppe of the Luftwaffe whose story has only recently come into the open. The B-17, mainly the G model, was its most important captured type, used for numerous long-range missions under the cover-designation Dornier Do 200. These machines carried out daring operations throughout Europe, from Norway to Jordan and the Western Desert. They were not specifically intended to deceive the Allies, and wore German markings; they were used just because they were better for the job than any German aircraft!

From a distance this B-17G, ship number 43-37716, merely looks a trifle dirty or weatherbeaten. On closer inspection it can be seen to be the famous 5 Grand, the 5,000th B-17 built by Boeing, covered with the names of every Seattle worker who found a space.

Boeing B-17 variants

Variants:
Boeing 299: prototype, with four 560-kW (750-hp) Pratt & Whitney Hornet engines; often called XB-17 but in fact had no military designation (total 1)
Y1B-17: service-test batch; four 694-kW (930-hp) Wright R-1820-39 engines, operational equipment, five 7.62-mm (0.3-in) guns, 2177-kg (4,800-lb) bombload; later redesignated B-17 (total 13)
Y1B-17A: single aircraft with R-1820-51 turbocharged Cyclone engines
B-17B: Boeing 299E, later styled 299M; first production model (total 39)
B-17C: Boeing 299H; four R-1820-65 engines; improved armament and equipment (total 38)

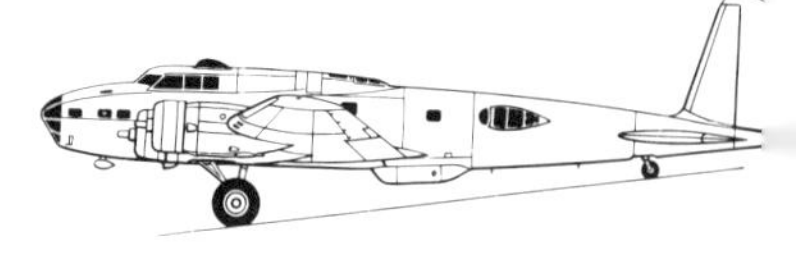

Boeing B-17C

B-17D: Boeing 299H; many further improvements (total 42)
B-17E: Boeing 299O; complete redesign and much heavier armament; first major production version (total 512)

B-17F: Boeing 299P; restressed for higher weights, R-1820-97 engines, frameless plastic nose (total 3,405)

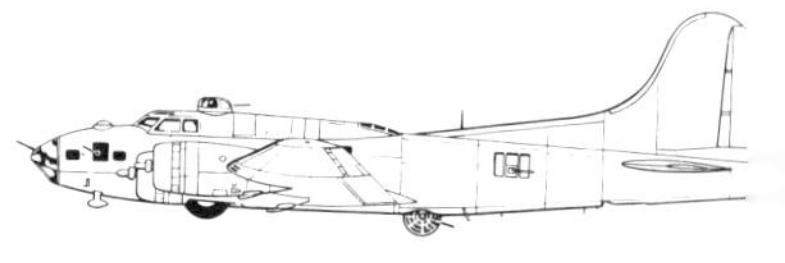

Boeing B-17F

B-17G: standard bomber from 1943, Dash-97 engines with B-2 (from late 1944, B-22) turbos, chin turret (normal defensive armament 13 12.7-mm (0.5-in) guns; basis for numerous conversions and post-war variants (total 8,680)

F4U Corsair

For an aircraft that accomplished so much, Vought's F4U Corsair entered service comparatively late in the war. It was not until well into 1943 that it began to enter service with the US Navy and Marines, but it made up for this by rapidly becoming the most effective aircraft in the Pacific theatre. A match for any Japanese fighter, it was also a supremely effective ground-attack aircraft. Easily the best carrier-based type of its day, the Corsair went on to underline its worth in Korea and elsewhere.

Design of the Corsair started in February 1938. The US Navy wanted a new, high-performance shipboard fighter to follow such machines as the Brewster F2A and Grumman G-36, the first of the fast US Navy monoplanes, with engines in the 671- to 746-kW (900- to 1,000-hp) class. The US Navy expected the new 1938 designs to use the latest Cyclone or Twin Wasp of 895 kW (1,200 hp), but Pratt & Whitney was running a larger engine, the R-2800 Double Wasp, already giving 1380 kW (1,850 hp) and good for 1492 kW (2,000 hp) with further development. Pratt & Whitney was one of the companies of United Aircraft Corporation in Connecticut. Another UAC company, formed by a shotgun marriage of two dissimilar members, was called Vought-Sikorsky Aircraft (before long they parted, January 1943 seeing Sikorsky go off to make helicopters and Chance Vought Aircraft putting all its effort into the F4U). Vought-Sikorsky's chief engineer, Rex Beisel, boldly submitted a proposal to meet the 1938 fighter requirement with a fighter powered by the new R-2800. In June this was accepted, and Vought Sikorsky received a contract for the prototype XF4U-1.

Design progressed swiftly, and the mock-up review was successfully passed in February 1939. The silver XF4U-1 was duly flown by Lyman A. Bullard Jr at Stratford on 29 May 1940. Though its empty weight of 3365 kg (7,418 lb) was a technical triumph it was, in fact, considerably heavier than the laden weight of all previous US Navy carrier fighters. Compared with most fighters of World War II, and especially those of the USSR and Japan, the Vought-Sikorsky team had created a monster. The 18-cylinder radial engine was the biggest and most powerful yet put into a fighter, and it drove a three-bladed Hamilton Standard (yet another UAC company) propeller with a diameter of 4.04 m (13 ft 4 in). This was easily the largest propeller so far fitted to a fighter, in comparison, for example, with 3.00 m (9 ft 10 in) for the Messerschmitt Bf 109. It was partly in order to provide ground clearance for this propeller that the wings were bent down in inverted-gull form. This made the main landing gears short enough to retract to the rear, the wheels turning 90° to lie flat in the angle of the wing just ahead of the large flaps.

The wing had to be large enough to provide for slow carrier landings, and this also conferred exceptional manoeuvrability. No less than 1046 litres (273 US gal) of fuel could be carried in some of the first-ever integral tanks formed by sealing bays in the wing. In the outer wings were compartments for 20 small anti-aircraft bombs, aimed via a sighting panel in the belly. Above the fuselage were two 7.62-mm (0.30-in) calibre synchronised guns, and two of the larger 12.7-mm (0.50-in) guns were in the outer wings. Structurally the new fighter was immensely strong, the skin of the fuselage being especially thick, and like that on the front of the wing it was attached

By far the most important operators of the Corsair in World War II were the fighter squadrons of the US Marine Corps, based on island airstrips in the Pacific. This bombing mission was photographed leaving parking areas on Majuro Atoll, in the Marshalls, on 29 August 1944. The squadron belongs to the 4th Marine Air Wing.

by a new spot-welding process. Aft of the main spar, however, the wing skin was fabric, and fabric also covered the control surfaces.

Performance was even better than that predicted, but on the fifth flight the valuable prototype was caught with tanks almost dry in heavy rain squalls. Pilot Boone T. Guyton decided to put it down on the Norwich golf course, but the heavy machine refused to slow down on the slippery wet grass, slammed into trees and came to rest almost demolished with just enough space under the inverted fuselage for Guyton to get out. It was then discovered that the XF4U was so strong it was repairable, though several months were lost. From September 1940 measured performance figures were taken, and on 1 October a true speed of 652 km/h (405 mph) was recorded in level flight. This was faster than any other fighter in the world, and one important spin-off of this performance was that Pratt & Whitney sought and won US Army Air Corps permission to abandon their large and costly programme of liquid-cooled sleeve-valve engines. After all, said the engine maker, what could these promised future engines do that the R-2800 was not doing already in the Corsair? This flight by the big US Navy fighter ensured that the Allies' biggest aero-engine maker stuck with air-cooled radials for the rest of the piston era, and it also put the Corsair in the no. 1 US Navy fighter spot, other proposals henceforth being judged against it.

Armament changes

The XF4U had still a very long way to go. After much argument the armament was made radically different. The fuselage guns were omitted, and the outer wings were given four extra 12.7-mm (0.50-in) guns, to make six in all. Bombs and the sighting panel were deleted. Unfortunately the heavy wing armament made it impossible to put integral tanks in the leading edge, and the rather retrograde decision was taken to put all fuel in a vast 896 litrc (237-US gal) tank in the fuselage. In turn this meant moving the cockpit 0.81 m (32 in) to the rear, which worsened the most vital forward field of view. There were many other changes, such as an increase in size of the ailerons to give more rapid roll, and a change to NACA-type slotted flaps. Much was done to add armour, bullet-proof windshield, protected self-sealing fuel-tank construction and British-invented IFF (radio identification friend or foe), as well as to improve the already outstanding engine installation – with 'jet thrust' exhaust stacks and

A combat formation of four Vought F4U-1 Corsair fighters (two two-ship elements) of the celebrated US Marine Corps 'Blacksheep' squadron (VMF-124) banks left over the island of Bougainville in the Solomons group. Operating in such an archipelago, the Corsair soon proved a potent and versatile fighter-bomber.

Vought F4U Corsair cutaway drawing key

1 Spinner
2 Three-bladed Hamilton Standard constant-speed propeller
3 Reduction gear housing
4 Nose ring
5 Pratt & Whitney R-2800-8 Double Wasp 18-cylinder two-row engine
6 Exhaust pipes
7 Hydraulically-operated cowling
8 Fixed cowling panels
9 Wing leading-edge unprotected integral fuel tank, capacity 235 litres (62 US gal)
10 Truss-type main spar
11 Leading-edge rib structure
12 Starboard navigation light
13 Wingtip
14 Wing structure
15 Wing ribs
16 Wing outer-section (fabric skinning aft of main spar)
17 Starboard aileron
18 Ammunition boxes (max total capacity 2,350 rounds)
19 Aileron trim tab
20 Aerial mast
21 Forward bulkhead
22 Oil tank, capacity 98 litres (26 US gal)
23 Oil tank forward armour plate
24 Fire suppressor cylinder
25 Supercharger housing
26 Exhaust trunking
27 Blower assembly
28 Engine support frame
29 Engine control runs
30 Wing mainspar carry-through structure
31 Engine support attachment
32 Upper cowling deflection plate (0.25 cm/0.1 in aluminium)
33 Fuel filler cap
34 Fuselage main fuel tank, capacity 897 litres (237 US gal)
35 Upper longeron
36 Fuselage forward frames
37 Rudder pedals
38 Heelboards
39 Control column
40 Instrument panel
41 Reflector sight
42 Armour-glass windshield
43 Rear-view mirror
44 Rearward-sliding cockpit canopy
45 Handgrip
46 Headrest
47 Pilot's head and back armour
48 Canopy frame
49 Pilot's seat
50 Engine control quadrant
51 Trim tab control wheels
52 Wing-folding lever
53 Centre/aft fuselage bulkhead
54 Radio shelf
55 Radio installation
56 Canopy track
57 Bulkhead
58 Aerial lead-in
59 Aerial mast
60 Aerials
61 Heavy-sheet skin plating
62 Dorsal identification light
63 Longeron
64 Control runs
65 Aft fuselage structure
66 Compass installation
67 Lifting tube
68 Access/inspection panels
69 Fin/fuselage forward attachment
70 Starboard tailplane
71 Elevator balance
72 Fin structure
73 Inspection panels
74 Rudder balance
75 Aerial stub
76 Rudder upper hinge
77 Rudder structure
78 Diagonal bracing
79 Rudder trim tab
80 Trim tab actuating rod
81 Access panel
82 Rudder post
83 Tailplane end rib
84 Elevator control runs
85 Fixed fairing root
86 Elevator trim tabs (port and starboard)
87 Tail cone
88 Rear navigation light
89 Port elevator
90 Elevator balance
91 Port tailplane structure
92 Arrester hook (stowed)
93 Tail section frames
94 Fairing
95 Tailwheel (retracted)
96 Arrester hook (lowered)
97 Tailwheel/hook doors
98 Tailwheel/hook attachment/pivot
99 Mooring/tie-down lug
100 Rearward-retracting tailwheel
101 Tailwheel oleo
102 Support strut
103 Arrester hook actuating strut
104 Aft/tail section bulkhead
105 Arrester hook shock-absorber
106 Tailwheel/arrester hook cylinder
107 Tailwheel retraction strut
108 Bulkhead attachment points
109 Fuselage skinning
110 Bulkhead frame
111 Elevator/rudder control runs
112 Entry hand/foothold
113 Hydraulically-operated flap inboard section
114 Wing fold line
115 'Flap gap' closure plate
116 Hydraulically-operated flap outboard section

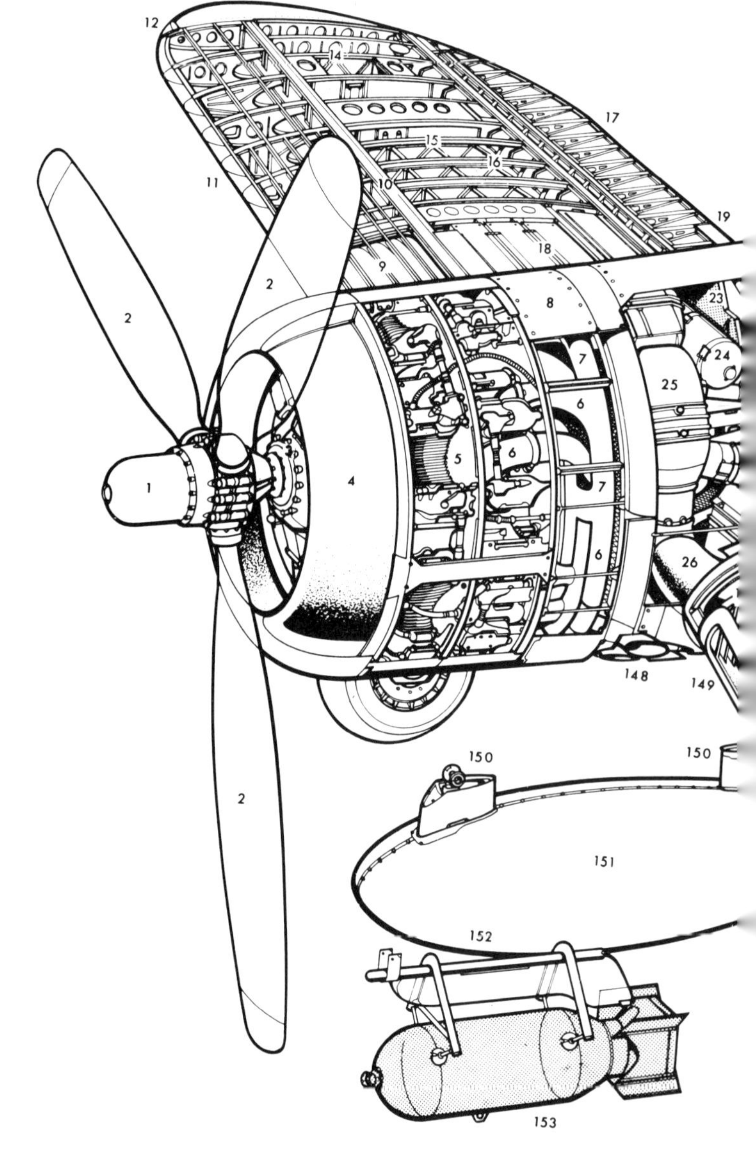

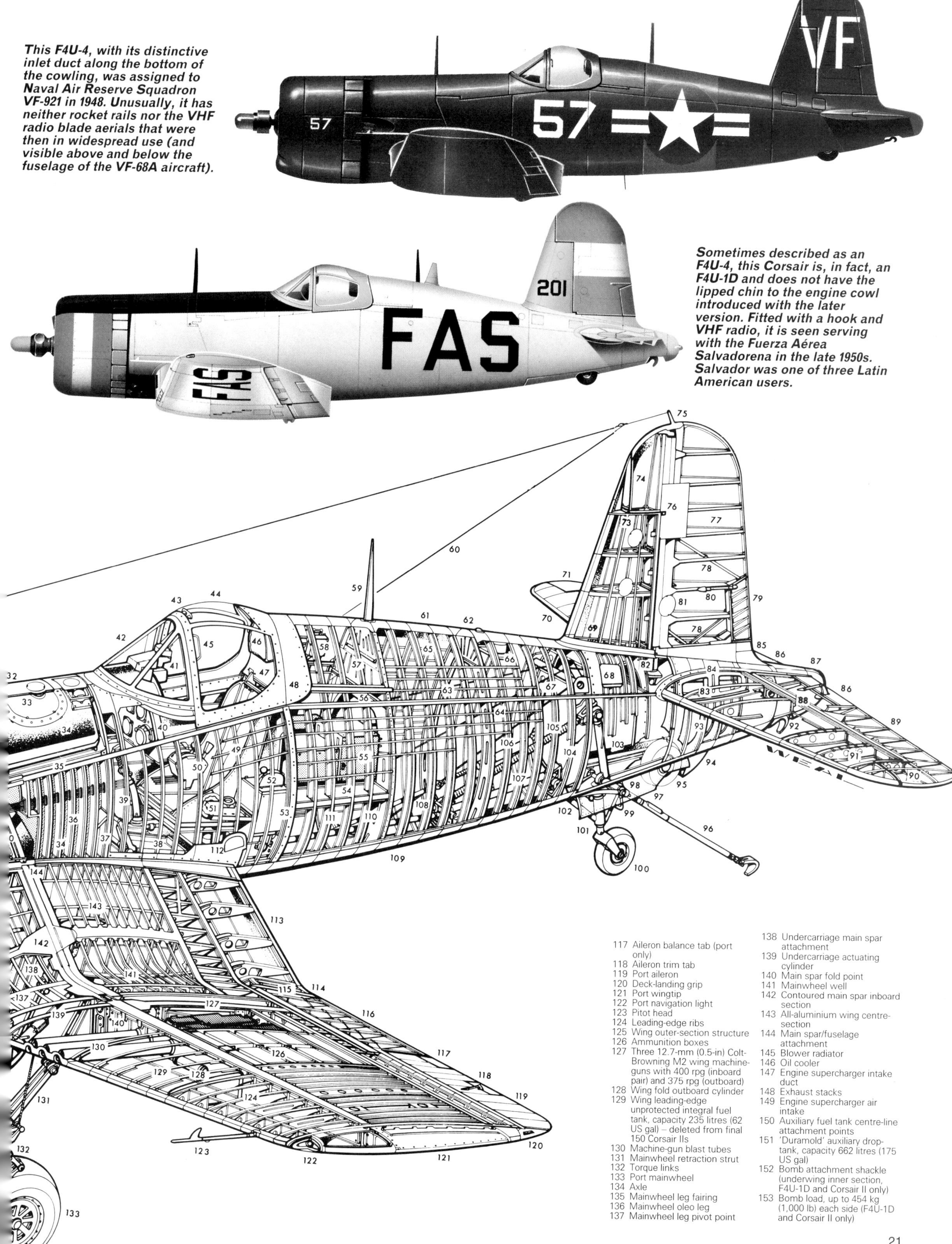

This F4U-4, with its distinctive inlet duct along the bottom of the cowling, was assigned to Naval Air Reserve Squadron VF-921 in 1948. Unusually, it has neither rocket rails nor the VHF radio blade aerials that were then in widespread use (and visible above and below the fuselage of the VF-68A aircraft).

Sometimes described as an F4U-4, this Corsair is, in fact, an F4U-1D and does not have the lipped chin to the engine cowl introduced with the later version. Fitted with a hook and VHF radio, it is seen serving with the Fuerza Aérea Salvadorena in the late 1950s. Salvador was one of three Latin American users.

117 Aileron balance tab (port only)
118 Aileron trim tab
119 Port aileron
120 Deck-landing grip
121 Port wingtip
122 Port navigation light
123 Pitot head
124 Leading-edge ribs
125 Wing outer-section structure
126 Ammunition boxes
127 Three 12.7-mm (0.5-in) Colt-Browning M2 wing machine-guns with 400 rpg (inboard pair) and 375 rpg (outboard)
128 Wing fold outboard cylinder
129 Wing leading-edge unprotected integral fuel tank, capacity 235 litres (62 US gal) – deleted from final 150 Corsair IIs
130 Machine-gun blast tubes
131 Mainwheel retraction strut
132 Torque links
133 Port mainwheel
134 Axle
135 Mainwheel leg fairing
136 Mainwheel oleo leg
137 Mainwheel leg pivot point
138 Undercarriage main spar attachment
139 Undercarriage actuating cylinder
140 Main spar fold point
141 Mainwheel well
142 Contoured main spar inboard section
143 All-aluminium wing centre-section
144 Main spar/fuselage attachment
145 Blower radiator
146 Oil cooler
147 Engine supercharger intake duct
148 Exhaust stacks
149 Engine supercharger air intake
150 Auxiliary fuel tank centre-line attachment points
151 'Duramold' auxiliary drop-tank, capacity 662 litres (175 US gal)
152 Bomb attachment shackle (underwing inner section, F4U-1D and Corsair II only)
153 Bomb load, up to 454 kg (1,000 lb) each side (F4U-1D and Corsair II only)

Vought F4U Corsair variants

XF4U-1: prototype, with R-2800-4 engine of 1380 kW (1,850 hp) and all fuel in wings
F4U-1: principal production version; usually 1492-kW (2,000-hp) R-2800-8 engine (later versions, 1679-kW/2,250-hp); six 12.7-mm (0.50-in) guns or (-1C) four M2 cannon (total 9,441)
F4U-2: first night fighter version, with APS-4 radar on right wing; usually only four or five 12.7-mm (0.50-in) guns (all conversions)
F4U-3: high-altitude version with turbocharged R-2800-16 (no production)
F4U-4: major F4U-1 successor; R-2800-18W or -42W engine rated at 1828 kW (2,450 hp); improved cockpit and other changes (total 2,357)
F4U-5: post-war model with 2126-kW (2,850-hp) R-2800-32W, metal-skinned wings and tail, and many other changes (total in several sub-types 568)
AU-1 (F4U-6): dedicated low-level attack version (total 111)
F4U-7: version for French, basically AU with F4U-4 engine (total 94)

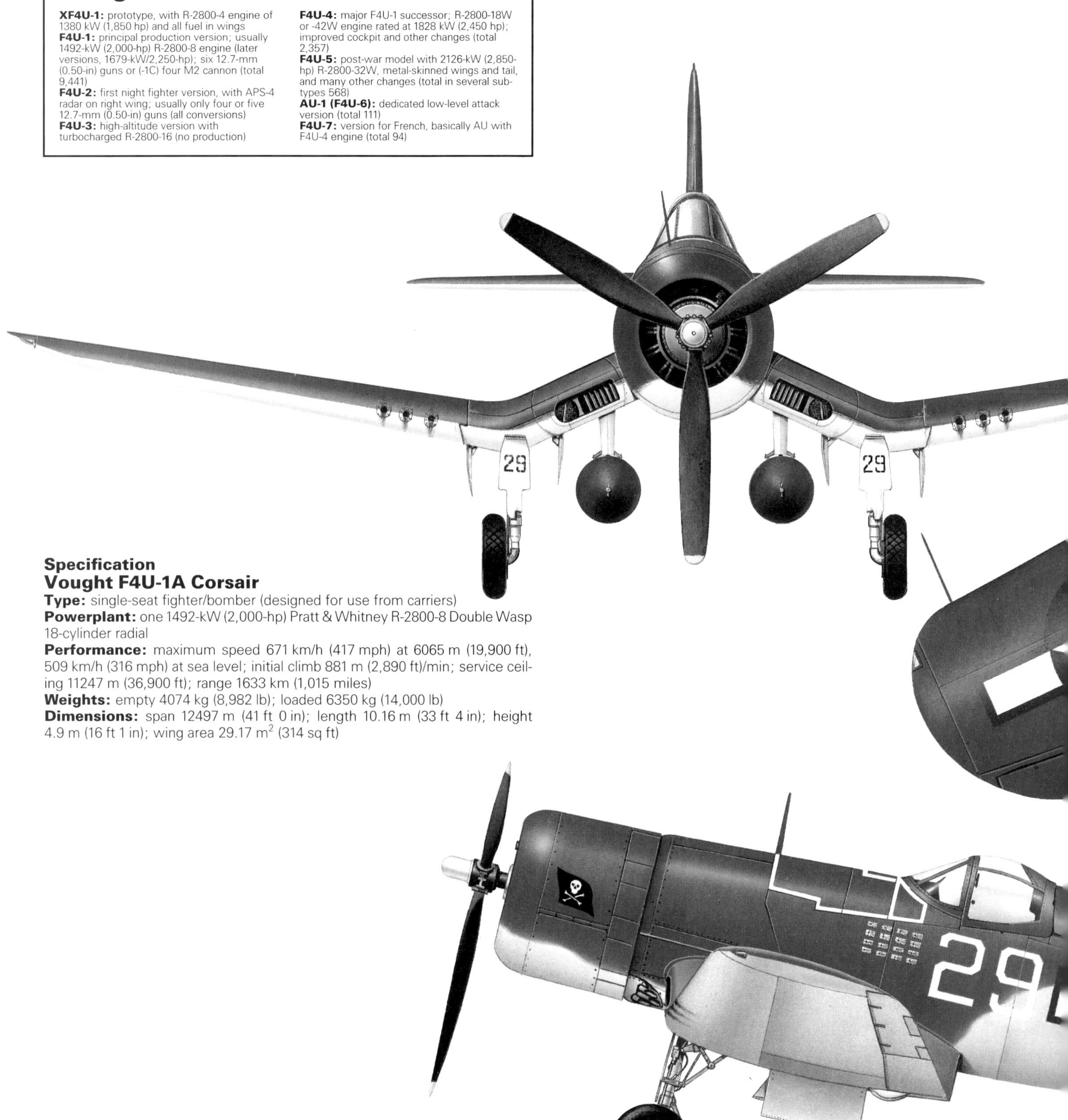

Specification
Vought F4U-1A Corsair

Type: single-seat fighter/bomber (designed for use from carriers)
Powerplant: one 1492-kW (2,000-hp) Pratt & Whitney R-2800-8 Double Wasp 18-cylinder radial
Performance: maximum speed 671 km/h (417 mph) at 6065 m (19,900 ft), 509 km/h (316 mph) at sea level; initial climb 881 m (2,890 ft)/min; service ceiling 11247 m (36,900 ft); range 1633 km (1,015 miles)
Weights: empty 4074 kg (8,982 lb); loaded 6350 kg (14,000 lb)
Dimensions: span 12497 m (41 ft 0 in); length 10.16 m (33 ft 4 in); height 4.9 m (16 ft 1 in); wing area 29.17 m^2 (314 sq ft)

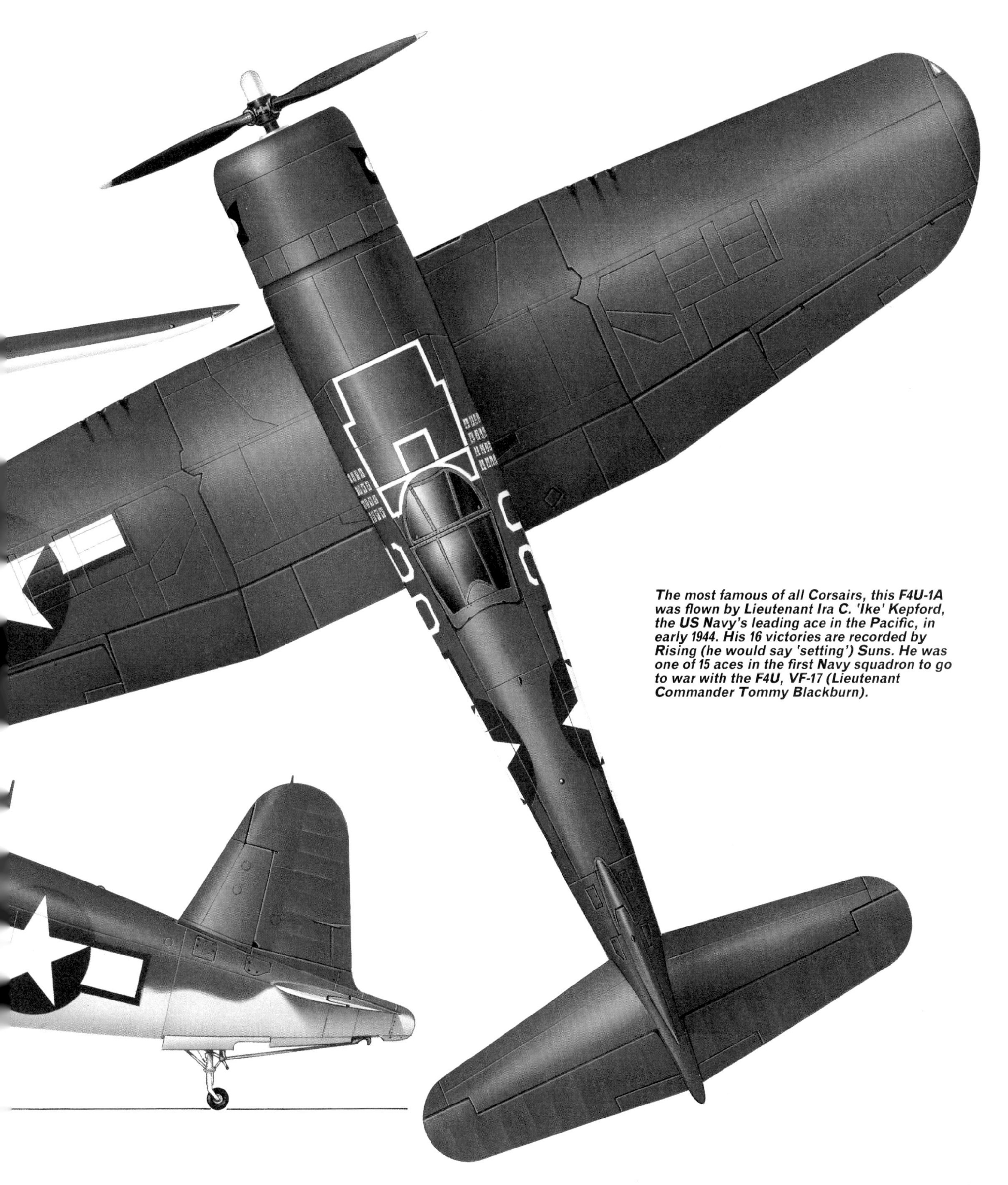

The most famous of all Corsairs, this F4U-1A was flown by Lieutenant Ira C. 'Ike' Kepford, the US Navy's leading ace in the Pacific, in early 1944. His 16 victories are recorded by Rising (he would say 'setting') Suns. He was one of 15 aces in the first Navy squadron to go to war with the F4U, VF-17 (Lieutenant Commander Tommy Blackburn).

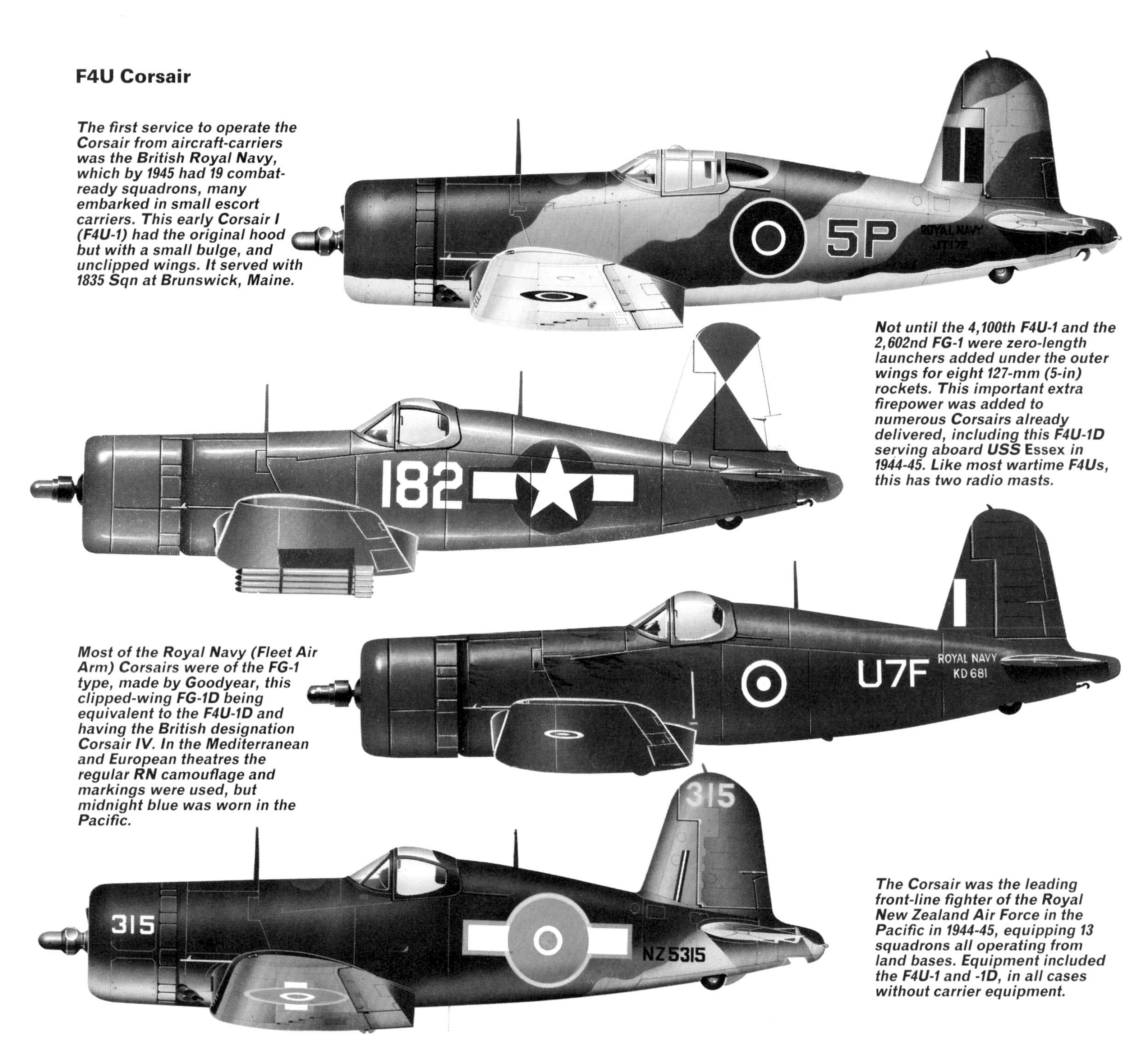

The first service to operate the Corsair from aircraft-carriers was the British Royal Navy, which by 1945 had 19 combat-ready squadrons, many embarked in small escort carriers. This early Corsair I (F4U-1) had the original hood but with a small bulge, and unclipped wings. It served with 1835 Sqn at Brunswick, Maine.

Not until the 4,100th F4U-1 and the 2,602nd FG-1 were zero-length launchers added under the outer wings for eight 127-mm (5-in) rockets. This important extra firepower was added to numerous Corsairs already delivered, including this F4U-1D serving aboard USS Essex in 1944-45. Like most wartime F4Us, this has two radio masts.

Most of the Royal Navy (Fleet Air Arm) Corsairs were of the FG-1 type, made by Goodyear, this clipped-wing FG-1D being equivalent to the F4U-1D and having the British designation Corsair IV. In the Mediterranean and European theatres the regular RN camouflage and markings were used, but midnight blue was worn in the Pacific.

The Corsair was the leading front-line fighter of the Royal New Zealand Air Force in the Pacific in 1944-45, equipping 13 squadrons all operating from land bases. Equipment included the F4U-1 and -1D, in all cases without carrier equipment.

efficient leading-edge ram inlets for the carburettor and oil coolers – and to add power-folding wings and a tail arrester hook. Final demonstrations took place in early 1941, and the first production contract, for 584 F4U-1 Corsairs, was received in June 1941. The first F4U-1 flew a year later and was handed to the US Navy on 31 July 1942, one day after the first of the rival Grumman F6F Hellcats made its first flight, with a similar engine.

It so happened that the F6F was rushed into carrier service, while the US Navy found much to criticise in the potentially greater F4U-1. Stalling behaviour was dangerous, and a sharp-edged metal strip was eventually added on the outer right leading edge to make that wing stall at the same time as the left. A sudden yaw – called 'rudder kick' – near the point of touchdown was corrected by making the tailwheel leg longer, but this made it impossible to use the full wing lift and so land more slowly. An especially tricky problem on a carrier deck was the severe tendency to bounce. The upshot of these factors was that the F4U was not accepted for carrier service, and all the first batches went to units of the US Marine Corps. These fine squadrons, beginning with VMF-124, all fought from narrow airstrips on Pacific islands. By the end of 1943 everyone, certainly including the Japanese, knew the F4U to be the premier air combat fighter in the Pacific; subsequent tests in the USA showed it on most counts to be the best everywhere else.

Pictured on 8 October 1940, soon after the 652 km/h (405 mph) level speed record, the XF4U-1 prototype was not only quite unlike any previous fighter but also different from all production Corsairs. The forward cockpit was possible because of the fuel tankage in the wings, which housed only onc gun on each side.

Production slowly got into its stride, and whereas 178 were built in 1942, the total for 1943 was 2,294, of which 378 were FG-1s produced by Goodyear Aircraft and 136 F3As by the inefficient Brewster company. At the 1,550th Corsair the more powerful R-2800-8W engine was fitted, with water injection to give 1679 kW (2,250 hp). This resulted in the designation F4U-1A (plus Goodyear FG-1A, with non-folding wings, and Brewster F3A-1A). By this time pilot view had been improved by a small bulge in the top of the sliding canopy, followed by elimination of the original 'birdcage' in favour of a clear-view raised canopy in conjunction with a raised seat. The F4U-1B was a variant for the British Fleet Air Arm. The F4U-1C was a batch of 200 with four 20-mm M2 (Hispano) cannon. The F4U-1D was the first model with pylons under the inner wings for two 606-litre (160-US gal) drop tanks or two 454-kg (1,000-lb) bombs, an exceptional load for a fighter. Twelve F4U-1s were rebuilt as F4U-2 night fighters, with only four guns but radar, an autopilot and other special gear; these Corsairs achieved a remarkable combat record from carriers and shore bases as the first radar-equipped naval night fighters.

Carrier flying was still prohibited in the US Navy, but the 2,012 Corsairs supplied under lend-lease to the British Fleet Air Arm were used aboard carriers from the start in 1943, and by April 1944 both HMS *Victorious* and *Illustrious* were in action against the enemy (the first against *Tirpitz* off Norway and the other ship off Sumatra). The FAA had to clip 20 cm (8 in) off each wing, squaring off the tip, to provide below-decks stowage on small carriers, yet despite this reduction in wing area the Corsair was cleared for deck operations as soon as a curving landing pattern had been devised to keep the deck in view. Altogether no fewer than 500 major and over 2,500 minor engineering changes were made to the F4U-1 during production of 4,102 by Vought, 3,808 by Goodyear and 735 by Brewster.

Combat record

Only a handful of F4U-3 high-altitude fighters were produced, with the XR-2800-16 engine and turbosupercharger, ram air being admitted via a large ventral duct. The F4U-4, however, did go into production as the final wartime model, stemming from the F4U-4XA flown in April 1944. Differences were relatively minor, including a new R-2800-18W or -42W engine (rated at up to 1828 kW/2,450 hp with water injection and driving a 4.01 m/13 ft 2 in four-bladed Hydromatic propeller) with the carburettor air duct moved from the leading edge to a new duct under the engine, which in turn meant rerouting the exhaust stacks. The F4U-4B had four M3 cannon, and all F4U-4s could carry any of the profusion of external loads then available including eight 12.7-cm (5-in) rockets or two of the monster Tiny Tim rockets. The F4U-4 was being built by Vought at the rate of 300 a month by 1945, and it stayed in production until 1947, by which time 2,365 had been delivered. By VJ-Day the F4U had flown 64,051 sorties, with a combat record of 2,140 confirmed enemy aircraft destroyed in air combat (plus at least as many more destroyed on the ground) for the loss in air combat of only 189 Corsairs.

Despite its relatively large size and considerable weight, the Vought F4U Corsair was quickly revealed as a fighter possessing great combat manoeuvrability as well as phenomenal flight performance even with a useful underwing armament.

Post-war production

Unlike almost all other US piston-engined fighters, the F4U remained a busy development and production programme after VJ-Day. On 4 April 1946 Chance Vought Aircraft flew the XF4U-5, powered by the R-2800-32W with a two-stage variable-speed supercharger and visually identified by cheek inlets on the cowling at 4 and 8 o'clock instead of one larger supercharger inlet at 6 o'clock. At last the entire wing was skinned in metal, markedly reducing drag, and the elevators were given spring-tab control to reduce pilot effort at the higher airspeeds now possible with this splendid machine. The cockpit, already greatly improved in the F4U-4, was further updated and the canopy bulged sideways to give a view almost directly to the rear. A combustion heater was added to warm the cockpit and defrost the windshield, and electric heaters were provided for the gun bays and pitot head. More fundamental was the 2.75° downward tilt of the engine to improve stability and forward field of view. One felt many of these changes could have been effected in 1941 instead

The worst thing about the entire F4U programme was the time it took to get this world-beating aircraft into production. Not until mid-1942 was there an assembly line, well over two years after first flight. Here are some of the original large order for 584 F4U-1s in the Stratford plant on 23 December 1942.

Three of the first production F4U-1 Corsairs photographed in late 1942 before the addition of white rectangles and red (later blue) border to the national insignia. These aircraft had the big fuselage tank, rear cockpit and six wing guns but were still fairly rudimentary compared with the F4U-1D and F4U-4 of 1944.

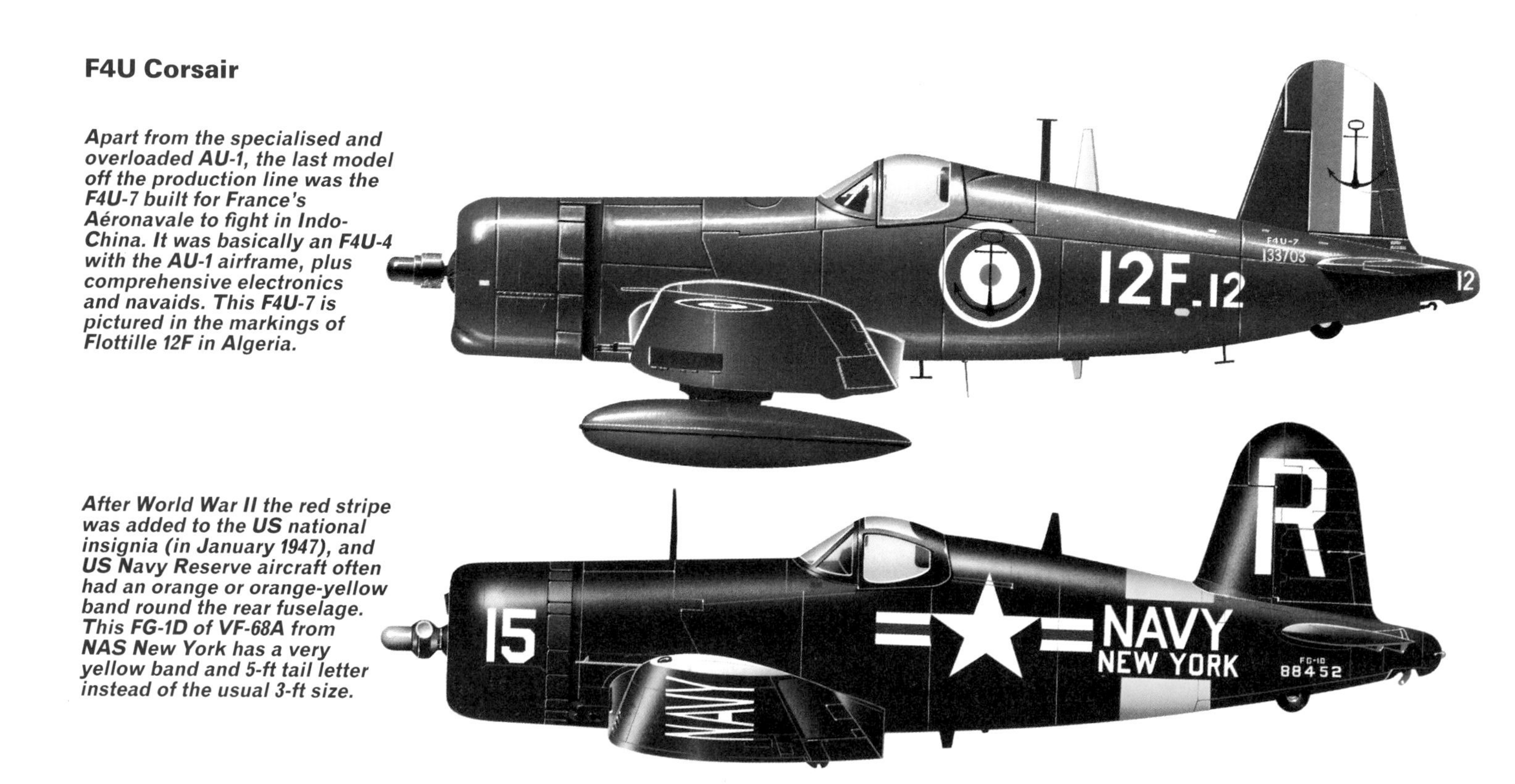

Apart from the specialised and overloaded AU-1, the last model off the production line was the F4U-7 built for France's Aéronavale to fight in Indo-China. It was basically an F4U-4 with the AU-1 airframe, plus comprehensive electronics and navaids. This F4U-7 is pictured in the markings of Flottille 12F in Algeria.

After World War II the red stripe was added to the US national insignia (in January 1947), and US Navy Reserve aircraft often had an orange or orange-yellow band round the rear fuselage. This FG-1D of VF-68A from NAS New York has a very yellow band and 5-ft tail letter instead of the usual 3-ft size.

of on this post-war model, whose armament comprised four M3 cannon as well as a wide range of stores up to a unit size of 907 kg (2,000 lb). As in the case of the F4U-4 there were -5N radar night fighters and -5P photo-reconnaissance versions, and the bitter winter in Korea led to a further variant, the -5NL night fighter with wing and tail de-icer boots of the Goodrich flexible pattern; de-icer shoes along the leading edges of the propeller and further improved thermal de-icing of the pilot windscreen. Vought produced 101 of this special winterised model, as well as 223 of the basic F4U-5 day fighter-bomber, 214 F4U-5N night fighters and 30 F4U-5Ps. US Marine Corps squadrons flew the bulk of the Corsair missions in Korea, though it was a US Navy carrier-based unit that opened the campaign only eight days after the war began. Corsairs were in intensive action to the last day of that war, 27 July 1953.

Attack bomber

In 1950 Vought began studying a dedicated attack version of the Corsair and was awarded a contract for the F4U-6 in January 1951. By the time it flew, in January 1952, the F4U-6 had been redesignated AU-1. As a true attack bomber it was a direct ancestor of today's A-7 Corsair II. The engine was an R-2800-83WA with a simple supercharger installation giving high power at low levels and with no auxiliary inlets around the cowling. The oil coolers were moved inboard to reduce vulnerability, and the whole aircraft was given the highest possible degree of protection against hostile AA fire. Though the loaded weight was the same as that of the F4U-5 fighter (5851 kg/12,900 lb normal or 6032 kg/13,297 lb maximum), the overload take-off weight of the AU-1 could be as high as 8799 kg (19,398 lb) with over 2032 kg (4,480 lb) of offensive stores under wings and fuselage, plus drop tanks. During the Korean War even the earlier F4U-4 and F4U-5 fighters had regularly flown combat missions – from both airstrips and carrier decks – with one 1136-litre (300-US gal) tank and 907 kg (2,000 lb) of bombs (typically one 454-kg/1,000-lb on the left inboard pylon and eight 113-kg/250-lb weapons under the outer wings). With no drop tanks the AU-1 could carry greater loads, a common arrangement being two 454-kg (1,000-lb) bombs inboard and six 227-kg (500-lb) bombs on the outer wing racks.

MiG killer

During the Korean War Corsairs scored many air-combat victories. Some were achieved at night by F4U-5N and -5NL night fighters using the APS-19A radar, and the Corsair was able to intercept and destroy slow-flying North Korean aircraft such as the Yakovlev Yak-18 and Polikarpov Po-2 that were almost impossible targets for the USAF Lockheed F-94 Starfires. At the other end of the speed scale the Corsair frequently met the Mikoyan-Gurevich MiG-15 and scored its first victory over a swept-wing jet in August 1952 (though on that occasion the F4U was itself shot down by another MiG seconds later).

Vought delivered the last of 111 AU-1 Corsairs in October 1952, but had still not reached the end of the line. Since 1949 the company had broken away from United Aircraft and been relocated in a US Navy plant at Dallas, Texas, where all the Korean Corsairs were built. The last model was for France's Aéronavale, which needed modern multi-role tactical aircraft for service in Indo-China. The result was the F4U-7, basically an F4U-4 with the Dash-18W engine and the AU-1 wing, and so able to carry the same heavy attack loads. The French received 94 F4U-7s under the US Mutual Defense Assistance Program, the last being delivered in January 1953. It had come off the Dallas line the preceding month, the last of 12,571 Corsairs of all versions and the last piston-engined fighter in production in the world apart from the S-49 in Yugoslavia and the Hispano Ha 1112 (Merlin-Messerschmitt) in Spain.

Large numbers of F4U-4 and -5 Corsairs operated from Navy carriers during the war in Korea, 1950-53. Here a Dash-4 of USN Reserve Squadron VF-791 makes spiral vortices as the pilot guns the R-2800 on take-off from USS* Boxer *(CVE-21). Cockpits were always open for carrier take-offs and landings but closed at other times.

Douglas A-26 Invader

The Invader is a timeless aircraft. A detractor might argue that it had no 'stretch' potential and was not amenable to modernisation, but men who flew the well-loved, unsung and, at times, troublesome A-26 would put it another way: right from the start the machine was so good in the right hands that there was no sense in tampering with its perfection.

The plain fact is that the A-26 fought in more wars than any other aircraft type. Americans flew it in World War II, Korea and Vietnam. Others flew it in Indo-China, Algeria, Biafra, Cuba, the Congo, and in a dozen other dirty little conflicts. And if it does not spring instantly to mind as the most important of American combat aircraft, the A-26 was, at least, a remarkably durable and potent light bomber that lasted four decades or more.

Designed as a replacement for the A-20 Havoc by the superb engineering team under Edward H. Heinemann at Douglas' El Segundo, California facility, the prototype XA-26 (42-19504) took to the air on 10 July 1942 with Ben Howard at the controls. The outward appearance of the Invader would change little, but the first machine was unusual in having camouflage and large propeller spinners.

Heinemann began from the outset with three variants: the XA-26 (later A-26C) bomber with a glazed nose for the bomb-aimer, the A-26A night-fighter with radar and four ventral 20-mm cannon, and the XA-26B with a solid gun-nose for the ground-attack role. The night-fighter version was short-lived (though the French air force later resurrected a night-fighter Invader in the 1950s), but bombers churned from the Douglas production lines at Long Beach, California and Tulsa, Oklahoma.

The A-26B had six 0.5-in (12.7-mm) machine-guns in the nose (later increased to eight), remotely controlled dorsal and ventral turrets each with two 0.5-in (12.7-mm) guns and up to 10 more 12.7-mm (0.5-in) guns in underwing and underfuselage packs. Heavily armoured and able to carry up to 1814 kg (4,000 lb) of bombs, the A-26B with its maximum speed of 571 km/h (355 mph) at 4570 m (15,000 ft) was the fastest Allied bomber of World War II. Some 1,355 A-26B models were followed by 1,091 A-26C machines with a bomb-aimer's glazed nose.

Operations by Douglas B-26 Invaders of the 5th Air Force played a significant part in the Korean War. Here a B-26 prepares for a belly landing after Communist small-arms fire had disabled the hydraulic system. Note the upper canopy panels open for a quick crew exit.

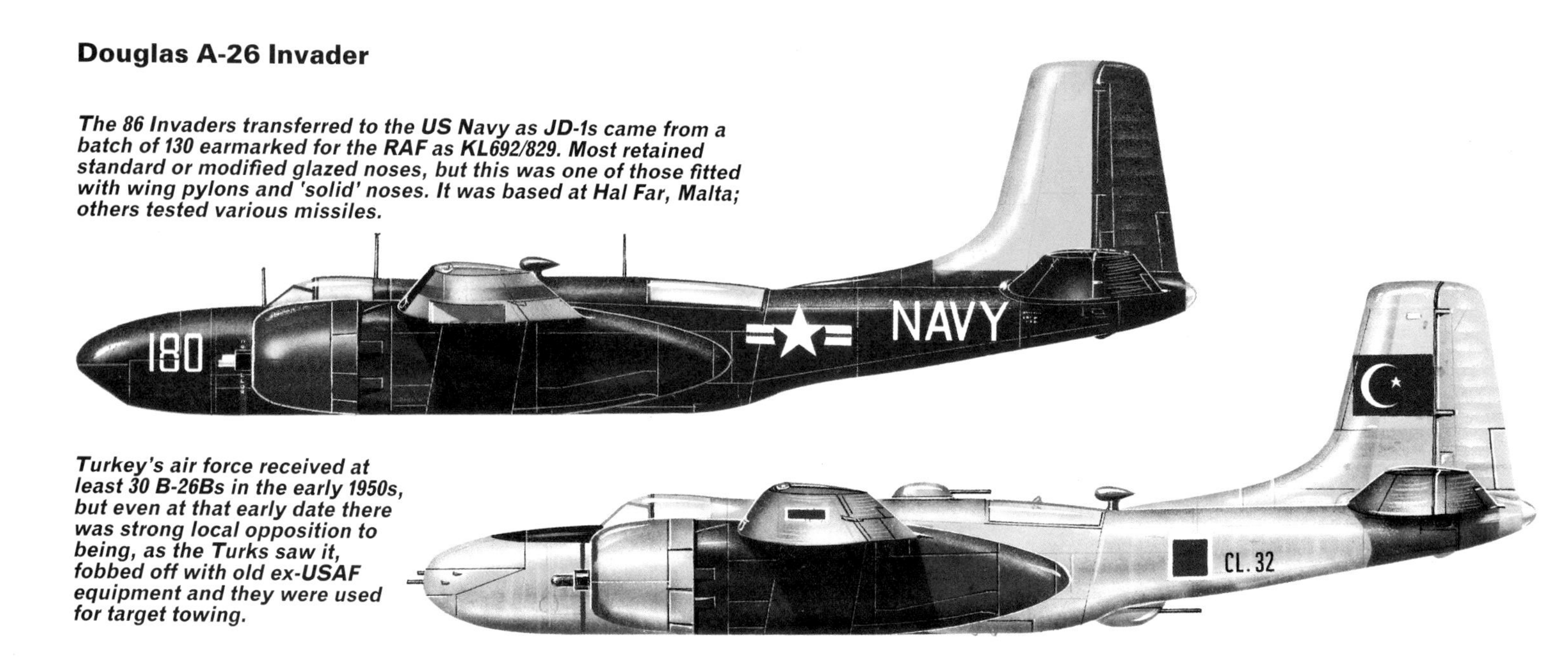

The 86 Invaders transferred to the US Navy as JD-1s came from a batch of 130 earmarked for the RAF as KL692/829. Most retained standard or modified glazed noses, but this was one of those fitted with wing pylons and 'solid' noses. It was based at Hal Far, Malta; others tested various missiles.

Turkey's air force received at least 30 B-26Bs in the early 1950s, but even at that early date there was strong local opposition to being, as the Turks saw it, fobbed off with old ex-USAF equipment and they were used for target towing.

Invader in combat

Rushed into combat with the 553rd Bomb Squadron at Great Dunmow in England by September 1944 and soon also operating in France and Italy, the Invader was flying air-to-ground missions against the Germans before its bugs were ironed out. Pilots were delighted with its manoeuvrability and ease of handling, but the A-26 began life with a needlessly complex and fatiguing instrument array, a weak nose gear that collapsed easily, and an early cockpit canopy that was difficult to hold in the 'open' position for bail-out. Time and attention resolved these problems, and A-26 pilots took pride in mastering a demanding but effective bombing machine.

In the European theatre of operations, Invaders flew 11,567 sorties and dropped 18,054 tons of bombs. The A-26 was also nimble enough to hold its own when intercepted by fighters. Major Myron L. Durkee of the 386th Bomb Group at Beaumont in France was credited with the probable kill of a Messerschmitt Me 262 jet fighter on 19 February 1945. Some 67 Invaders were lost to all causes in the European theatre, but A-26s also chalked up seven confirmed air-to-air kills.

Two Invaders were supplied briefly to the Royal Air Force, but the RAF apparently saw no significant benefit over other types then in service, such as the de Havilland Mosquito.

In the Pacific war, the Invader also progressed from an inauspicious beginning to respectable achievement. With its 1491-kW (2,000-hp) Pratt & Whitney R-2800-27 Double Wasp engines and sea-level speed of no less than 600 km/h (373 mph), the Invader was a potent anti-shipping and ground-attack weapon, but crews did not immediately take to it. A-20 pilots who had reigned supreme in their high, single-seat cabins now found themselves with a YOT ('you over there') in the navigator's right-hand jump-seat, essentially a co-pilot without controls. When rockets and bombs were expended in unison in a low-level pass, debris from the rockets' explosions damaged the underside of the Invader. In the belief that the new machine was unsuited for low-level work, the 5th Air Force commander, General George Kenney, actually requested not to convert from the A-20 to the A-26. But conversions went ahead, the A-26 also replacing North American B-25 Mitchells in some units. The A-26 served with the USAAF's 3rd, 41st and 319th Bomb Groups in operations against Formosa, Okinawa and Japan itself. Invaders were active near Nagasaki when it was razed by the war's second atomic bomb on 9 August 1945. After VJ Day the aircraft which may have arrived one war too soon became a familiar sight at Far East air bases, including those in Korea.

One-off prototypes

The XA-26D and XA-26E were one-off prototypes for Invader variants cancelled at the war's end, the latter variant being described by historian James C. Fahey as 'an X article no data released', though now known to have been a glazed-nose high-performance model with R-2800-83 radials and designed to match the performance of the XA-26D solid-nose model with 1566-kW (2,100-hp) R-2800-83s. In a post-war attempt to capitalise on the jet engine, a single Invader (44-34586) was converted to XA-26F with the addition of a 726-kg (1,600-lb) thrust General Electric I-16 (or J31) jet engine in the rear fuselage. This machine was also fitted with four-blade Hamilton Standard propellers, initially with large hub-type spinners. The natural-metal XA-26F apparently flew for several years but the jet

USAAF no. 41-39186 was one of the first to come off the Long Beach line, being an A-26B-15-DL. It is shown in combat service in 1944 with the US 553rd BS, 386th BG, based at Great Dunmow and then Beaumont-sur-Oise. Like most A-26 units it converted from the original B-26, the Martin Marauder.

Often omitted from development histories are the numerous 50-plus late production A-26Cs completed for night attack and reconnaissance. Painted black, they had either the lower or both turrets deleted and nav/bombing radar in the forward part of the bomb bay. They were active between 1946-55.

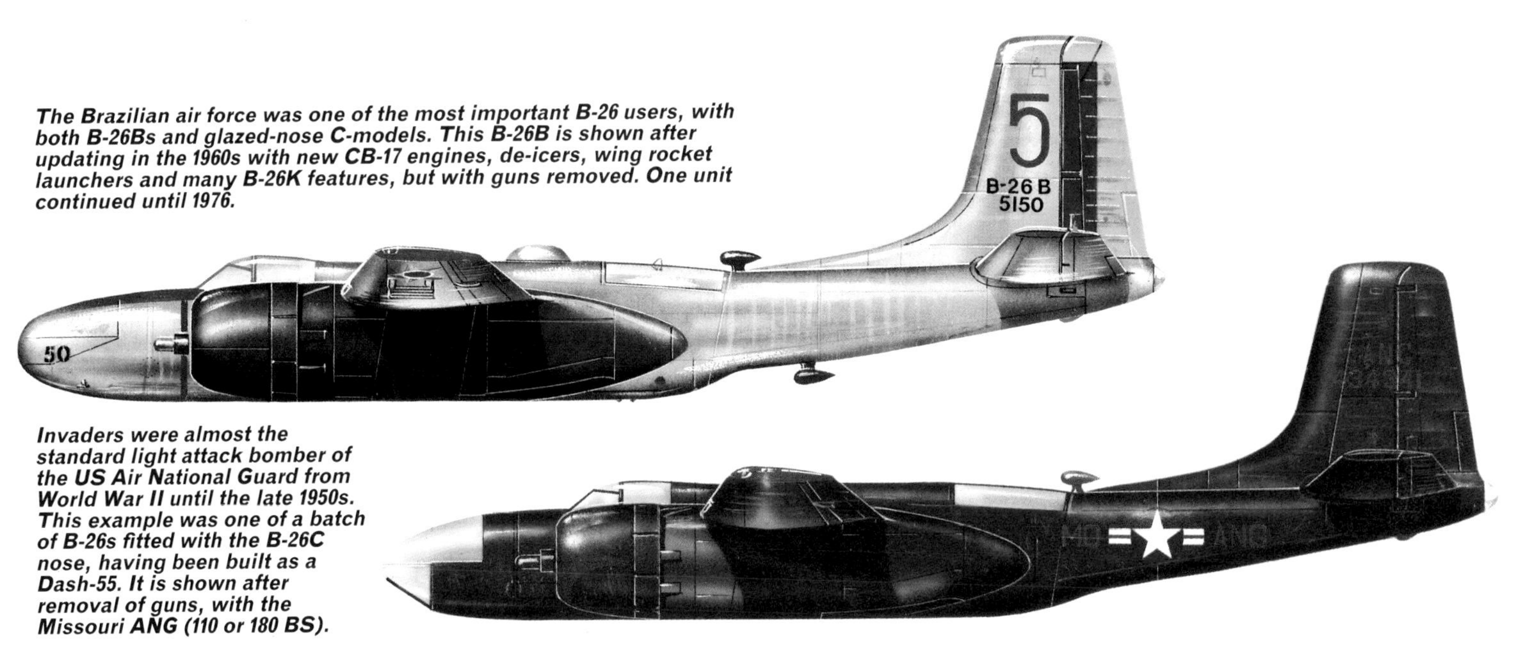

The Brazilian air force was one of the most important B-26 users, with both B-26Bs and glazed-nose C-models. This B-26B is shown after updating in the 1960s with new CB-17 engines, de-icers, wing rocket launchers and many B-26K features, but with guns removed. One unit continued until 1976.

Invaders were almost the standard light attack bomber of the US Air National Guard from World War II until the late 1950s. This example was one of a batch of B-26s fitted with the B-26C nose, having been built as a Dash-55. It is shown after removal of guns, with the Missouri ANG (110 or 180 BS).

engine installation, which markedly reduced the Invader's range, never found practical application.

The North Korean assault on South Korea on 25 June 1950 followed by massive Chinese intervention in November, created a war of relatively short distance and intense battlefield environments where the durability and load-carrying capability of the B-26 Invader were all-important. The B-26 (as it had been redesignated in 1947) proved effective against tanks and truck convoys and was later unleashed on more general, high-altitude bombing missions. Solid-nosed B-26B and glazed-nosed B-26C Invaders also flew night intruder missions against Communist rail lines and other targets. At first, only crude searchlights and flares were available. On 14 September 1951, flying a B-26B (43-49770), Captain John Walmsley attacked a large convoy, hit a train, and when out of ordnance and ammunition loitered in the area under heavy fire illuminating targets for his wingman. Walmsley was shot down and killed, the inevitable consequence for his acceptance of enormous risk; he became one of only four airmen in the 1950-3 Korean War to received the highest American award, the Medal of Honor.

The USAF's 3rd, 17th, 47th and 452nd Bomb Groups flew B-26 Invaders in the bulk of Korean operations. The 67th Tactical Reconnaissance Wing flew RB-26C aircraft, with dorsal turret removed, on photo missions. In Korea, the Invader performed well in all regimes, including low-level strikes, and scored several probable air-to-air kills against Chinese Mikoyan-Gurevich MiG-15s.

The most important foreign user of the Invader was the French Armée de l'Air, which had up to 180 B-26B, B-26C and RB-26C aircraft, most of them committed to the Indo-China war. France's 1946-54 struggle with Viet Minh forces tested the B-26 Invader under crude, difficult tropical conditions, culminating in the siege at Dien Bien Phu where Invaders bombed and strafed Communist forces in the surrounding hills. French pilots liked the Invader for its toughness, firepower and handling characteristics. They flew B-26s again in their 1956-62 conflict in Algeria.

Nine ex-USAF B-26Bs were provided to Saudi Arabia in 1955 to make up the first operational squadron in that country's fledgling air force. A 1961 survey found Invaders in no fewer than 21 countries, mostly in Latin America but also in the Congo and Indonesia. 1961 also saw American UN Ambassador Adlai Stevenson hold up a photo of a B-26 in the General Assembly and claim that free Cubans had escaped from Castro's air force in the bomber. Stevenson had been purposely kept in the dark on the CIA-supported, White House-approved invasion by Cuban exiles at the Bay of Pigs, and was enraged to learn that he had been telling UN delegates a fake story designed to justify B-26 pounding of the insurgents' beach-head. Apart from being a total fiasco, the Bay of Pigs invasion was the only instance when B-26 Invaders fought each other – CIA-backed exiles battling members of Castro's air arm.

'Counter Invader' in Vietnam

War clouds were gathering elsewhere. In 1962, the US supplied B-26B and RB-26C Invaders to South Vietnam, where they were flown in combat with American crews and South Vietnamese mark-

Because of its all-round excellence, fully appreciated by VJ Day, the A-26 was used for many 'hack' duties in post-war years. Here Tulsa-built 44-35350 is seen after conversion as a DB-26C (D for Drone director), with two of the first Ryan Firebee turbo-jet-engined targets under its wings.

When Beech Aircraft was developing its inflight-refuelling hosereel pod, as used under the wingtips of 707 aircraft, it used a company-owned B-26C with the pod carried under the fuselage. The recipient here is another company aircraft, the MS.760 Paris, used from 1959.

ings. Wing stress problems, resulting in the loss of one airframe and its crew when a wing was literally ripped off, brought an end to B-26 operations in Vietnam in early 1964. However, the US Air Force had decided that the type could have a rebirth if low-hour airframes could be converted for the special combat conditions of the South East Asia war. The On Mark Engineering Company, one of several firms which had also produced executive transport versions of the B-26, made the conversion and produced a virtually new machine, the YB-26K, first flown in production form in May 1964.

The B-26K was outwardly similar to the Invaders which had come before it, but on the inside it was a new aeroplane. The fuselage was remanufactured and had the twin turrets removed, while the wings were rebuilt and strengthened, the tail section was enlarged, and new Pratt & Whitney R-2800-52W engines with reversible propellers and feathering controls were installed. The YB-26K had eight underwing hardpoints and six wing guns in addition to the nose guns. Wing guns were deleted on the 40 B-26K machines which followed, all but one with solid noses. While the camouflaged B-26K was being tested at Edwards AFB, California, in the Congo and in the Panama Canal Zone, the USAF completely obfuscated the situation by redesignating the 40 B-26K aircraft (63-17630/17679) as the A-26A. The A-26A (B-26K) was moderately successful in the conventional strike role in South Vietnam and was used for 'black cover' operations by the USAF's 609th Special Operations at Nakhom Phanom AB, Thailand as late as 1970.

Flying the Invader

Piloting the A-26 Invader was an experience. 'It was graceful, potent and extremely unforgiving' says Lieutenant-Colonel Clifford Erly, who flew the A-26C with the 416th Bomb Group in the European theatre. Wide-track mainwheels and tricycle gear gave the A-26 excellent ground-handling characteristics. On take-off, it tended to 'eat up runway' says Erly, especially with a full ordnance load, 'but once you rotated and started to climb out, there was no ambiguity about it.' A revised instrument layout made the aircraft easy to handle and the Invader's tall single tail assured responsiveness in turns.

Visibility was not as good as on the A-20 because the engines were placed closer inboard and further forward, but the pilot remained able to see ahead and above remarkably well. Flight controls were provided for the pilot only (until the dual-control B-26K) and the flight deck was roomy but cluttered. The 'YOT' in the right seat (navigator or flight engineer depending on the mission) was less comfortable than those for the pilot or the dorsal radio operator/gunner. The pilot had a heavy control yoke and throttles rather far forward for his right-hand reach. The bomb-aimers' station on the glazed-nose A-26C, reached through a nosewheel hatch, provided a Norden bombsight and a hand-held bomb-release button attached to a long chord to permit movement.

Best-looking of many of the executive conversions, the L. B. Smith Tempo II had a stretched fuselage seating up to 13 in pressurised accommodation. With R-2800-CB17 engines and much extra fuel the Tempo II could fly coast-to-coast at 482 km/h (300 mph). Note the leading-edge de-icer boots.

'Once rid of the bombs it was a real fighter,' says Erly. 'Not only were we almost as fast as any fighter in the air, we were almost as manoeuvrable. We had studies showing that at some altitudes, under some conditions, we could turn inside a Messerschmitt 109. I never heard of a fighter successfully engaging an A-26 because we had the choice. We could run away from him in the straightaway, or we could turn and fight . . .'

Although executive transport conversions of the Invader abounded in the 1950s, in the era before executive transports were designed as such from the outset, relatively few Invaders survive today. A couple are flying with 'warbird' groups in the USA. An example of the B-26K stands as a gate guardian outside Hulbert Field, Florida, home of the US Air Force Special Operations, a fitting memorial to a type flown in combat by men not born when it was designed.

Douglas A-26B Invader cutaway drawing key

1 Starboard wing tip
2 Starboard navigation light
3 Water tank
4 Water tank filler cap
5 Aileron hinge control
6 Starboard aileron
7 Aileron tab
8 Landing and taxiing light
9 Control cables
10 Bombardier nose configuration, A-26C
11 Optically flat bomb sight window
12 Bomb bay doors
13 Ventral periscope gunsight
14 Ventral turret
15 Starboard outboard flap
16 Wing access panels
17 Chordwise stiffeners
18 Double slotted flap segments
19 Oil cooler radiator
20 Cooler intake ducting
21 Ram air intake to oil cooler
22 Nacelle fuel tank, capacity 300 US gal (1136 litres)
23 Wing inboard fuel tank, capacity 100 US gal (379 litres)
24 Control runs
25 Oil tank filler
26 Oil tank
27 Carburettor intake ducting
28 Exhaust stubs
29 Cowling air flaps
30 Pratt & Whitney R-2800-27 Double Wasp, two-row 18-cylinder radial engine
31 Carburettor ram air intake
32 Propeller reduction gearbox
33 Propeller hub mechanism
34 Three-bladed propeller
35 Detachable engine cowlings
36 General purpose nose configuration, A-26B
37 Machine-gun barrels
38 Four 0.5-in (12.7-mm) machine-guns, starboard side
39 Spent cartridge case chutes
40 Gun bay bracing strut
41 Two 0.5-in (12.7-mm) machine-guns, port side
42 Ammunition feed chutes
43 Ammunition boxes
44 Pitot tube
45 Nosewheel torque scissors
46 Rearward retracting nosewheel
47 Shock absorber leg strut
48 Nosewheel doors
49 Nosewheel bay/flight deck floor support construction
50 Rudder pedals
51 Interchangeable nose joint bulkhead
52 Autopilot controls
53 Back of instrument panel
54 Fixed foresight
55 Windscreen panels
56 Instrument panel shroud
57 Reflector sight
58 Clear vision panel
59 Control column
60 Pilot's seat
61 Pilot's side window panel/entry hatch
62 Bomb release controls
63 Bombardier/navigator's seat
64 Canopy hatch handles
65 Bombardier/navigator's side canopy/entry hatch
66 Oxygen regulator
67 Radio racks
68 Radio receivers and transmitters
69 Bomb-bay armoured roof panel
70 Wing root fillet
71 Armoured wing spar bulkhead
72 Hydraulic accumulators
73 Air filter
74 De-icing valve
75 Aerial mast
76 Double slotted flap inboard section
77 Wing de-icing fluid reservoir
78 De-icing fluid pump
79 Starboard bomb rack, five 100-lb (45-kg) HE bombs

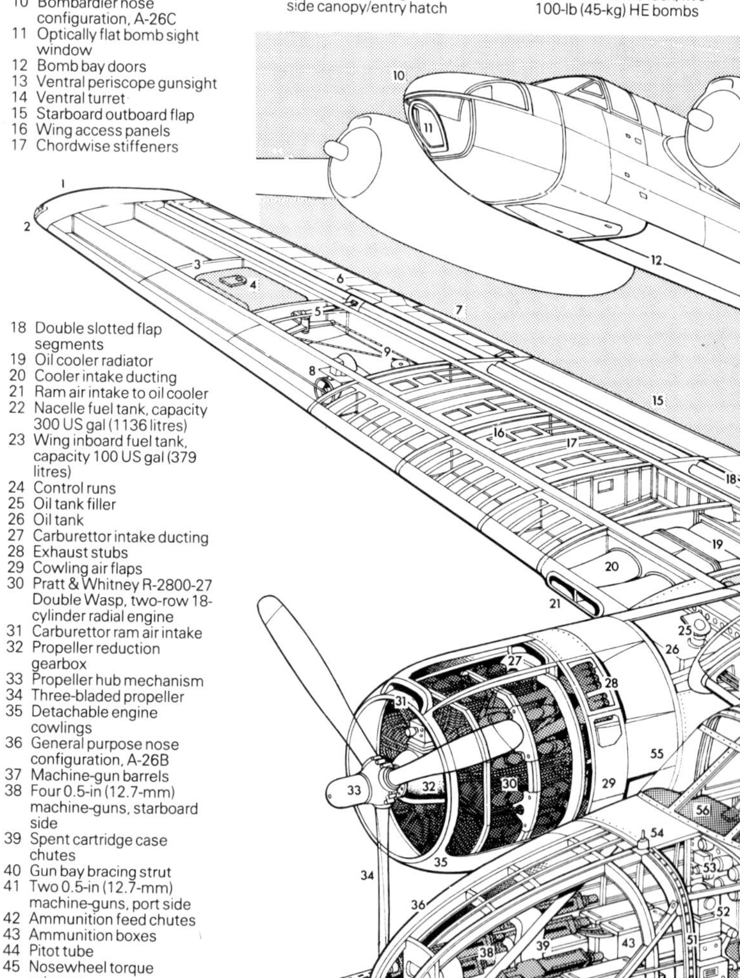

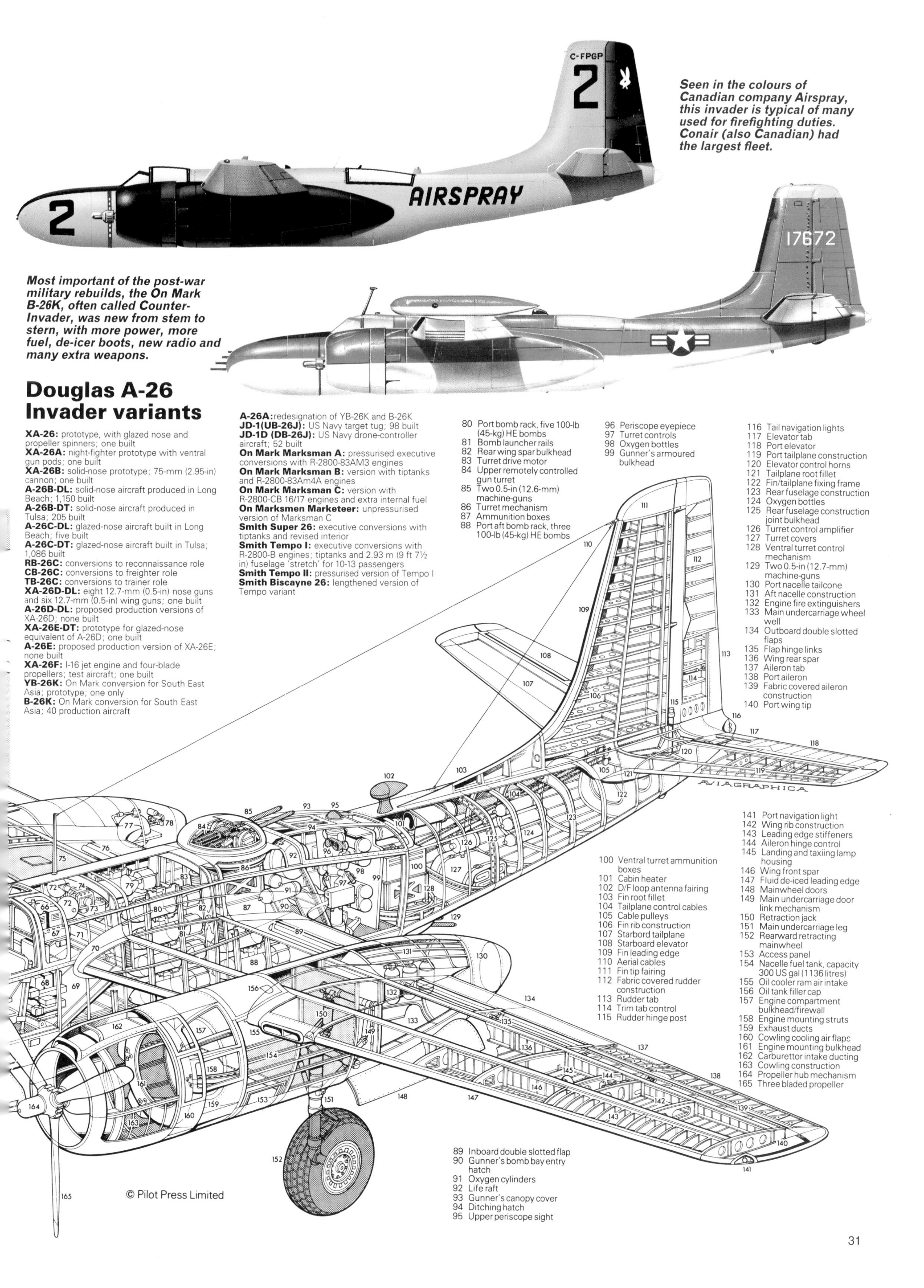

Seen in the colours of Canadian company Airspray, this invader is typical of many used for firefighting duties. Conair (also Canadian) had the largest fleet.

Most important of the post-war military rebuilds, the On Mark B-26K, often called Counter-Invader, was new from stem to stern, with more power, more fuel, de-icer boots, new radio and many extra weapons.

Douglas A-26 Invader variants

XA-26: prototype, with glazed nose and propeller spinners; one built
XA-26A: night-fighter prototype with ventral gun pods; one built
XA-26B: solid-nose prototype; 75-mm (2.95-in) cannon; one built
A-26B-DL: solid-nose aircraft produced in Long Beach; 1,150 built
A-26B-DT: solid-nose aircraft produced in Tulsa; 205 built
A-26C-DL: glazed-nose aircraft built in Long Beach; five built
A-26C-DT: glazed-nose aircraft built in Tulsa; 1,086 built
RB-26C: conversions to reconnaissance role
CB-26C: conversions to freighter role
TB-26C: conversions to trainer role
XA-26D-DL: eight 12.7-mm (0.5-in) nose guns and six 12.7-mm (0.5-in) wing guns; one built
A-26D-DL: proposed production versions of XA-26D; none built
XA-26E-DT: prototype for glazed-nose equivalent of A-26D; one built
A-26E: proposed production version of XA-26E; none built
XA-26F: I-16 jet engine and four-blade propellers; test aircraft; one built
YB-26K: On Mark conversion for South East Asia; prototype; one only
B-26K: On Mark conversion for South East Asia; 40 production aircraft
A-26A: redesignation of YB-26K and B-26K
JD-1(UB-26J): US Navy target tug; 98 built
JD-1D (DB-26J): US Navy drone-controller aircraft; 52 built
On Mark Marksman A: pressurised executive conversions with R-2800-83AM3 engines
On Mark Marksman B: version with tiptanks and R-2800-83Am4A engines
On Mark Marksman C: version with R-2800-CB 16/17 engines and extra internal fuel
On Marksmen Marketeer: unpressurised version of Marksman C
Smith Super 26: executive conversions with tiptanks and revised interior
Smith Tempo I: executive conversions with R-2800-B engines; tiptanks and 2.93 m (9 ft 7½ in) fuselage 'stretch' for 10-13 passengers
Smith Tempo II: pressurised version of Tempo I
Smith Biscayne 26: lengthened version of Tempo variant

Douglas A-26 Invader

Specification

On Mark A-26A (B-26K) Counter Invader

Type: two-seat attack bomber

Powerplant: two 1864-kW (2,500-hp) Pratt & Whitney R-2800-103 W Double Wasp 18-cylinder piston engines

Performance: maximum speed (clean) 587 km/h (365 mph) at medium altitudes; service ceiling (maximum weight) 6555 m (21,500 ft); typical range 2140 km (1,330 miles)

Weights: empty equipped 10748 kg (23,695 lb); loaded (maximum external stores) 19677 kg (43,380 lb)

Dimensions: span 21.34 m (70 ft 0 in); length 15.6 m (51 ft 2 in), 1 in longer with bombardier nose; height 5.6 m (18 ft 5 in); wing area 50.17 m^2 (540 sq ft)

Armament: in version illustrated, eight 12.7-mm (0.5-in) nose guns (two more in dorsal turret if fitted) plus internal bay and eight wing pylons for wide range of stores up to overall limit of 5443 kg (12,000 lb)

As rebuilt by On Mark Engineering in 1965-7, the B-26K was to all intents and purposes a new aircraft, though the original airframe was older than many of its pilots. This example, USAF 64-17645, was one which saw much action in South East Asia, its main operating unit being the 609th SOS (Special Operations Squadron), 56th SOW, based at Nakhon Phanom AB, Thailand, in 1966. Visible features include the bigger main tyres to support the greatly increased weights, steerable nose gear, tip tanks, extra avionics aerials (antennae) and roof fairing over the observer cockpit instead of a turret. Not visible are the Hytrol anti-skid brakes, fittings and connectors for a six-camera weapon-bay pack and attachments for six 454-kg (1,000-lb) thrust assisted take-off rockets under the rear fuselage. The installations of six or eight guns in the wings were not fitted in Vietnam.

Boeing B-29 Superfortress

No other aircraft ever combined so many technological advances as the B-29. Designed for a specific strategic task, it later spawned the double-deck Stratocruiser airliner, the KC-97 tanker/transport and laid the foundations for the super-successful Boeing airliner series. It also provided the Soviet Union with the starting block for the entire Tupolev heavy aircraft lineage.

It is probable that a detailed analysis of the Soviet 'Blackjack' swing-wing bomber of the 1980s would unearth design features that can be traced right back to the B-29. And the Boeing B-29 Superfortress was started more than three years before the USA entered World War II, in October 1938. In one of his last acts before he was killed in a crash at Burbank the US Army Air Corps Chief of Staff, General Oscar Westover, had officially established a requirement for a new super-bomber to succeed the Boeing B-17, at a time when the B-17 itself was being denied funds by the Congress. Despite a totally negative reaction from the War Department, procurement chief General Oliver Echols never gave up in his fight to keep the super-bomber alive, and it had the backing of 'Hap' Arnold, Westover's successor. The bomber was to be pressurised to fly very fast at high altitude: the figures for speed (628 km/h; 390 mph), range (8582 km; 5,333 miles) and military load were staggering.

At the Boeing Airplane Company in Seattle there was, at least, experience of large pressurised aircraft, unlike all other companies, but there seemed no way to reconcile the conflicting factors. For most of 1939 the answer seemed to be to fit Pratt & Whitney's slim sleeve-valve liquid-cooled engines inside the wing, but newly hired George Schairer soon pointed out that as the biggest drag item was the wing, the best course was to make the wing as small as possible and not try to put engines inside it. (Thus began a basic philosophy which saw sharp contrast between the Boeing B-47 and the British V-bombers, and has continued to today's Boeing Models 757 and 767.) How does one pressurise a fuselage containing enormous bomb doors? The answer here was to make the colossal bomb bays unpressurised and link the front and rear pressure cabins by a sealed tunnel. Chief engineer Wellwood Beall was first to crawl through the mock-up tunnel in January 1940.

By March 1940 the demands had increased, including 7258 kg

Dave's Dream ***was built as B-29-40-MO 44-27354, but it is pictured here with Major W. P. Swancutt in command, heading for Bikini Atoll on 1 July 1946, where the modified aircraft dropped the first post-war nuclear weapon. The 509th Composite Group named the aircraft for bombardier Dave Semple, killed in a B-29.***

(16,000 lb) of bombs for short-range missions, powered turrets, and far more protection including armour and self-sealing tanks. Weight had already leapt in stages from 21773 to 38556 kg (48,000 to 85,000 lb), and with the fresh demands the design finally rounded out at a daunting 54432 kg (120,000 lb). With just 161.55 m^2 (1,739 sq ft) of wing, the wing loading was going to be 336.9 kg/m^2 (69 lb/sq ft), about double the figure universally taken in 1940 as the desirable limit. Test pilot Eddie Allen was happy that the Boeing Model 345 would be flyable (just) if it had the biggest and most powerful high-lift flaps ever thought of, to reduce take-off and landing speeds to about 257 km/h (160 mph), which was about double the equivalent speed of such familiar machines as the B-17 and Supermarine Spitfire.

Funds from USAAC

As the the BEF was rescued from the beaches at Dunkirk the new bomber was designated the B-29, and in August the US Army Air Corps provided funds for two (later three) prototypes. Work was rushed ahead, but nobody knew how to stop guns and propeller mechanisms from freezing at far over 9145 m (30,000 ft), which Boeing was confident the aircraft could reach. The intense wing loading was all against the designers, but using four monster Wright R-3350 Duplex Cyclones, each with not one but two of General Electric's best turbochargers and driving 5.05-m (16-ft 7-in) Hamilton Standard four-blade propellers, the propulsion was equal to the task.

Behind the nose section were two giant bomb bays, from which an electric sequencing system released bombs alternately from front and rear to preserve the centre of gravity position. Between the two bays was a ring forming the structural heart of the aircraft and integral with the main wing box, the strongest aircraft part built up to that time. On the wing were four monster nacelles, which Schairer showed to have less drag than engines buried in a bigger wing. After four main gears had been studied, a way was found to fold simple two-wheel gears into the inboard nacelles. Fowler flaps were screwed out electrically to add 21 per cent to area of the wing, fighting a wing loading which by September 1940 reached 351.1 kg/m^2 (71.9 lb/sq ft) and climbed to a frightening 396 kg/m^2 (81.1 lb/sq ft) by the time of the first combat mission.

Behind the wing the rear pressure cabin had three sighting stations linked to two upper and two lower turrets, each with twin 12.7-mm (0.5-in) machine-guns. The electric fire control was

Boeing B-29 Superfortress cutaway drawing key

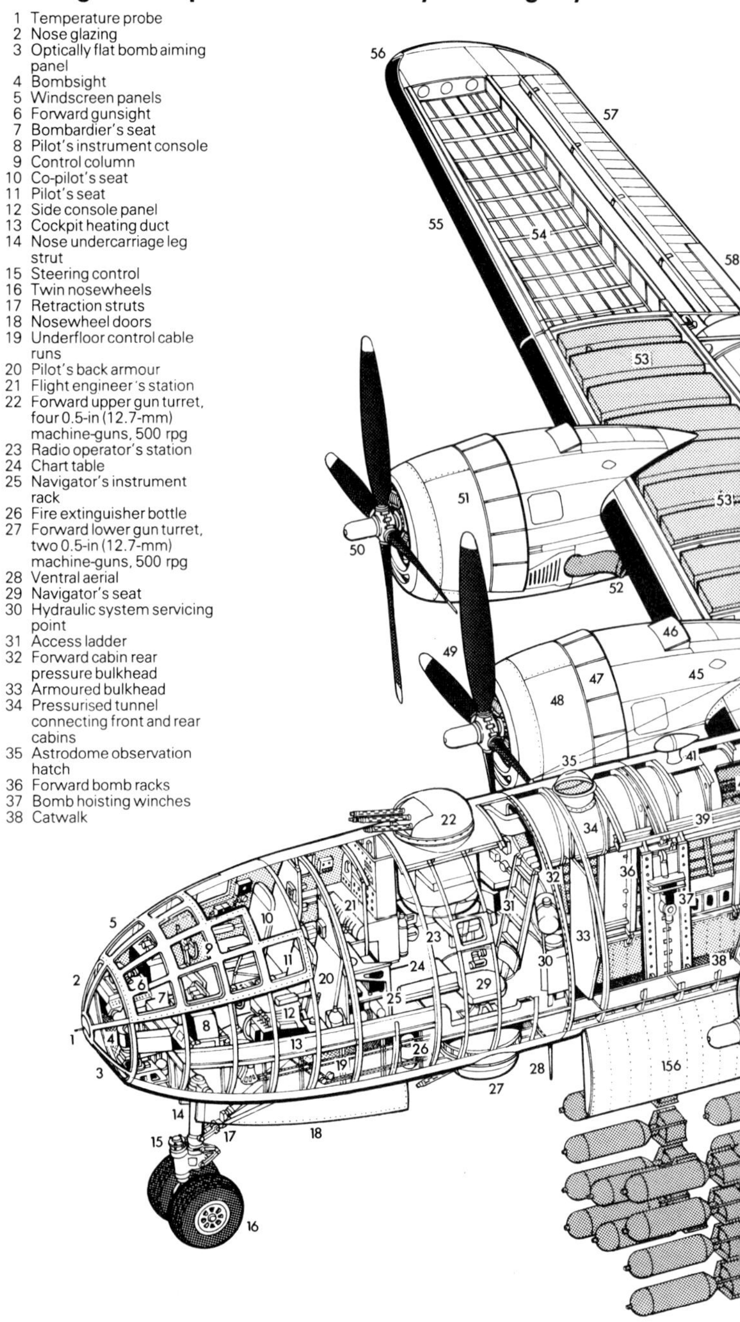

1 Temperature probe
2 Nose glazing
3 Optically flat bomb aiming panel
4 Bombsight
5 Windscreen panels
6 Forward gunsight
7 Bombardier's seat
8 Pilot's instrument console
9 Control column
10 Co-pilot's seat
11 Pilot's seat
12 Side console panel
13 Cockpit heating duct
14 Nose undercarriage leg strut
15 Steering control
16 Twin nosewheels
17 Retraction struts
18 Nosewheel doors
19 Underfloor control cable runs
20 Pilot's back armour
21 Flight engineer's station
22 Forward upper gun turret, four 0.5-in (12.7-mm) machine-guns, 500 rpg
23 Radio operator's station
24 Chart table
25 Navigator's instrument rack
26 Fire extinguisher bottle
27 Forward lower gun turret, two 0.5-in (12.7-mm) machine-guns, 500 rpg
28 Ventral aerial
29 Navigator's seat
30 Hydraulic system servicing point
31 Access ladder
32 Forward cabin rear pressure bulkhead
33 Armoured bulkhead
34 Pressurised tunnel connecting front and rear cabins
35 Astrodome observation hatch
36 Forward bomb racks
37 Bomb hoisting winches
38 Catwalk

One of very few surviving pictures of 'parasiting', this photograph was taken during trials in 1949-51 to see if a bomber really could tow fighters over long ranges. ETB-29A-60 44-62093 was much modified for Project Tom Tom, towing F-84D-1 Thunderjets 48-641 and 48-661. Another B-29 carried the XF-85 Goblin.

Boeing B-29 variants

XB-29: Boeing Model 345 prototypes (41-002, 41-003 and 41-18335)
YB-29: service-test aircraft with armament (41-36954/36967); total 14
B-29: main production by BW (Boeing Wichita), BA (Bell Airplane) and MO (Martin Omaha); total 1,62 BW, 357 BA and 204 MO
B-29A: span 43.36 m (142 ft 3 in), R-3350-57 or -59 engines, and four-gun forward upper turret; built Boeing Renton (BN); total 1,119
F-13A: conversions as strategic reconnaissance aircraft with large camera installations and long-range tanks; total 117
RB-29A: redesignation in 1948 of F-13A
TB-29A: conversions as crew trainers
ETB-29A: TB-29A modified for parasite attachments of F-84 jet fighters at wingtips (44-62093)
B-29B: R-3350-51 engines, defensive armament removed except tail turret; built by Bell (BA); total 3
EB-29B: conversion to launch XF-85 Goblin parasite jet from trapeze (44-84111)
B-29D: ex-XB-44, later became B-50
XB-29E: conversion to test different electronic defensive fire-control
B-29F: Arctic conversions of six aircraft
XB-29G: conversion (44-84043) to test experimental turbojets in pod extended below bomb bay
XB-29H: conversion of B-29A for different defensive armament
YB-29J: conversions (six) to test commercial R-3350 powerplants
RB-29J: conversions (two YB-29J) as multi-sensor reconnaissance aircraft; also called **FB-29J**
YKB-29J: conversions (two YB-29J) for tests of Boeing Flying Boom inflight-refuelling system
CB-29K: conversion to military cargo aircraft
B-29L: original designation of B-29MR
KB-29M: major programme of rebuilds as inflight-refuelling tankers (92) with British looped hose method
B-29MR: conversions (74) as receivers to link with inflight-refuelling hose
KB-29P: major programme of conversions (116) as inflight-refuelling tankers with Flying Boom for SA
YKB-29T: single conversion of KB-29M (45-21734) as triple-point tanker
DB-29: various conversions as drone and target directors
GB-29: conversions to launch the XS-1, X-1, X-2 and X-3 supersonic research aircraft

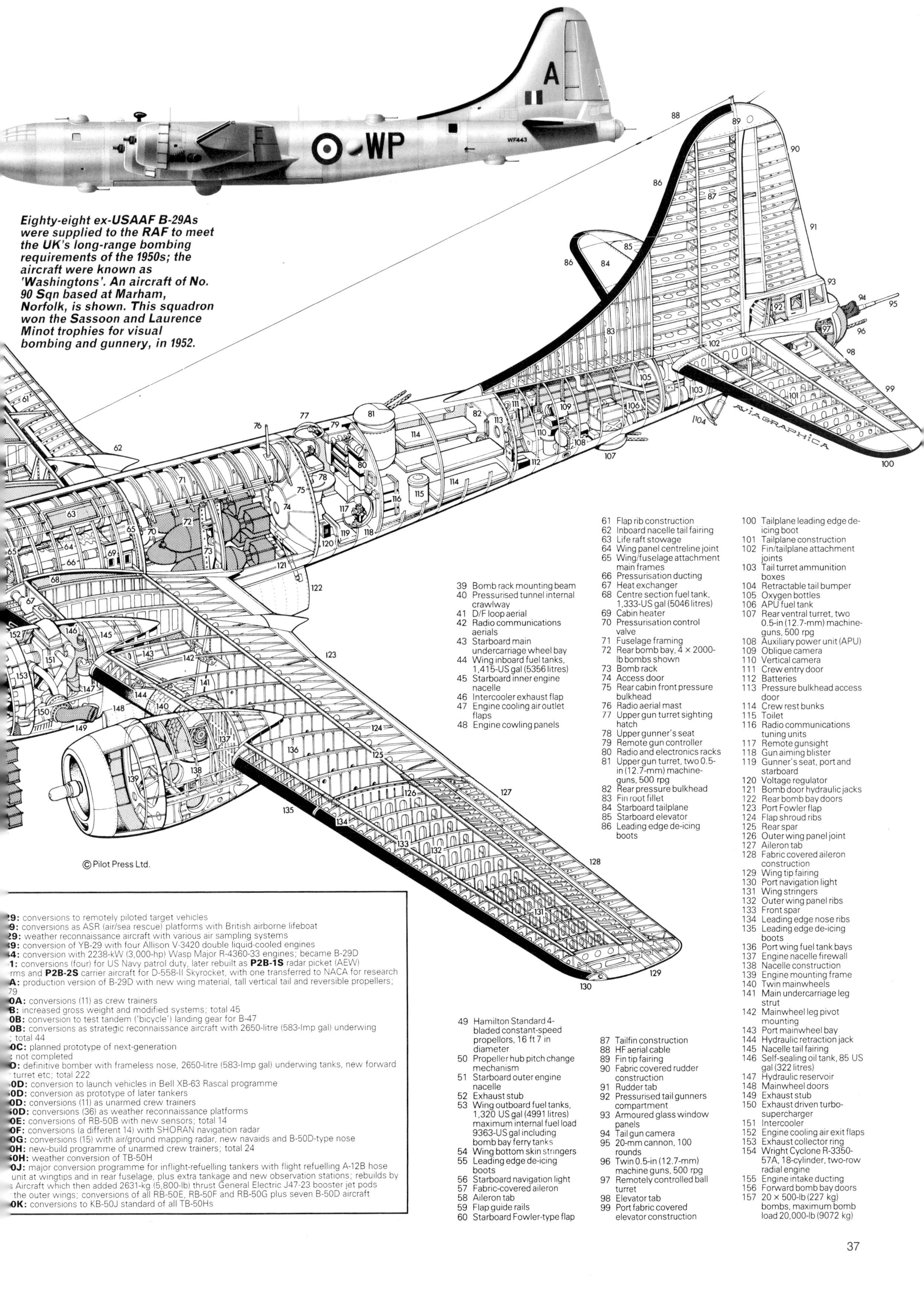

Eighty-eight ex-USAAF B-29As were supplied to the RAF to meet the UK's long-range bombing requirements of the 1950s; the aircraft were known as 'Washingtons'. An aircraft of No. 90 Sqn based at Marham, Norfolk, is shown. This squadron won the Sassoon and Laurence Minot trophies for visual bombing and gunnery, in 1952.

39 Bomb rack mounting beam
40 Pressurised tunnel internal crawlway
41 D/F loop aerial
42 Radio communications aerials
43 Starboard main undercarriage wheel bay
44 Wing inboard fuel tanks, 1,415-US gal (5356 litres)
45 Starboard inner engine nacelle
46 Intercooler exhaust flap
47 Engine cooling air outlet flaps
48 Engine cowling panels
49 Hamilton Standard 4-bladed constant-speed propellers, 16 ft 7 in diameter
50 Propeller hub pitch change mechanism
51 Starboard outer engine nacelle
52 Exhaust stub
53 Wing outboard fuel tanks, 1,320 US gal (4991 litres) maximum internal fuel load 9363-US gal including bomb bay ferry tanks
54 Wing bottom skin stringers
55 Leading edge de-icing boots
56 Starboard navigation light
57 Fabric-covered aileron
58 Aileron tab
59 Flap guide rails
60 Starboard Fowler-type flap
61 Flap rib construction
62 Inboard nacelle tail fairing
63 Life raft stowage
64 Wing panel centreline joint
65 Wing/fuselage attachment main frames
66 Pressurisation ducting
67 Heat exchanger
68 Centre section fuel tank, 1,333-US gal (5046 litres)
69 Cabin heater
70 Pressurisation control valve
71 Fuselage framing
72 Rear bomb bay, 4 × 2000-lb bombs shown
73 Bomb rack
74 Access door
75 Rear cabin front pressure bulkhead
76 Radio aerial mast
77 Upper gun turret sighting hatch
78 Upper gunner's seat
79 Remote gun controller
80 Radio and electronics racks
81 Upper gun turret, two 0.5-in (12.7-mm) machine-guns, 500 rpg
82 Rear pressure bulkhead
83 Fin root fillet
84 Starboard tailplane
85 Starboard elevator
86 Leading edge de-icing boots
87 Tailfin construction
88 HF aerial cable
89 Fin tip fairing
90 Fabric covered rudder construction
91 Rudder tab
92 Pressurised tail gunners compartment
93 Armoured glass window panels
94 Tail gun camera
95 20-mm cannon, 100 rounds
96 Twin 0.5-in (12.7-mm) machine guns, 500 rpg
97 Remotely controlled ball turret
98 Elevator tab
99 Port fabric covered elevator construction
100 Tailplane leading edge de-icing boot
101 Tailplane construction
102 Fin/tailplane attachment joints
103 Tail turret ammunition boxes
104 Retractable tail bumper
105 Oxygen bottles
106 APU fuel tank
107 Rear ventral turret, two 0.5-in (12.7-mm) machine-guns, 500 rpg
108 Auxiliary power unit (APU)
109 Oblique camera
110 Vertical camera
111 Crew entry door
112 Batteries
113 Pressure bulkhead access door
114 Crew rest bunks
115 Toilet
116 Radio communications tuning units
117 Remote gunsight
118 Gun aiming blister
119 Gunner's seat, port and starboard
120 Voltage regulator
121 Bomb door hydraulic jacks
122 Rear bomb bay doors
123 Port Fowler flap
124 Flap shroud ribs
125 Rear spar
126 Outer wing panel joint
127 Aileron tab
128 Fabric covered aileron construction
129 Wing tip fairing
130 Port navigation light
131 Wing stringers
132 Outer wing panel ribs
133 Front spar
134 Leading edge nose ribs
135 Leading edge de-icing boots
136 Port wing fuel tank bays
137 Engine nacelle firewall
138 Nacelle construction
139 Engine mounting frame
140 Twin mainwheels
141 Main undercarriage leg strut
142 Mainwheel leg pivot mounting
143 Port mainwheel bay
144 Hydraulic retraction jack
145 Nacelle tail fairing
146 Self-sealing oil tank, 85 US gal (322 litres)
147 Hydraulic reservoir
148 Mainwheel doors
149 Exhaust stub
150 Exhaust driven turbo-supercharger
151 Intercooler
152 Engine cooling air exit flaps
153 Exhaust collector ring
154 Wright Cyclone R-3350-57A, 18-cylinder, two-row radial engine
155 Engine intake ducting
156 Forward bomb bay doors
157 20 × 500-lb (227 kg) bombs, maximum bomb load 20,000-lb (9072 kg)

29: conversions to remotely piloted target vehicles
9: conversions as ASR (air/sea rescue) platforms with British airborne lifeboat
29: weather reconnaissance aircraft with various air sampling systems
39: conversion of YB-29 with four Allison V-3420 double liquid-cooled engines
4: conversion with 2238-kW (3,000-hp) Wasp Major R-4360-33 engines; became B-29D
1: conversions (four) for US Navy patrol duty, later rebuilt as **P2B-1S** radar picket (AEW)
rms and **P2B-2S** carrier aircraft for D-558-II Skyrocket, with one transferred to NACA for research
A: production version of B-29D with new wing material, tall vertical tail and reversible propellers;
79
0A: conversions (11) as crew trainers
B: increased gross weight and modified systems; total 45
0B: conversion to test tandem ('bicycle') landing gear for B-47
0B: conversions as strategic reconnaissance aircraft with 2650-litre (583-Imp gal) underwing
; total 44
0C: planned prototype of next-generation
: not completed
D: definitive bomber with frameless nose, 2650-litre (583-Imp gal) underwing tanks, new forward
turret etc; total 222
0D: conversion to launch vehicles in Bell XB-63 Rascal programme
0D: conversion as prototype of later tankers
0D: conversions (11) as unarmed crew trainers
0D: conversions (36) as weather reconnaissance platforms
0E: conversions of RB-50B with new sensors; total 14
0F: conversions (a different 14) with SHORAN navigation radar
0G: conversions (15) with air/ground mapping radar, new navaids and B-50D-type nose
0H: new-build programme of unarmed crew trainers; total 24
0H: weather conversion of TB-50H
0J: major conversion programme for inflight-refuelling tankers with flight refuelling A-12B hose
unit at wingtips and in rear fuselage, plus extra tankage and new observation stations; rebuilds by
s Aircraft which then added 2631-kg (5,800-lb) thrust General Electric J47-23 booster jet pods
the outer wings; conversions of all RB-50E, RB-50F and RB-50G plus seven B-50D aircraft
0K: conversions to KB-50J standard of all TB-50Hs

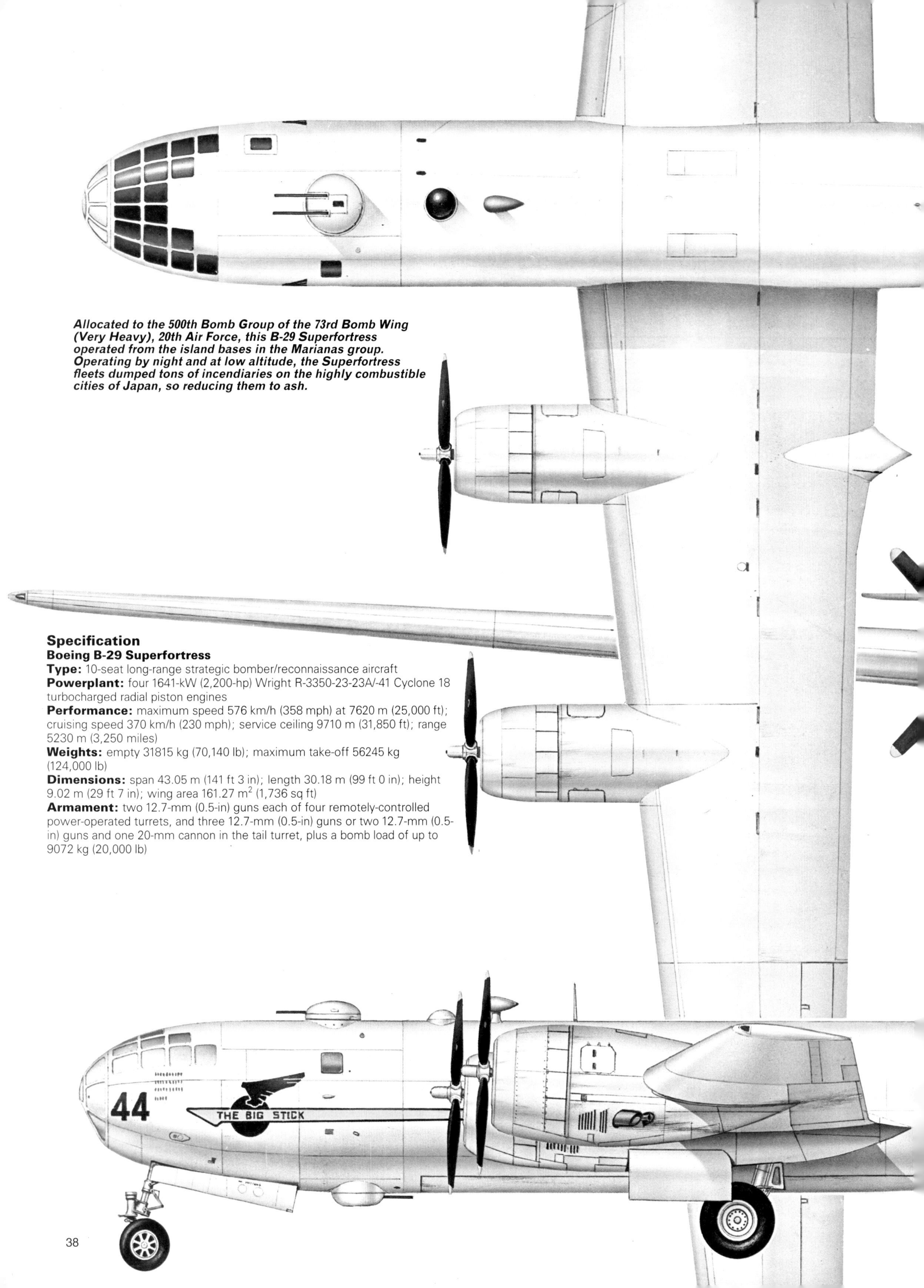

Allocated to the 500th Bomb Group of the 73rd Bomb Wing (Very Heavy), 20th Air Force, this B-29 Superfortress operated from the island bases in the Marianas group. Operating by night and at low altitude, the Superfortress fleets dumped tons of incendiaries on the highly combustible cities of Japan, so reducing them to ash.

Specification

Boeing B-29 Superfortress

Type: 10-seat long-range strategic bomber/reconnaissance aircraft

Powerplant: four 1641-kW (2,200-hp) Wright R-3350-23-23A/-41 Cyclone 18 turbocharged radial piston engines

Performance: maximum speed 576 km/h (358 mph) at 7620 m (25,000 ft); cruising speed 370 km/h (230 mph); service ceiling 9710 m (31,850 ft); range 5230 m (3,250 miles)

Weights: empty 31815 kg (70,140 lb); maximum take-off 56245 kg (124,000 lb)

Dimensions: span 43.05 m (141 ft 3 in); length 30.18 m (99 ft 0 in); height 9.02 m (29 ft 7 in); wing area 161.27 m^2 (1,736 sq ft)

Armament: two 12.7-mm (0.5-in) guns each of four remotely-controlled power-operated turrets, and three 12.7-mm (0.5-in) guns or two 12.7-mm (0.5-in) guns and one 20-mm cannon in the tail turret, plus a bomb load of up to 9072 kg (20,000 lb)

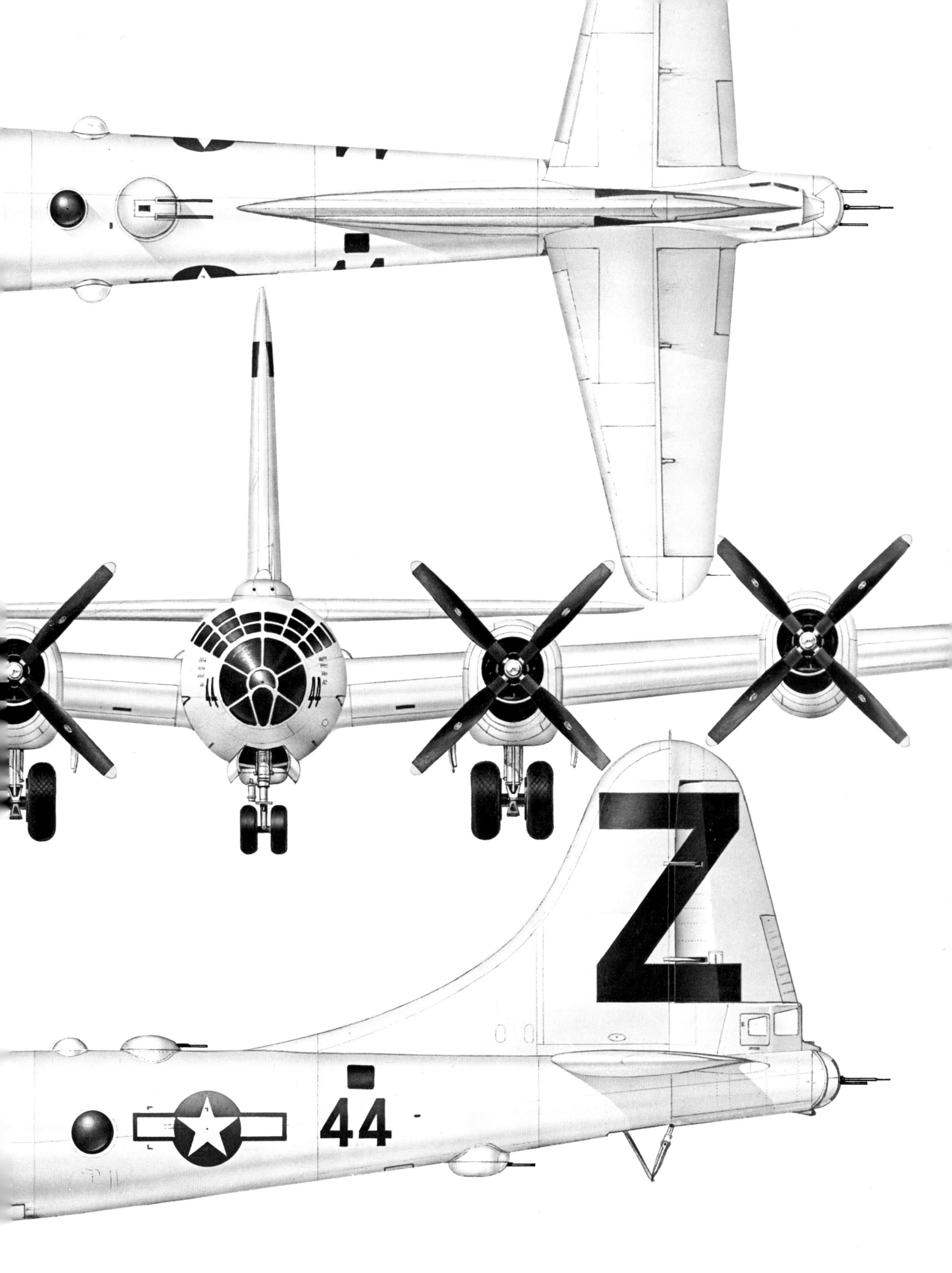
Z
44

Boeing B-29 Superfortress

Together with Consolidated C-87s and other modified B-24s, the B-29 was pressed into service as a tanker to bring to Chinese B-29 airbases the fuel needed for the missions over Japan. Many were permanently modified as tankers, an example being B-29-1-BW 42-6242, one of the first production block, which served with the 486th BG.

normally set so that the top station controlled either or both of the upper turrets, the side stations the lower rear turret, and the bombardier the forward lower turret, but control could be overridden or switched (because gunners could be knocked out in action). In the extreme tail was another gunner driving a turret with two 12.7-mm (0.5-in) guns and a 20-mm cannon.

In any case, over 2,000 B-29s were to be built before this turret could come into production, because immediately after Pearl Harbor a colossal manufacturing programme was organised, involving vast new plants across the nation. Major parts were made in over 60 new factories, the enormous nacelles, each as big as a P-47, coming from a new Cleveland facility operated by the Fisher Body Division of General Motors. Final assembly was organised at three of the world's largest buildings, Boeing at Wichita, Martin at Omaha and Bell at Marietta (today the same building houses the Lockheed-Georgia Company). Later yet another line was set up at Boeing Renton. All this had been organised before the olive-drab XB-29 (41-002) had even flown, but from the first flight, on 21 September 1942 (initially using three-blade propellers), it was clear that the B-29 was going to be a winner. It could so easily have been what test pilots then called 'a dog'; and one of the firms delegated to build B-29s was convinced Boeing's figures were far too optimistic and that the whole programme was a giant mistake. What made the B-29, by 1942 named Superfortress, now vitally important was that it was obviously going to be the only aircraft with the range to attack Japan.

To say that the good results of ship 41-002 were a relief would be an understatement. Far more money (three billion dollars) had been invested in the B-29 programme long before its wheels left the ground than in any other project in the history of any nation. At the same time the technical snags were severe, and multiplied. Many, such as powerplant fires and runaway propellers, were highly dangerous, and three months into the flight programme the prototypes had logged just 31 of the 180 hours scheduled.

Even when the Superfortresses trickled and then poured off the lines, they were so complex that nobody in uniform fully understood them. All went to a modification centre at Salina, Kansas, where over 9,900 faults in the first 175, urgently needed for the new 20th Bomb Wing, were bulldozed right by a task force of 600 men in 'The Battle of Kansas'. Sheer manpower and the USA's mighty industrial power forced the obstacles out of the way, and the B-29s not only began racking up the hours but their baffled crews gradually learned how to manage them, how to fly straight and level in a goldfish bowl without continuously using instruments, and above all how to get something faintly resembling the published range with heavy bombloads. Air miles per pound of fuel were improved by exactly 100 per cent between January and March 1944. And the complex systems grew reliable in the ultra-cold of 10060 m (33,000 ft).

The very first Superfortress was XB-29 no. 41-002, design of which took place in 1939-40, ready for a first flight on 21 September 1942. Olive-drab and grey, it had three-blade propellers, no defensive turret system and numerous details which were later altered, yet the basic airframe was almost identical to production B-29s.

On 5 June 1944 the first combat mission was flown from Kharagpur, India, to Bangkok; the worst problem was an unexpected tropical storm. On 15 June the first of the raids on Japan was mounted, from Chengtu (one of many newly bulldozed B-29 strips in China) to the Yawata steel works. The specially created 20th Air Force grew in muscle, and in October 1944 the first B-29s arrived on newly laid runways on the Marianas islands of Tinian, Saipan and Guam, just taken from the enemy. Swiftly the numbers grew as the mighty plants back home poured out B-29s and B-29As with 0.3 m (12 in) more span and the four-gun front turret, while Bell added 311 B-29Bs with all armament stripped except that in the tail, making a considerable difference in reduced weight and complexity. The B-29B was made possible by the patchy fighter opposition, and many Superfortresses were similarly stripped in the field.

Moreover, the commander of the XXI Bomber Command, Major-General Curtis LeMay, boldly decided to bomb Tokyo by night from low level, with a full load of incendiaries. There were many reasons for this, but the chief ones were that it promised much greater bombloads and the elimination of bombing errors attributable to jetstream winds. This policy, totally at variance with the idea of high-altitude day formations, resulted in the greatest firestorms the world has ever seen, and the biggest casualties ever caused by air attack. They were far greater than the 75,000 of Hiroshima, hit by the 20-kiloton 'Little Boy' atom bomb dropped on 6 August 1945 from Colonel Paul Tibbetts' B-29 *Enola Gay,* or the 35,000 of Nagasaki hit by the 20-kiloton 'Fat Man' dropped on 9 August from *Bock's Car.* The war ended five days later.

Many modifications

Only by the incredibly bold decision to go into the biggest multi-company production programme ever organised long before the first flight, did the B-29 manage to make so large a contribution to World War II. By VJ Day more than 2,000 were actually with combat crews, and though 5,000-plus were cancelled days later the manufacturing programme was slowed progressively, and did not close until May 1946, by which time 3,960 B-29s had been built. Hundreds were modified for different tasks, and many were launched on new careers as air/sea rescue aircraft, turbojet test-beds or tankers, which kept them busy for another decade or more. Back in 1942 Boeing had begun to work on the Model 367 transport version with a much larger upper lobe to a 'double bubble' fuselage, the first XC-97 flying on 15 November 1944. Various improved bomber versions were cancelled but the B-29D, with new engines, was continued and

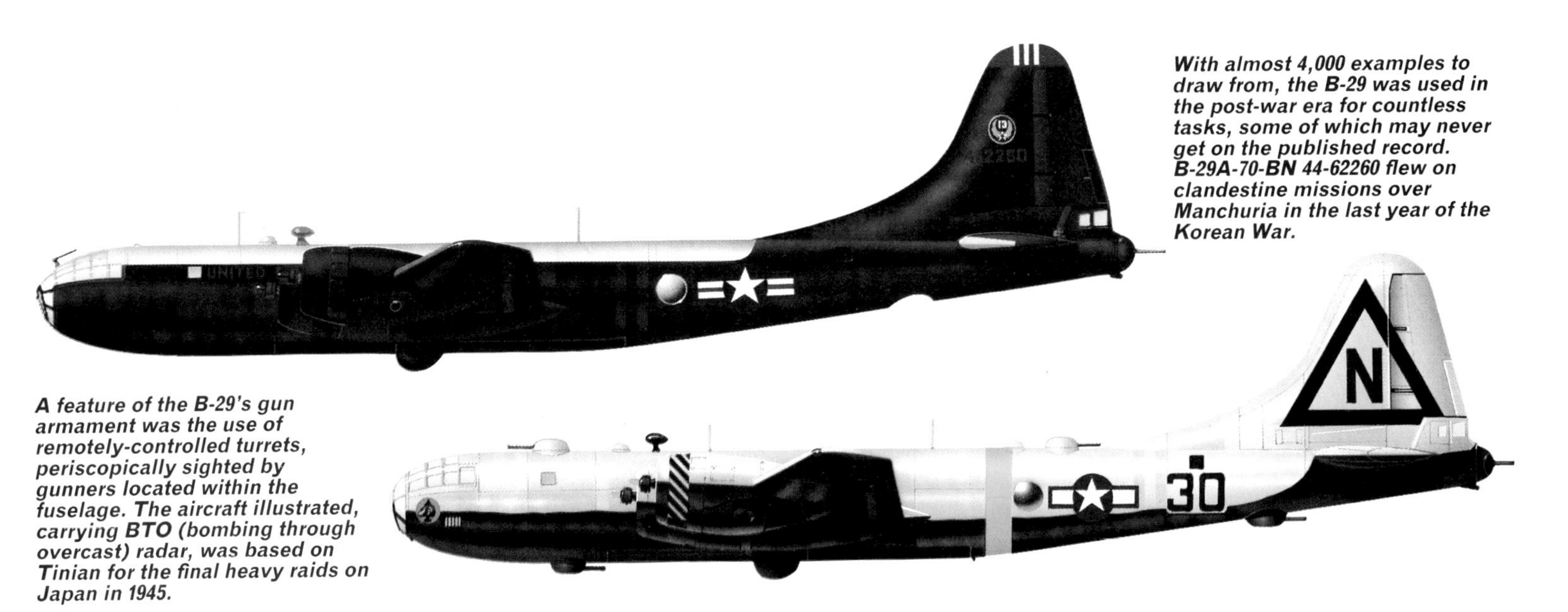

With almost 4,000 examples to draw from, the B-29 was used in the post-war era for countless tasks, some of which may never get on the published record. B-29A-70-BN 44-62260 flew on clandestine missions over Manchuria in the last year of the Korean War.

A feature of the B-29's gun armament was the use of remotely-controlled turrets, periscopically sighted by gunners located within the fuselage. The aircraft illustrated, carrying BTO (bombing through overcast) radar, was based on Tinian for the final heavy raids on Japan in 1945.

became the B-50.

A B-29A (42-093845) was flown with the 28-cylinder Pratt & Whitney R-4360 Wasp Major engine in early 1944 as the XB-44, and the 2238-kW (3,000-hp) engine made such a difference that other changes were made, including a wing made of 75ST aluminium alloy giving much greater strength with 295 kg (650 lb) less weight, and a taller vertical tail. There were many systems changes, and the propellers were made reversible. The new bomber, the B-29D, went into production at Renton in July 1945. Manufacture continued, at a reduced pace, with the changed designation B-50. The first production B-50A finally emerged in June 1947, and Boeing built 79, followed by 45 strengthened B-50Bs (all but one being rebuilt as unarmed RB-50B reconnaissance aircraft with 2650-litre (583-Imp gal) underwing tanks), 222 of the definitive B-50D and finally 24 TB-50H crew trainers.

In the 1950s hundreds of B-29s kept flying, almost all modified for different roles but including 88 ordinary B-29 bombers handed to the RAF and used as the Boeing Washington by Bomber Command's Nos 15, 35, 44, 57, 90, 115, 149 and 207 Squadrons. In the USAF the jet-assisted KB-50J went on tanking until the last pair were struck off charge in Vietnam in 1963. But this is not really the end of the story.

Back in 1943 Josef Stalin began a major campaign to get B-29s. He never succeeded, and work began on a Soviet copy, though smaller and without the complex armament. Then out of the blue, on 29 July 1944, a B-29 made an emergency landing in the Soviet Union near Vladivostok after bombing Japan. Two more arrived later (one of them was the *General H. H. Arnold Special,* the 175th to be built and picked out on the Wichita line by the USAAF chief of staff, who said "This is the one I want as soon as you can build it; it will complete our first Bomb Group"), and within weeks they were all being carefully taken apart. In an operation without parallel, the Russian technicians studied every part of the B-29 to the extent of preparing their own production drawings, establishing material specifications, manufacturing tolerances and production procedures. The vast Tupolev bureau finally went into production, trying to short-cut some areas by buying tyres and brakes in the USA. These purchases did not succeed, but they did make the US government believe the previously incredible rumours of what the Soviets were doing.

First the Tupolev bureau built much simpler aircraft, the big-bodied Tu-70 and Tu-75 transports, both of which incorporated the complete wing and many other parts of the 'captured' B-29s. The Tu-70 flew on 27 November 1946. On Aviation Day, 3 August 1947, three Soviet copies of the B-29, designated Tu-4 by the VVS (air force), thundered over Moscow. They were followed by over 300 others. Like the B-29 four years earlier, the Tu-4 test programme in 1947-9 was marked by plenty of problems, but the Tu-4 eventually matured and not only comprised the core of a formidable nuclear strike force but, to a far greater extent than the B-29 itself, led to versions of much greater power and capability including the Tu-80 and Tu-85 which represented the all-time pinnacle of piston-engine bomber development to the traditional formula. Very considerable amounts of B-29 technology were carried straight across to the Tu-88 (Tu-16 'Badger') and Tu-95 (Tu-20 'Bear'), and small features can no doubt be distinguished in today's Tu-22M 'Backfire'.

Though three RAF Meteors had been refuelled by a triple-point KB-29 years earlier, this test near Eglin AFB was the first by a triple-point KB-50D, in 1956. Aircraft 48-123, formerly a B-50D-105, was later boosted with underwing jet pods to become a KB-50J. The receiver aircraft were F-100Cs of TAC from Foster AFB.

Externally indistinguishable from the B-29, the Tupolev Tu-4 made its public debut at the 1947 Soviet Aviation Day held at Tushino, Moscow. This photograph of the original aircraft was taken in 1983 at Monino, which was closed to the public shortly afterwards.

Bell P-39 Airacobra

Featuring an unusual mid-engine arrangement, then-novel tricycle undercarriage and heavy cannon armament, the P-39 was an unusual fighter which did not quite match its promise. Unpopular with Western allies, it was well-liked by the Soviets, who used it with great expertise.

The P-39 Airacobra was one of the outstanding examples of an aircraft which, on paper, seemed likely to be a world-beater but which, in practice, turned out to be an also-ran. Radical in arrangement, it did have some excellent qualities, and eventually matured as an excellent ground-attack fighter which saw much action in different parts of the world.

Bell Aircraft was formed in 1935 by three key men who remained behind in Buffalo after the Consolidated Company moved to San Diego. In June 1936 they began to design a revolutionary new fighter, which they named the Airacobra. The two most unusual (but not unique) features were that the engine was mounted on the centre of gravity, above the wing and behind the pilot, and the new 'tricycle' type of landing gear was fitted. The unusual location of the engine was expected to confer several advantages. One obvious benefit was improved manoeuvrability, the heavy engine being located in the centre of the aircraft instead of being swung round on an extremity. All-round pilot vision was considerably improved, especially when taxiing, conventional fighters having a giant nose completely blocking forward view. The new form of landing gear was expected to offer many advantages, including much easier handling on take-off and landing and eliminating the possibility of nosing over, which was increasingly becoming a major problem with high-power fighters with large propellers. It also facilitated the installation of concentrated firepower in the nose, including a large cannon firing through the hub of the propeller.

Bell put together a detailed proposal to the US Army Air Corps. The list of advantages looked impressive, and the Army was especially eager to find a fighter that could carry the powerful T-9 cannon of 37-mm calibre developed by AAC (American Armament Corporation). Such a gun could go in the nose of the Lockheed P-38, but this was a big aircraft with two engines. The Bell proposal fitted the heavy gun into a small agile machine. On 7 October 1937 the Army ordered a prototype of the Airacobra as the XP-39. There has been much confusion over the date of the first flight, but the XP-39 actually flew on 6 April 1938.

It was a beautiful-looking aircraft, with a shiny metal skin and almost perfect streamlining. The 858-kW (1,150-hp) Allison V-1710-17 liquid-cooled V-12 engine was installed just behind the cockpit, where it provided protection against attack from astern. On the left was a big air inlet and fairing over a General Electric B-5 turbosupercharger. On the right side was a smaller air duct housing the coolant radiator and oil cooler. The roomy cockpit offered almost perfect all-round visibility, and its most unusual feature (apart from being in a level attitude on the ground) was that it had a car-type door on each side, with a wind-down window. The landing gear and split flaps were electrically operated, all control surfaces were fabric-covered, and all exterior riveting was of the flush type.

The XP-39 carried no armament or armour, and weighed only 2517 kg (5,550 lb) in flying trim. Together with the turbo-equipped engine this resulted in scintillating performance, the maximum

The Bell P-39 Airacobra was a promising project, which in its initial form would have made a superb fighter. However, extra weight, unreliability and the removal of the all-important turbocharger cut its performance to merely adequate.

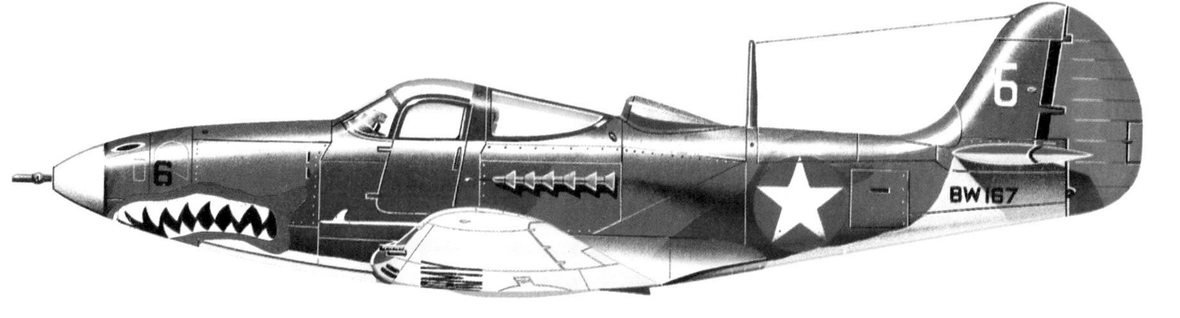

Bell P-400 (ex-RAF aircraft returned to USAAF) of the 67th Fighter Squadron, 35th Fighter Group, serving in New Caledonia in 1942. Note the retention of RAF serial.

speed being 628 km/h (390 mph) at a height of 6100 m (20,000 ft), this being reached in only five minutes. It is not surprising that, on 27 April 1939, the Army ordered 12 YP-39A service-test aircraft, plus one YP-39A without turbosupercharger. However, the XP-39 was lent to the National Advisory Committee for Aeronautics at Langley Field, and NACA (predecessor of NASA) recommended over 60 modifications. The most significant was the elimination of the turbosupercharger. The United States considered that its geographic position made it invulnerable to attack by high-altitude bombers, so that the only possible missions for an American fighter would be close support and ground (or anti-ship) attack. Accordingly, the engine was changed to a V-1710-39 rated at 4054 m (13,300 ft).

The chief other changes were to move the coolant radiators to the roots of the wings, with leading-edge inlets, and the carburettor air inlet to the top of the fuselage; to reduce the span and increase the length; to redesign the canopy to have greater length and reduced height; and to add fairing doors over the main-wheel wells. Altogether the NACA changes resulted in a significant reduction in drag, but the deletion of the turbo greatly reduced the maximum speed and all high-altitude performance, the time to 6100 m (20,000 ft) being increased to 7.5 minutes. At low levels there was little difference, and manoeuvrability was improved, so all 13 service-test aircraft were built as YP-39Bs with the recommended changes.

When the first YP-39B (40-27) flew on 13 September 1940 it also featured a significantly broader fin. The engine was a V-1710-37, rated at 813 kW (1,090 hp) at 4054 m (13,300 ft), and armament was installed, together with cockpit armour. The armament comprised a 37-mm T-9 cannon with 15 rounds, two 12.7-mm guns with 200 rounds each and two 7.62-mm guns each with 500 rounds. The four machine-guns were mounted in the top of the nose. All the modifications increased the gross weight to 3282 kg (7,235 lb), further reducing maximum speed to 592 km/h (368 mph). This did not greatly bother the Army, which on 10 August 1939 ordered 80 production aircraft. These were to be designated P-45, but the political climate did not allow what seemed to be a 'new' fighter, so the designation was changed to P-39C.

This line-up of early P-39s displays the unique arrangement of the Airacobra. With the engine mounted in the central fuselage, the nose was left clear for a retractable nosewheel and heavy armament. The engine was aspirated by the large airscoop behind the cockpit.

The first P-39C (40-2971) flew in January 1941. By this time, however, the Army had studied combat reports from Europe and decided that the Airacobra was inadequately protected. Thus, only 20 of the first 80 were completed as P-39Cs. On 13 September 1940, the day on which the YP-39B first flew, the Army ordered 344 P-39Ds. On the following day it ordered the last 60 C models to be completed as Ds. Among the changes were the provision of improved armour, self-sealing fuel tanks (reducing capacity from 645 to 454 litres/142 to 100 Imp gal), a bullet-proof windscreen, and revised armament. The 7.62-mm guns were removed, but four similar guns, each with 1,000 rounds, were fitted in the outer wings. The ammunition box for the 37-mm gun was doubled in capacity, to 30

Ground crew in the Aleutians strip a P-39 for maintenance, revealing the engine position and nose armament. The 37-mm cannon firing through the propeller spinner was allied to six machine-guns, four in the wings and two in the upper fuselage decking.

Bell P-39 Airacobra

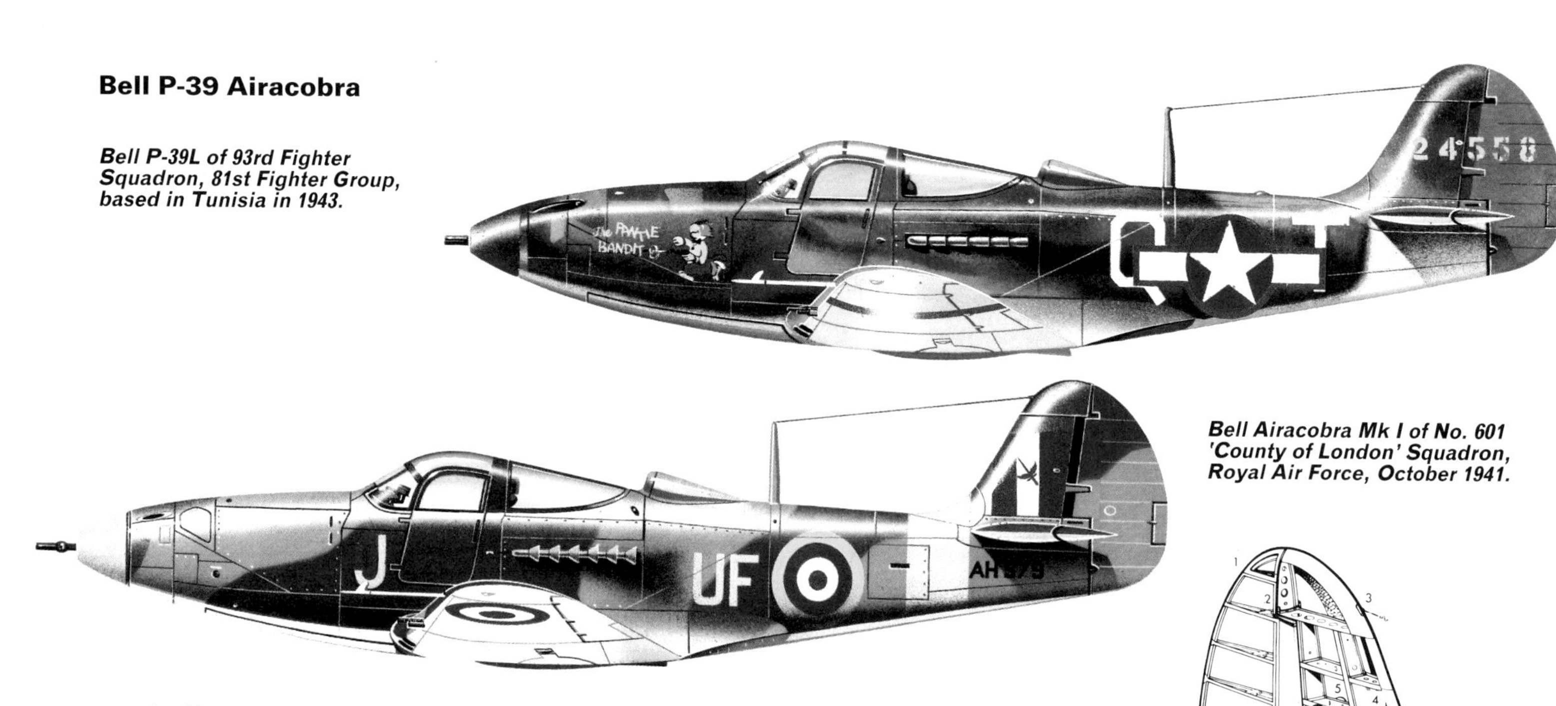

Bell P-39L of 93rd Fighter Squadron, 81st Fighter Group, based in Tunisia in 1943.

Bell Airacobra Mk I of No. 601 'County of London' Squadron, Royal Air Force, October 1941.

rounds. Empty weight was increased by 111 kg (245 lb), and performance fell further.

Back on 13 April 1940 the British had ordered no fewer than 675 of what seemed to be a wonderful aircraft (having believed Bell's XP-39 figures were typical of production aircraft). Originally to be called Bell Caribou I, the RAF Airacobra I was similar to the P-39D apart from the cannon being a long-barrelled Hispano 20-mm with 60 rounds, and all six machine-guns being Brownings of 7.7 mm. The first aircraft was test-flown in England on 6 July 1941, and by September 601 Squadron had re-equipped with the unusual US fighter. By this time it was realised that it was useless as a fighter for the RAF, being 53 km/h (33 mph) slower than advertised and having totally inadequate high-altitude performance. On 10 October 1941 four of 601's aircraft flew a strafing mission over northern France, shooting up invasion barges. There were 19 other deficiencies including lethal carbon monoxide concentration in the cockpit after firing the guns, random errors in the compass after firing the cannon, and an unacceptably long take-off run of 686 m (2,250 ft). The Airacobra was withdrawn, and of the British order 212 were diverted to the Soviet Union, 54 were lost at sea and 179 were taken over by the US Army as P-400s, most of the P-400s being rushed to bolster the defences of northern Australia and New Guinea. Nearly all the remainder, about 200 aircraft, were handed to the US 8th Air Force in England in 1942.

Production in 1941-42 centred on P-39D-1s, D-2s, D-3s and D-4s. All had provision for a 284-litre (62.5-Imp gal) drop tank or 227-kg (500-lb) bomb, and they respectively introduced a dorsal fin fillet and 20-mm M-1 gun; V-1710-63 engine of 988-kW (1,325-hp); armoured oil and glycol radiators (these were earlier Ds rebuilt); and two cameras in the rear fuselage. There were still such deficiencies as lack of high-altitude gun heaters and gun hydraulic chargers and a

Bell P-39D Airacobra cutaway drawing key

1 Aluminium sheet rudder tip
2 Rudder upper hinge
3 Aerial attachment
4 Fin forward spar
5 Tall navigation lights
6 Fin structure
7 Rudder middle hinge
8 Rudder
9 Rudder tab
10 Rudder tab flexible shaft
11 Elevator control quadrant
12 Rudder control quadrant
13 Starboard elevator
14 Starboard tailplane
15 Rudder lower hinge
16 Control cables
17 Fuselage aft frame
18 Diagonal brace
19 Fin root fillet
20 Elevator hinge fairing
21 Elevator tab (port only)
22 Port elevator
23 Aerial
24 Aerial mast
25 Port tailplane
26 Aft fuselage semi-monocoque structure
27 Radio installation
28 Access panel
29 Radio equipment tray
30 Control quadrant
31 Oil tank armour plate
32 Aft fuselage/central chassis bulkhead
33 Engine oil tank
34 Prestone (cooler) expansion tank
35 Carburettor intake fairing
36 Carburettor intake shutter housing
37 Engine accessories
38 Central chassis web
39 Frame
40 Starboard longitudinal fuselage beam
41 Exhaust stubs
42 Allison V-1710-35 Vee 12-cylinder engine
43 Engine compartment decking
44 Aft-vision glazing
45 Crash turnover bulkhead
46 Turnover bulkhead armour plate
47 Auxiliary air intake
48 Ventral Prestone (coolant) radiator
49 Rear main spar/centre section attachment
50 Cylindrical oil radiator
51 Ventral controllable shutters
52 Auxiliary spar/centre section attachment

This interesting attempt to provide a carrier-borne fighter for the Navy was designated the XFL-1 Airabonita. Based on the Airacob featured a retractable tailwheel and a 'sting'-type arrester hook ur the rear fuselage.

Bell P-39Q (1943044) of the Soviet air force, on the southern sector of the Russian Front. This aircraft is the one flown by Major Aleksandr Pokryshkin, second highest-scoring Soviet ace.

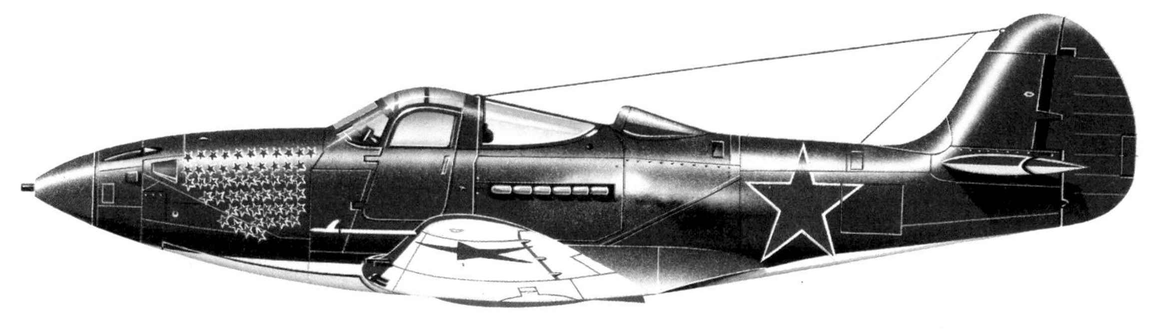

53 Hoses
54 Shutter control rod access doors
55 Starboard mainwheel well
56 Mainwheel leg/rear main spar attachment point
57 Wing structure
58 Port flap structure
59 Aileron tab control link fairing
60 Aileron trim tab
61 Aileron servo tab
62 Wing rib
63 Starboard navigation light
64 Ammunition tanks
65 Two 0.3-in (7.62-mm) machine-guns
66 Inboard gun ammunition feed chute
67 Machine-gun barrels
68 Mainwheel door fairing
69 Starboard mainwheel
70 Axle
71 Mainwheel fork
72 Torque links
73 Mainwheel oleo leg
74 Wing fuel cells (6)
75 Fuel filler cap
76 Mainwheel retraction spindle
77 Fuel tank gauge capacity plate
78 Fuel tank access plate
79 Forward main spar
80 Oil cooler intakes
81 Intake duct rib cut-out
82 Wing centre-section
83 Aileron control cables
84 Undercarriage gear motor
85 Aileron control quadrant
86 Undercarriage emergency handcrank
87 Coolant radiator/oil temperature shutter controls
88 Sutton harness
89 Pilot's seat
90 Armoured glass turnover bulkhead frame
91 Cockpit entry doors
92 Internal rear-view mirror
93 Gunsight
94 Armoured glass windscreen
95 Steel plate armour overlap
96 Instrument panel frame
97 Control column
98 Control column yoke/drive shaft
99 Nosewheel retraction chain coupling

The Royal Air Force had an unhappy time with the Airacobra, equipping only one squadron briefly before withdrawing the type from service and redistributing the aircraft to the Soviet Union and the USAAF. The winged sword insignia was that of No. 601 'County of London' Squadron.

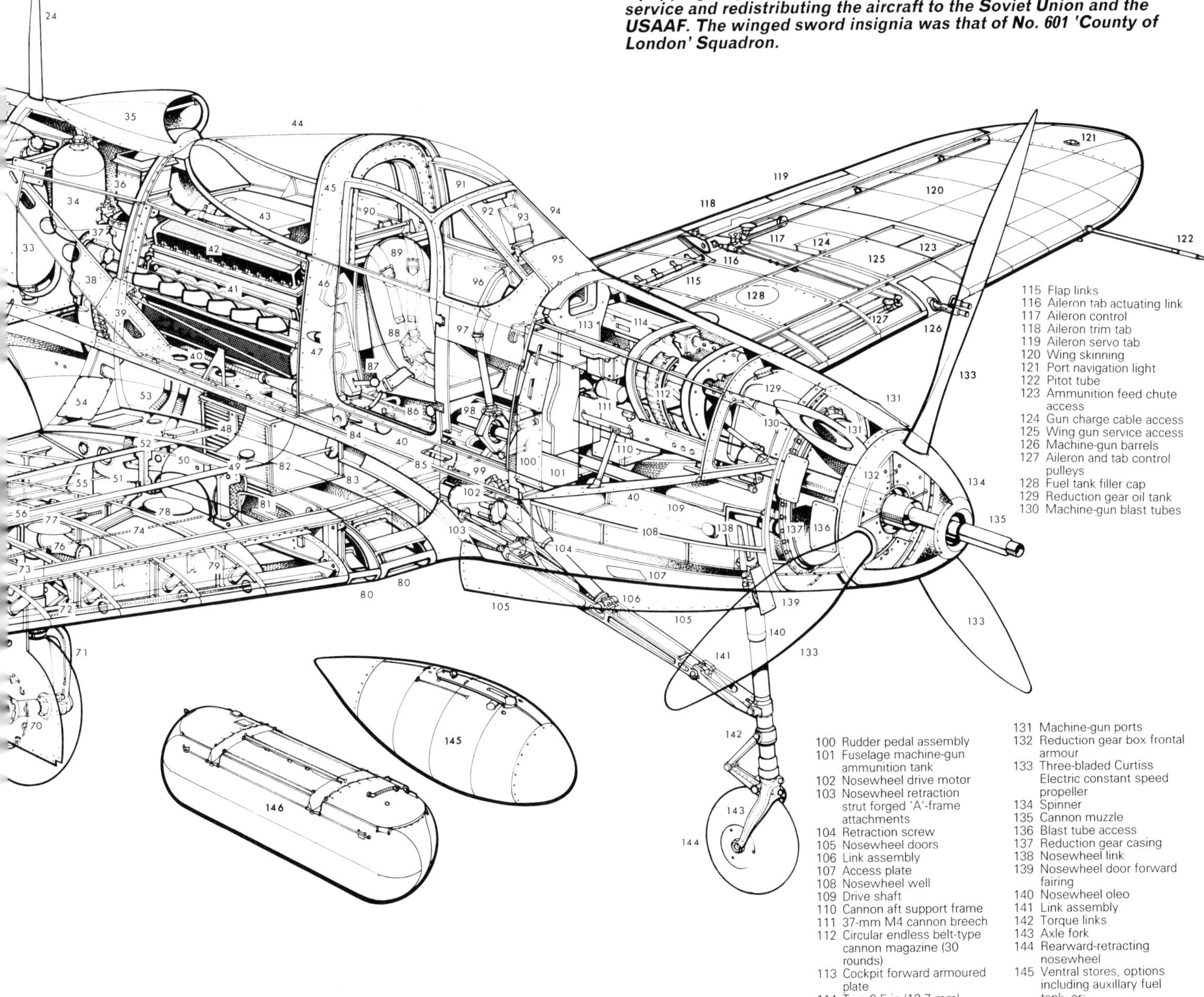

115 Flap links
116 Aileron tab actuating link
117 Aileron control
118 Aileron trim tab
119 Aileron servo tab
120 Wing skinning
121 Port navigation light
122 Pitot tube
123 Ammunition feed chute access
124 Gun charge cable access
125 Wing gun service access
126 Machine-gun barrels
127 Aileron and tab control pulleys
128 Fuel tank filler cap
129 Reduction gear oil tank
130 Machine-gun blast tubes

100 Rudder pedal assembly
101 Fuselage machine-gun ammunition tank
102 Nosewheel drive motor
103 Nosewheel retraction strut forged 'A'-frame attachments
104 Retraction screw
105 Nosewheel doors
106 Link assembly
107 Access plate
108 Nosewheel well
109 Drive shaft
110 Cannon aft support frame
111 37-mm M4 cannon breech
112 Circular endless belt-type cannon magazine (30 rounds)
113 Cockpit forward armoured plate
114 Two 0.5-in (12.7-mm) fuselage machine-guns
131 Machine-gun ports
132 Reduction gear box frontal armour
133 Three-bladed Curtiss Electric constant speed propeller
134 Spinner
135 Cannon muzzle
136 Blast tube access
137 Reduction gear casing
138 Nosewheel link
139 Nosewheel door forward fairing
140 Nosewheel oleo
141 Link assembly
142 Torque links
143 Axle fork
144 Rearward-retracting nosewheel
145 Ventral stores, options including auxiliary fuel tank, or;
146 Two-man life raft

The Soviet air force was one of the few to welcome the Bell P-39 into service, enjoying its considerable sophistication when compared with indigenous types. Initial equipment was 212 Airacobra Mk Is transferred from the Royal Air Force, and a further 49 were lost in transit. Later, huge numbers of P-39s were supplied on Lend-Lease from the United States, and were much used in ground attack and air-to-air fighting. The leading exponent of the latter was Aleksandr Pokryshkin, who downed 48 of his 59 victories in the P-39 with the 16th Guards Polk, before moving to the Yak-9. Shot down four times, he was thrice a Hero of the Soviet Union.

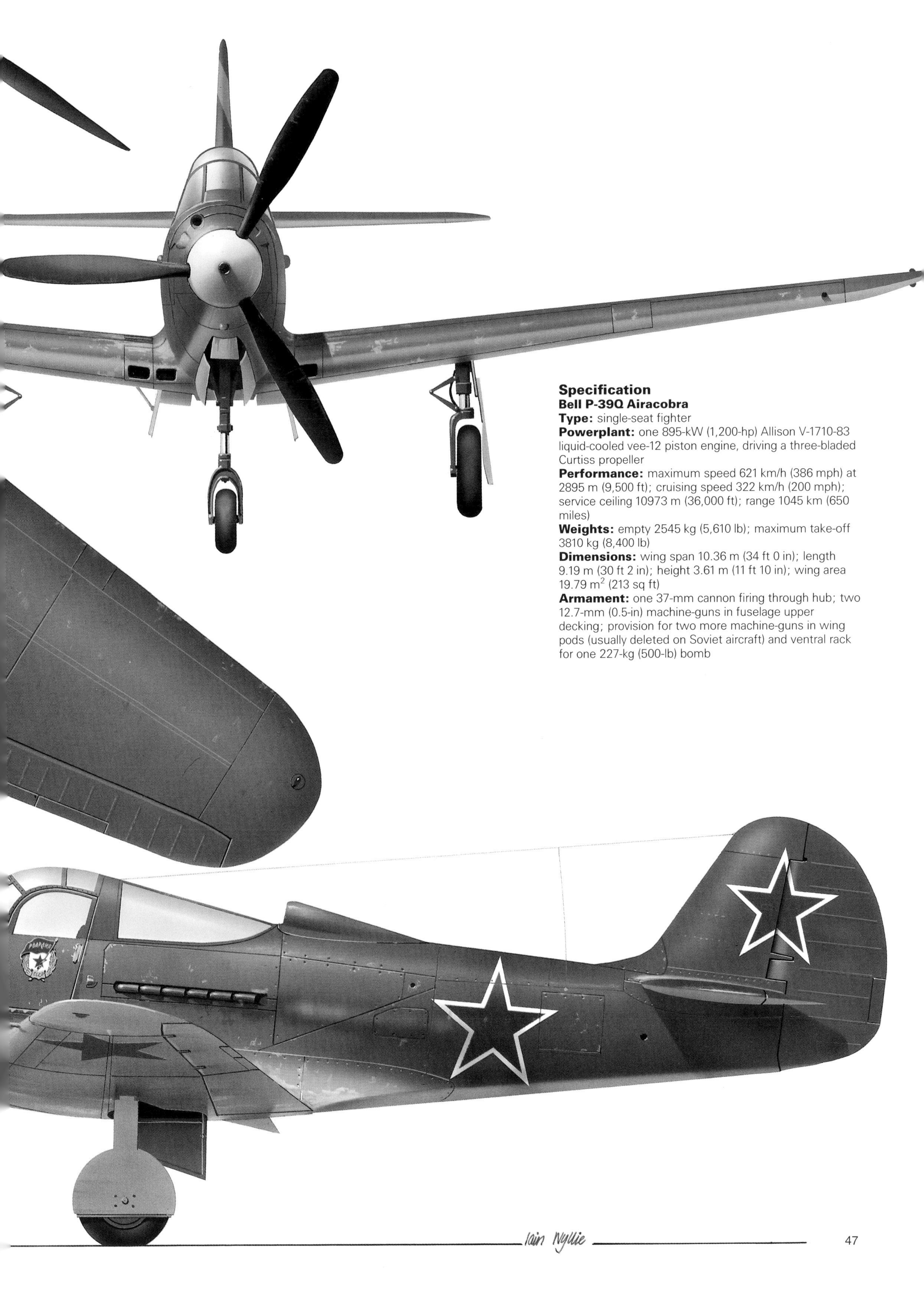

Specification

Bell P-39Q Airacobra

Type: single-seat fighter

Powerplant: one 895-kW (1,200-hp) Allison V-1710-83 liquid-cooled vee-12 piston engine, driving a three-bladed Curtiss propeller

Performance: maximum speed 621 km/h (386 mph) at 2895 m (9,500 ft); cruising speed 322 km/h (200 mph); service ceiling 10973 m (36,000 ft); range 1045 km (650 miles)

Weights: empty 2545 kg (5,610 lb); maximum take-off 3810 kg (8,400 lb)

Dimensions: wing span 10.36 m (34 ft 0 in); length 9.19 m (30 ft 2 in); height 3.61 m (11 ft 10 in); wing area 19.79 m^2 (213 sq ft)

Armament: one 37-mm cannon firing through hub; two 12.7-mm (0.5-in) machine-guns in fuselage upper decking; provision for two more machine-guns in wing pods (usually deleted on Soviet aircraft) and ventral rack for one 227-kg (500-lb) bomb

Following on from 20 P-39Cs, the P-39D was the first major production model, with 554 built. The majority were built with a 20-mm cannon (note the longer, narrower barrel) firing through the spinner in place of the 37-mm weapon.

While the P-39's retractable undercarriage was easy to use, it was prone to some trouble. Manual retraction was difficult, achieved by a large crank handle. This lucky pilot performs a good belly landing, keeping the aircraft straight during the run.

tendency for oil to seep over the canopy from the propeller gearbox.

The P-39E tested the laminar-flow wings later used on the P-63 Kingcobra. The P-39F, 229 of which were built, had an Aeroproducts (instead of Curtiss) propeller and had the 12-stub exhaust first seen on the P-400. No G/H/I versions were built, but there were 25 Js with automatic engine boost control and most features similar to the F. Bell delivered 210 Ks and 250 Ls, all ordered as Gs but with small differences, all having the 988-kW (1,325-hp) Dash-63 engine. The next 240 of the G order were built as P-39Ms with an engine giving better performance at height, but worse performance lower down.

The first really massive production comprised 2,095 P-39Ns. Almost all went to the Soviet Union where they were popular as ground-attack aircraft, being found tough and able to return after suffering very severe battle damage. Most had the four wing fuel cells supplied as an optional kit, so that if range was unimportant the low-level performance could be marginally increased. Armour replaced a rear sheet of curved armour-glass, and altogether gross weight was reduced from 4128 to 3969 kg (9,100 to 8,750 lb).

The most important production variant of all was the P-39Q, output of which totalled 4,905, bringing total Airacobra production to 9,558. The initial Q-1 sub-type replaced the four wing machine-guns by two underwing gondolas housing single 12.7-mm weapons. Fuel capacity and weight of armour shuttled between previous values, while some sub-types had four-bladed propellers. From the Q-20 block the underwing guns were often omitted, the Soviet authorities considering one 37-mm and two 12.7-mm sufficient, and the small gain in performance and agility to be valuable.

By 1943 the P-39 was rapidly being replaced in US Army Air Force

Most of the Airacobras supplied to the Soviet Union were the P-39Q variant, although many others of earlier versions were delivered. This is a P-39M, complete with Allison V-1710-83 engine, developing some 1,200 hp. The underfuselage tank was used for ferrying.

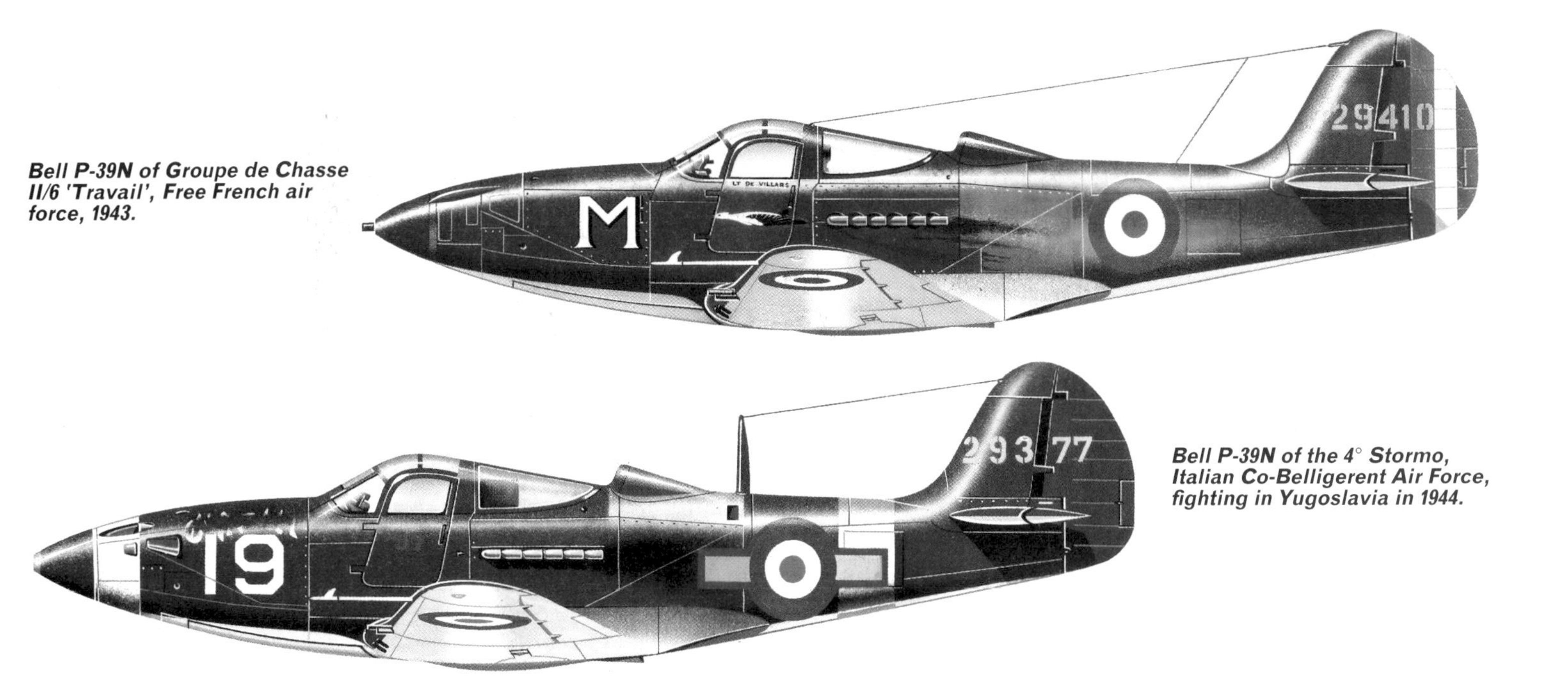

Bell P-39N of Groupe de Chasse II/6 'Travail', Free French air force, 1943.

Bell P-39N of the 4° Stormo, Italian Co-Belligerent Air Force, fighting in Yugoslavia in 1944.

units, but it was being delivered to numerous units in other Allied air forces. By far the most important remained the IAP fighter regiments of the Soviet air forces, including many elite Guards units. The P-39Q served on all sectors of the Eastern Front right up to the final Battle of Berlin. A total of 165, almost all of them Q-models, were supplied to the Free French air force, serving in Italy and southern France in 1944-45. The last USAAF unit was the 332nd Fighter Group which, equipped with 75 P-39Qs, joined the 15th Air Force in Italy in February 1944. Over 220 Ns and Qs were supplied to units of the Italian Co-Belligerent Air Force in 1944, operating mainly in northern Italy and over the Balkans. Even Portugal put the P-39 into service, using at least nine P-39Fs which landed in Portugal in November 1942. The aircraft had been *en route* from England to North Africa to take part in Operation Torch. Whether due to navigational error or mechanical failure (or deliberate action by the pilot) is now difficult to determine, but the aircraft all landed in serviceable condition and, following a period of internment, were formally commandeered by the Portuguese air force.

Bell did considerable work on the P-76, intended to be powered by the Continental IV-1430 inverted engine. The laminar-wing XP-39E was planned to test this engine, but the programme was dropped. Much earlier, in 1938, Bell had schemed the XFL-1 Airabonita for the US Navy, with a shorter fuselage, tailwheel landing gear, carrier equipment and many other changes. Carrier trials (which were failed) took place in February 1941. Later in the war, however, the US Navy did receive seven F2L Airacobras and a P-39Q-10 modified as the XTDL-1. All these were target drones, though much of the flight testing took place with human pilots. The production radio-controlled target was to have been the A-7, but this was never completed.

The last versions were two-seaters, almost all converted at service units. Most were TP-39Fs and RP-39Qs, the former being a dual-control version. In each case the extra cockpit was added in front of the first, the armament being removed, and the canopy hinging to the side. To maintain directional stability the dorsal fin fillet was enlarged and a long shallow ventral fin was added.

Designed as a fighter, the P-39 found more fame as a ground attack aircraft, for which its heavy armament of 37-mm cannon and 0.50-in machine-guns were widely used. Bomb racks could also be carried on the centreline, although only a small weapon load was possible.

P-47 Thunderbolt: Fighter-Bomber Supreme

Built in larger numbers than any other US fighter in history, the P-47 Thunderbolt was at first thought to be clumsy and overlarge. Later the 'Jug' did as much to win World War II as any other Allied aircraft, proving ideal for the ground-attack role and more than adequate in air combat.

Built in larger numbers than any other fighter in American history, the mighty P-47 – popularly called the Jug, short for Juggernaut – was the exact opposite of the Russian philosophy of making fighters small and agile. Today even the smallest fighters make the P-47 look like a midget, but in World War II it was a monster. RAF pilots said the driver of a P-47 could escape enemy fire by running about in the cockpit, and the shock its laden weight of 6124 kg (13,500 lb) provoked would have been turned to amazement had people then (1942) known that by 1945 later versions would turn the scales at 9390 kg (20,700 lb) – considerably heavier than a loaded Dornier Do 17 bomber! One can argue indefinitely about small and large fighters, but the 'T-bolt' was to prove itself one of the most useful Allied aircraft, in all theatres.

Certainly the question of small or large fighters was far from resolved in the US Army Air Corps in 1940. One of its chief fighter builders, Republic Aviation Corporation (successor to Seversky Aircraft) had a heritage of rotund radial-engined fighters with elliptical wings and tails, and was in production with the P-35 and about to produce the P-43 Lancer with inward-retracting landing gear and a turbocharged Twin Wasp engine. For the future there were various AP-4 projects with the 1044-kW (1,400-hp) R-2180 or the massive new 1380-kW (1,850-hp) R-2800 Double Wasp, as well as the lightweight AP-10 with liquid-cooled Allison engine and two 12.7-mm

Five of the first P-47s to be delivered to a fighting unit. The unit, of course, was the 56th Fighter Group; the aircraft in the background were with the 61st FS, led by the Group CO. Still equipped with early P-47Bs, this group (under the famed Colonel Hubert Zemke) arrived in England at the end of 1942 to prove the P-47 in combat.

A fine portrait of a P-47D (Evansville-built) on a combat mission in the Europe theatre. This unit is the 82nd Fighter Squadron, 78th Fighter Group, based at Duxford. The photograph was taken after D-Day because in addition to the famed black/white check cowl the aircraft carries black/white 'invasion stripes'.

(0.5-in) machine-guns. Combat reports from Europe suggested none would make the grade, and on 12 June 1940 chief engineer Alex Kartveli submitted a dramatically more formidable machine which technically was probably the most advanced then in existence. It was quickly accepted by the worried Army Air Corps and allotted the designation XP-47B, the original XP-47 and XP-47A having been versions of the totally different AP-10.

Big-engined inspiration

The new fighter was an exceptionally severe challenge. For a start, the engine installation was so complex Kartveli designed this first, and then schemed the rest around it! The chosen engine, the big 18-cylinder R-2800, was supplied by a turbocharger which, for various aerodynamic and efficiency reasons, was mounted under the rear fuselage instead of close to the engine. The multiple exhausts were grouped into two monster pipes, which at their upstream ends glowed red-hot at full power and which led back beneath the wing to the turbocharger itself. Here a variable valve system called a waste gate either expelled the hot gas to the atmosphere or, as altitude was increased, diverted it to drive the turbine. The latter spun a centrifugal compressor at some 60,000 rpm to feed high-pressure air to the engine via even larger ducts which incorporated intercoolers to increase the density of the air, and thus give further-enhanced engine power. The mass of large pipes and ducts made the fuselage deep, and put the wing well above its bottom.

This was just what Kartveli did not want, because the great power of the engine needed an enormous propeller: even with the novel use of four blades in a constant-speed Curtiss electric propeller, the diameter had to be no less than 3.71 m (12 ft 2 in). To provide safe clearance between the tips and the ground on take-off, the landing gear had to be exceptionally long, especially because the wing was not in the low position and had to have dihedral. Long landing gears are not only very heavy (if they are not to get a reputation for breaking) but also need long spaces in the wings when retracted. Again, this was just what Kartveli did not want, because he proposed to use the phenomenal armament of not two but eight of the big 12.7-mm (0.5-in) Browning guns, all in the wings outboard of the landing gear legs. It was a technical triumph to design main gears which on retraction shortened by 22.86 cm (9 in) to fit into normal-size bays in the wing between the spars. Immediately outboard of the landing gears were four guns in each wing, staggered so that the four bulky ammunition belts (each of at least 350 rounds) could lie in boxes side-by-side extending very nearly to the tip of the wing.

Distinct shape in the sky

The bluff nose cowl was not circular but extended below into a pear shape to accommodate the ducts for left and right oil coolers and for the bulky intercooler air which was then discharged through a large rectangular valve on each side of the rear fuselage. It was then necessary to find somewhere to put an exceptionally large fuel capacity, and main and auxiliary tanks for 776 and 379 litres (205 and 100 US gal), both of self-sealing construction, were installed above the wing between the supercharger air ducts and in the rear fuselage

First of the Thunderbolts, the XP-47B is seen here shortly after being rolled out on to the Farmingdale field late in April 1941. It had a canopy that hinged open sideways. After ground testing it was flown by Lowry L. Brabham on 6 May. Leaking gas from the exhaust ducts almost forced Brabham to bale out.

Of 15,683 P-47s just two had liquid-cooled engines. Two P-47D-15-RAs were held back to serve as testbeds for the Chrysler XIV-2200-1, a remarkable 1865-kW (2,500-hp) unit comprising front and rear halves each made up of four inverted-vee twins (16 cylinders in all) with drive gears in the centre. Note the radiator/turbo duct.

under the cockpit. The cockpit was extremely well equipped: it was packed with controls for systems and devices not then found in other fighters, such as electric fuel-contents transmitters, cabin air-conditioning, variable gun-bay heating and anti-icing by an Eclipse pump. There was a deep Vee windscreen, upward-hinged canopy and sharp upper line to the rear fuselage which caused all early P-47s later to be called 'razorbacks'.

Completely unpainted, the prototype XP-47B flew on 6 May 1941, exactly eight months after it was ordered. It was clearly a potential world-beater, but gave a lot of trouble. Handicapped by its sheer size and weight, it suffered problems with fabric-covered flight-control surfaces, canopies which jammed, and snags with the guns, fuel system and engine installation. Despite agonised misgivings, the US Army ordered 171 of the new fighters and soon followed with orders for 602 of an improved model, designated P-47C. The first production P-47B left the assembly line at Farmingdale, Long Island, in March 1942. This had a sliding canopy with jettison system, metal-skinned control surfaces (not yet standard), sloping radio mast mounted farther aft, blunt-nose ailerons, balance/trim rudder tab and production R-2800-21 engine. The first deliveries went to the 56th Fighter Group of what by this time was the US Army Air Force. After suffering severely from control problems, tyre bursts and other difficulties, the 56th FG went on to become the top-scoring fighter group in all US forces, with a final air-combat score of 674½. With the 78th FG, the 56th joined the 8th Air Force in England and flew its first escort mission on 13 April 1943. With 1155 litres (305 US gal), the big fighters could not accompany the bombers very far, and they found life tough in close combat with the smaller Messerschmitt Bf 109s and Focke-Wulf Fw 190s. The unmatched diving speed of the P-47 meant they could always break off, but that after all was not the basic objective, which was to shoot down the Luftwaffe.

Recognition problems

The last P-47B had a pressurised cockpit and was designated XP-47E. The 172nd was the first P-47C, with a fundamental problem of balance removed by mounting the engine nearly 0.305 m (1 ft) further forward and for the first time fitted with an attachment under the fuselage for a 227-kg (500-lb) bomb or a 757-litre (200-US gal) drop tank, a most important addition. Externally the most obvious change was the shorter vertical radio mast. Recognising the P-47 should have presented no problem, but in the European theatre standards of recognition were so poor that the first Thunderbolts (which were painted olive-drab overall) were given white bands across the tail surfaces, and a white nose, so they would not be shot down by mistake for the totally different Fw 190. (The equally different British Typhoon was likewise given distinctive markings very

Four more aircraft of the 56th FG pictured in the Connecticut/Long Island area in mid-1942 whilst in the painful process of ironing out the remaining 'bugs' in this potentially great fighter. This photograph emphasises the sharp dorsal spine which led to these early models of Thunderbolt becoming known as 'razorbacks'.

Republic P-47D-10 Thunderbolt cutaway drawing key

1 Rudder upper hinge
2 Aerial attachment
3 Fin flanged ribs
4 Rudder post/fin aft spar
5 Fin front spar
6 Rudder trim tab worm and screw actuating mechanism (chain driven)
7 Rudder centre hinge
8 Rudder trim tab
9 Rudder structure
10 Tail navigation light
11 Elevator fixed tab
12 Elevator trim tab
13 Starboard elevator structure
14 Elevator outboard hinge
15 Elevator torque tube
16 Elevator trim tab worm and screw actuating mechanism
17 Chain drive
18 Starboard tailplane
19 Tail jacking point
20 Rudder control cables
21 Elevator control rod and linkage
22 Fin spar/fuselage attachment points
23 Port elevator
24 Aerial
25 Port tailplane structure (two spars and flanged ribs)
26 Tailwheel retraction worm gear
27 Tailwheel anti-shimmy damper
28 Tailwheel oleo
29 Tailwheel doors
30 Retractable and steerable tailwheel
31 Tailwheel fork
32 Tailwheel mount and pivot
33 Rudder cables
34 Rudder and elevator trim control cables
35 Lifting tube
36 Elevator rod linkage
37 Semi-monocoque all-metal fuselage construction
38 Fuselage dorsal 'razorback' profile
39 Aerial lead-in
40 Fuselage stringers
41 Supercharger air filter
42 Supercharger
43 Turbine casing
44 Turbosupercharger compartment air vent
45 Turbosupercharger exhaust hood fairing (stainless steel)
46 Outlet louvres
47 Intercooler exhaust doors (port and starboard)
48 Exhaust pipes
49 Cooling air ducts
50 Intercooler unit (cooling and supercharged air)
51 Radio transmitter and receiver packs (Detrola)
52 Canopy track
53 Elevator rod linkage
54 Aerial mast
55 Formation light
56 Rearward-vision frame cut-out and glazing
57 Oxygen bottles
58 Supercharged and cooling air pipe (supercharger to carburettor) port
59 Elevator linkage
60 Supercharged and cooling air pipe (supercharger to carburettor) starboard
61 Central duct (to intercooler unit)
62 Wingroot air louvres
63 Wingroot fillet
64 Auxiliary fuel tank (100 US gal/379 litres)
65 Auxiliary fuel filler point
66 Rudder cable turnbuckle
67 Cockpit floor support
68 Seat adjustment lever
69 Pilot's seat
70 Canopy emergency release (port and starboard)
71 Trim tab controls
72 Back and head armour
73 Headrest
74 Rearward-sliding canopy
75 Rear-view mirror fairing
76 'Vee' windshields with central pillar
77 Internal bulletproof glass screen
78 Gunsight
79 Engine control quadrant (cockpit port wall)
80 Control column
81 Rudder pedals
82 Oxygen regulator
83 Underfloor elevator control quadrant
84 Rudder cable linkage
85 Wing rear spar/fuselage attachment (tapered bolts/bushings)
86 Wing supporting lower bulkhead section
87 Main fuel tank (205 US gal/776 litres)
88 Fuselage forward structure
89 Stainless steel/Alclad firewall bulkhead
90 Cowl flap valve
91 Main fuel filler point
92 Anti-freeze fluid tank
93 Hydraulic reservoir
94 Aileron control rod
95 Aileron trim tab control cables
96 Aileron hinge access panels
97 Aileron and tab control linkage
98 Aileron trim tab (port wing only)
99 Frise-type aileron
100 Wing rear (No. 2) spar
101 Port navigation light
102 Pitot head
103 Wing front (No. 1) spar
104 Wing stressed skin
105 Four-gun ammunition troughs (individual bays)
106 Staggered gun barrels
107 Removable panel
108 Inter-spar gun bay access panel
109 Forward gunsight bead
110 Oil feed pipes
111 Oil tank (28.6 US gal/108 litres)
112 Hydraulic pressure line
113 Engine upper bearers
114 Engine control correlating cam
115 Eclipse pump (anti-icing)
116 Fuel level transmitter
117 Generator
118 Battery junction box
119 Storage battery
120 Exhaust collector ring
121 Cowl flap actuating cylinder
122 Exhaust outlets to collector ring
123 Cowl flaps
124 Supercharged and cooling air ducts to carburettor (port and starboard)
125 Exhaust upper outlets
126 Cowling frame
127 Pratt & Whitney R-2800-59 18-cylinder twin-row engine
128 Cowling nose panel
129 Magnetos
130 Propeller governor
131 Propeller hub
132 Reduction gear casing
133 Spinner
134 Propeller cuffs
135 Four-blade Curtiss constant-speed electric propeller
136 Oil cooler intakes (port and starboard)
137 Supercharger intercooler (central) air intake
138 Ducting
139 Oil cooler feed pipes
140 Starboard oil cooler
141 Engine lower bearers
142 Oil cooler exhaust variable shutter
143 Fixed deflector
144 Excess exhaust gas gate
145 Belly stores/weapons shackles
146 Metal auxiliary drop tank (75 US gal/284 litres)
147 Inboard mainwheel well door
148 Mainwheel well door actuating cylinder
149 Camera gun port
150 Cabin air-conditioning intake (starboard wing only)
151 Wingroot fairing
152 Wing front spar/fuselage attachment (tapered bolts/bushings)
153 Wing inboard rib mainwheel well recess
154 Wing front (No. 1) spar
155 Undercarriage pivot point
156 Hydraulic retraction cylinder
157 Auxiliary (undercarriage mounting) wing spar
158 Gun bay warm air flexible duct
159 Wing rear (No. 2) spar
160 Landing flap inboard hinge
161 Auxiliary (No. 3) wing spar inboard section (flap mounting)

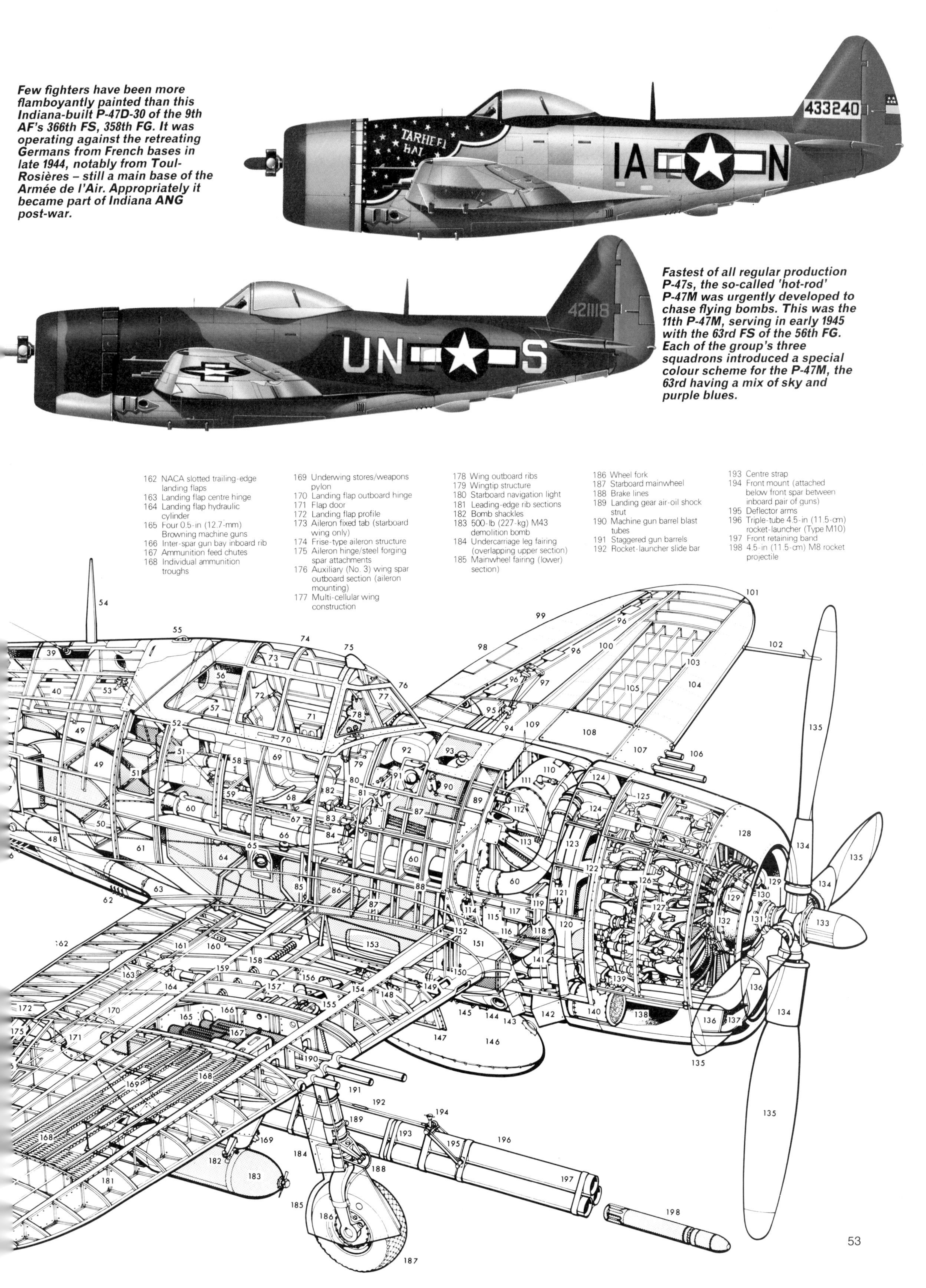

Few fighters have been more flamboyantly painted than this Indiana-built P-47D-30 of the 9th AF's 366th FS, 358th FG. It was operating against the retreating Germans from French bases in late 1944, notably from Toul-Rosières – still a main base of the Armée de l'Air. Appropriately it became part of Indiana ANG post-war.

Fastest of all regular production P-47s, the so-called 'hot-rod' P-47M was urgently developed to chase flying bombs. This was the 11th P-47M, serving in early 1945 with the 63rd FS of the 56th FG. Each of the group's three squadrons introduced a special colour scheme for the P-47M, the 63rd having a mix of sky and purple blues.

162 NACA slotted trailing-edge landing flaps
163 Landing flap centre hinge
164 Landing flap hydraulic cylinder
165 Four 0.5-in (12.7-mm) Browning machine guns
166 Inter-spar gun bay inboard rib
167 Ammunition feed chutes
168 Individual ammunition troughs
169 Underwing stores/weapons pylon
170 Landing flap outboard hinge
171 Flap door
172 Landing flap profile
173 Aileron fixed tab (starboard wing only)
174 Frise-type aileron structure
175 Aileron hinge/steel forging spar attachments
176 Auxiliary (No. 3) wing spar outboard section (aileron mounting)
177 Multi-cellular wing construction
178 Wing outboard ribs
179 Wingtip structure
180 Starboard navigation light
181 Leading-edge rib sections
182 Bomb shackles
183 500-lb (227-kg) M43 demolition bomb
184 Undercarriage leg fairing (overlapping upper section)
185 Mainwheel fairing (lower section)
186 Wheel fork
187 Starboard mainwheel
188 Brake lines
189 Landing gear air-oil shock strut
190 Machine gun barrel blast tubes
191 Staggered gun barrels
192 Rocket-launcher slide bar
193 Centre strap
194 Front mount (attached below front spar between inboard pair of guns)
195 Deflector arms
196 Triple-tube 4.5-in (11.5-cm) rocket-launcher (Type M10)
197 Front retaining band
198 4.5-in (11.5-cm) M8 rocket projectile

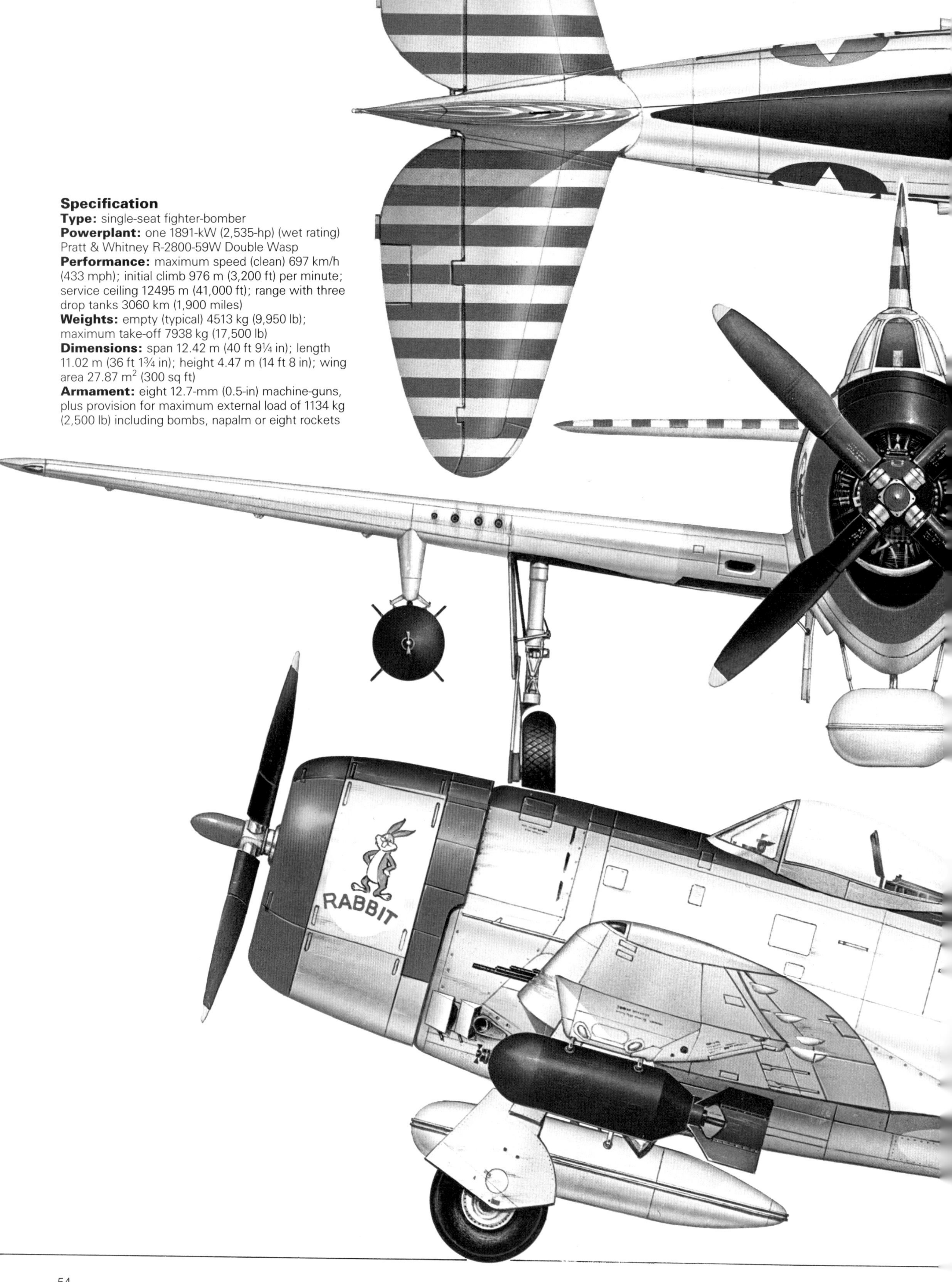

Specification
Type: single-seat fighter-bomber
Powerplant: one 1891-kW (2,535-hp) (wet rating) Pratt & Whitney R-2800-59W Double Wasp
Performance: maximum speed (clean) 697 km/h (433 mph); initial climb 976 m (3,200 ft) per minute; service ceiling 12495 m (41,000 ft); range with three drop tanks 3060 km (1,900 miles)
Weights: empty (typical) 4513 kg (9,950 lb); maximum take-off 7938 kg (17,500 lb)
Dimensions: span 12.42 m (40 ft 9¼ in); length 11.02 m (36 ft 1¾ in); height 4.47 m (14 ft 8 in); wing area 27.87 m^2 (300 sq ft)
Armament: eight 12.7-mm (0.5-in) machine-guns, plus provision for maximum external load of 1134 kg (2,500 lb) including bombs, napalm or eight rockets

Fighter-bomber par excellence, the P-47D is seen here with bombs of the 454-kg (1,000-lb) size hung under the wing pylons and one of the nine types of drop tank and napalm carried on the centreline. This particular aircraft, a P-47D-25-RE, served with the 527th Fighter Squadron of the 86th Fighter Group. This was one of the leading fighter groups in the Mediterranean theatre; it fought its way from North Africa through Sicily into Italy, and equipped with P-47Ds in 1944. It then operated intensively not only in ground attack on Kesselring's retreating forces in Italy but also over the Balkans and on long-range escort duties of B-24s (occasionally other bombers) as far as Berlin. The principal home base for 'Rabbit' was Pisa. Note that the stripes of the 86th FG have obliterated the USAAF tail number.

One of the last of the 'razorback' variety, this Evansville-built P-47D was assigned to the Pacific theatre and is pictured serving with the 19th Fighter Squadron, 318th Fighter Group, based on Saipan island in the summer of 1944. Though generally adequate, the original canopy produced a 20° blind spot at the rear.

At least 830 P-47s were supplied to the RAF, most of them late-block P-47Ds known to the Commonwealth air forces as Thunderbolt IIs. This P-47D-30 served with RAF No. 79 Sqn on the Burmese central front in late 1944, based at Wangjing. Allied aircraft engaged on any of the Japanese fronts avoided red in their insignia.

One of several captured P-47s, this P-47D was serving with the 358th FS of the 355th FG on escort and ground-attack missions over northern Europe when it made a forced landing in France. It was soon operating with sondAufklSt. 103 from Paris-Orly, still in its original livery and squadron markings and pilot's personal emblem.

like the 'invasion stripes' painted on all Allied machines a year later.) By mid-1943, when the first of the P-47D models reached front-line units, everyone had come to respect the P-47's great strength, which often enabled it to limp home with severe damage and to effect a self-destructive belly landing without injury to the pilot.

Most prolific version

Though the first order for the P-47D was placed on 13 October 1941, before the United States entered the war, it was mid-1943 before the flood of production had much effect. Eventually no fewer than 12,602 of this version were built, far more than of any other US fighter, and including output from a new factory at Evansville, Indiana. A further 354 identical machines were made by Curtiss-Wright as the P-47G. Basically the P-47D grouped a whole package of improvements, such as a refined engine with water injection for emergency combat boost, a better turbocharger installation, improved pilot armour, and multi-ply tyres (also retrofitted to earlier P-47s) which did not burst even on rough strips when the aircraft was carrying bombs and tanks. The ability to carry both loads together came with the P-47D-20 (and counterparts at the Evansville plant), which introduced a 'universal' wing having pylons for 454-kg (1,000-lb) bombs on each side or a 568-litre (150-US gal) tank, as well as the load on the centreline. With three tanks the P-47 could escort bombers deep into Germany, going all the way on most missions; on the return journey it became common practice to use unexpended ammunition shooting up targets of opportunity on the ground, and the P-47D became the chief ground-attack aircraft of the Allied air forces in Europe in the final year of war, as well as serving in large numbers in the Pacific and with the RAF (825, mainly in Burma), Soviet Union, Brazil and Mexico (and many other air forces post-war).

In July 1943 one aircraft was given a cut-down rear fuselage and the clear-view bubble canopy from a Typhoon. This XP-47K was so popular the new hood was immediately introduced to production, starting with the P-47D-25-RE and Evansville's P-47D-26-RA. Previously Farmingdale had delivered 3,962 P-47Ds and the Indiana plant 1,461; from the Dash-25 onwards the two factories produced 2,547 and 4,632. By this time the aircraft were being delivered unpainted, which slightly enhanced performance. Despite the great increase in weight (to some 7938 kg/17,500 lb), the boosted engine improved performance, which gained a further fillip (such as 122 m/400 ft per minute extra climb) as a result of the fitting of a broad paddle-blade propeller especially useful at high altitude. The lower rear fuselage caused slight loss in directional stability and from the D-27-RE batch the fin area was increased by a shallow dorsal

Last of the Thunderbolts, the P-47N was the largest and heaviest, with a new long-span wing with tankage tailored to the vast Pacific theatre. The prototype N was 42-27387, originally built as a D. These two are N-5-REs from the middle of the 1,667 built at Farmingdale. The dorsal fin was larger than that on the late P-47D.

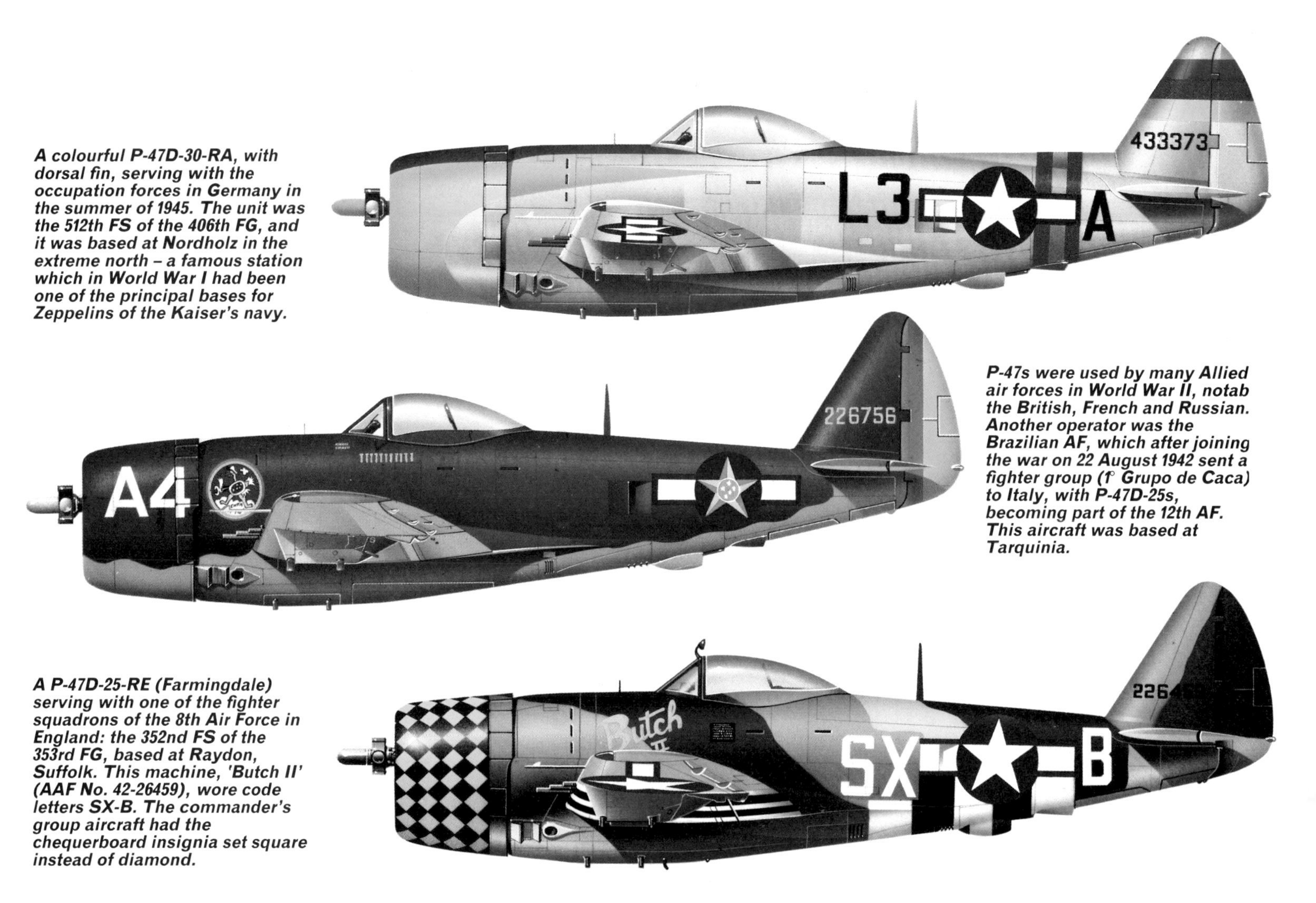

A colourful P-47D-30-RA, with dorsal fin, serving with the occupation forces in Germany in the summer of 1945. The unit was the 512th FS of the 406th FG, and it was based at Nordholz in the extreme north – a famous station which in World War I had been one of the principal bases for Zeppelins of the Kaiser's navy.

P-47s were used by many Allied air forces in World War II, notab the British, French and Russian. Another operator was the Brazilian AF, which after joining the war on 22 August 1942 sent a fighter group (1° Grupo de Caca) to Italy, with P-47D-25s, becoming part of the 12th AF. This aircraft was based at Tarquinia.

A P-47D-25-RE (Farmingdale) serving with one of the fighter squadrons of the 8th Air Force in England: the 352nd FS of the 353rd FG, based at Raydon, Suffolk. This machine, 'Butch II' (AAF No. 42-26459), wore code letters SX-B. The commander's group aircraft had the chequerboard insignia set square instead of diamond.

spine stretching most of the way to the canopy. From the D-35-RA block each wing was given zero-length attachments for five 12.7-cm (5-in) rocket projectiles on each side.

The only other service variants were the 'hot-rod' P-47M and the very long-range P-47N. The P-47M was quickly produced in the summer of 1944 to counter the menace of the 'V-1' flying bomb, which ordinary P-47s were hard-pressed to catch, and the various German jet and rocket fighters. Basically a late-model P-47D, the P-47M had the extra-powerful R-2800-57(C) engine with uprated CH-5 turbocharger which had previously been fitted to the experimental XP-47J to make it the fastest piston-engined fighter of all at 811 km/h (504 mph). The only other significant change was the fitting of airbrakes to the wings to assist slowing down behind slower aircraft before opening fire.

Pacific fighter

The P-47N, however, was almost a new aircraft because it had a long-span wing of totally new design which not only was tailored to much increased gross weights but also for the first time contained fuel. A 352-litre (93-US gal) tank was fitted in each, so that with external tanks no less than 4792 litres (1,266 US gal) could be carried. This resulted in a really capable long-range fighter for the Pacific war, though the loaded weight of up to 9616 kg (21,200 lb) required a strengthened landing gear and fairly good long airstrip. Features of the production P-47N included the Dash-77 engine, enlarged ailerons and square-tipped wings for rapid roll, and zero-length rocket launchers. Farmingdale built 1,667, Evansville also managing to deliver the first 149 of an order for 5,934. Farmingdale completed the last of the P-47N series not to be cancelled in December 1945, bringing the grand total of all versions to 15,683.

In typical US style, plenty of information was published not only about the 'Jug' but also about its accomplishments. P-47s flew 546,000 combat sorties between March 1943 and VJ-Day in August 1945. They had an outstanding combat record of only 0.7 per cent losses per mission, with 4.6 enemy aircraft destroyed for each P-47 lost. They dropped 119750 tonnes (132,000 US tons) of bombs, many thousands of gallons of napalm and fired 132 million rounds of 'fifty calibre' and over 60,000 rockets. They burned 774129000 litres (204,504,000 US gal) of fuel in 1,934,000 operational flight hours. The claims for ground targets knocked out were astronomic, but even more important were the European (excluding Italian front) claim of 3,752 aircraft destroyed in air combat and a further 3,315 on the ground. These losses to the Luftwaffe bled it white; they could not be replaced.

Republic P-47 Thunderbolt variants

XP-47B: prototype, first flown on 6 May 1941; powered by 1380-kW/1,850-hp (later 1492-kW/2,000-hp) XR-2800 radial; maximum weight 5482 kg (12,086 lb) and maximum speed 663 km/h (412 mph) (total 1)
P-47B: first production version, initial aircraft being flown in March 1942; 1492-kW (2,000-hp) R-2800-21 radial; sliding hood and metal-skinned control surfaces; maximum weight 6060 kg (13,360 lb) and maximum speed 674 km/h (419 mph) (total 171)
P-47C: revised production model, first flown in September 1942; initially same engine as P-47B, then (from P-47C-5-RE onwards) powered by 1716-kW (2,300-hp) R-2800-59; longer forward fuselage, and provision for belly/bomb tank; maximum weight 6770 kg (14,925 lb) and maximum speed 697 km/h (433 mph) (total 602)
P-47D: major production model, the first example being flown in December 1942; 1716-kW (2,300-hp) R-2800-21W or 1891-kW (2,535-hp) R-2800-59W water-injected radial; numerous modifications in various blocks; maximum weight 7938 kg (17,500 lb) and maximum speed, clean 697 km/h (433 mph) (total 12,602)
XP-47E: experimental 1943 version of P-47D with pressurised cockpit (total 1)
XP-47F: experimental 1943 version of P-47B with so-called laminar-flow wings (total 1)
P-47G: designation of P-47D razorback-model built by Curtiss-Wright (total 354)
XP-47H: experimental development of P-47D with 1716-kW (2,300-hp) Chrysler XIV-2220-1 liquid-cooled 16-cylinder inverted-Vee engine; totally different in appearance to other P-47 models; length 11.94 m (39 ft 2 in); and maximum speed 789 km/h (490 mph) (total 2)
XP-47J: experimental development based on the P-47D with lightened structure and special 2089-kW (2,800-hp) R-2800-57(C) radial with CH-5 turbocharger; fitted with six 12.7-mm (0.5-in) machine-guns; first flown in November 1943 and in August 1944 reached an instrumented level speed of 811 km/h (504 mph); maximum weight 6056 kg (13,350 lb) (total 1)
XP-47K: developed P-47D with clearview teardrop hood from a Hawker Typhoon; first flown on 3 July 1943 (total 1)
XP-47L: developed P-47D-20-RE with larger fuselage fuel tanks increasing standard capacity from 1155 to 1401 litres (305 to 370 US gal) (total 1)
P-47M: 'sprint' model based on P-47D but with 2089-kW (2,800-hp) R-2800-57(C) and CH-5 turbocharger; first flown in mid-1944; sometimes fitted with only six 12.7-mm (0.5-in) machine-guns; maximum weight 7031 kg (15,500 lb) and maximum speed 756 km/h (470 mph) (total 133, including 3 prototypes)
P-47N: long-range model for Pacific theatre; fitted with new wing with fuel tanks, broad ailerons and square-cut tips; stronger landing gear and other modifications; 2089-kW (2,800-hp) R-2800-57(C) radial; maximum weight up to 9616 kg (21,200 lb), maximum speed 740 km/h (460 mph) and maximum range 3540 km (2,200 miles) (total 1,816)

2
114180
114181
4

Curtiss P-40 Hawk family

Culmination of the famous Curtiss Hawk fighter family which spanned the years 1925-40, the P-40 Warhawk was numerically the most important American fighter at the time of Pearl Harbor. Although its development never kept pace with rival designs, it nevertheless compiled a creditable war record on many fronts.

Encouraged by the performance being demonstrated by European interceptors powered by liquid-cooled inline engines, the Curtiss-Wright Corporation decided, in 1938, to substitute an 865-kW (1,160-hp) supercharged Allison V-1710-19 in the current Wright radial-powered P-36A, retaining the 10th production example (30-18) for the trial installation. Redesignated the XP-40, this aircraft was first flown in October 1938 and evaluated at Wright Field the following May, in competition with the Bell XP-39 and Seversky XP-41. As originally flown, the XP-40 featured a radiator located under the rear fuselage, but this was moved forward to the nose, together with the oil cooler. In all respects other than the powerplant the new aircraft remained unchanged from the P-36A, being an all-metal, low-wing monoplane whose main landing gear units retracted rearwards into the wings, the mainwheels turning through 90° to lie flush with the undersurfaces. Armament remained the paltry pair of 7.62-mm (0.3-in) machine-guns in the wings.

Although the other prototypes evaluated with the XP-40 later led to successful service fighters, the Curtiss-Wright aircraft was selected for immediate production and a contract for 524 P-40s, worth almost $13 million and at that time the largest order ever placed for an American fighter, was signed. Production got under way late in 1939 with 200 aircraft known as the Hawk 81A for the USAAC, powered by the 776-kW (1,040-hp) Allison V-1710-33 engine and distinguishable by the absence of wheel disc plates and by the carburettor air intake above the nose. The first three aircraft served as prototypes (occasionally known as YP-40s) and subsequent machines were delivered to the 33rd Pursuit Squadron, moved to Iceland on 25 July 1941.

Meanwhile France had ordered 140 examples of an export version of the P-40, designated Hawk 81A-1, but these were not ready by the time of the French collapse in June 1940 so were diverted to the UK, where the RAF took them over with the designation Tomahawk Mk I late that year. British contracts at that time totalled 1,000 aircraft (of which most were transferred to later versions), and the first RAF squadron to be equipped with Tomahawk Mk Is (with four wing guns) was No. 2 (Army Co-operation) Squadron based at Sawbridgeworth in England in August 1941. Subsequent aircraft were shipped to Takoradi in West Africa for service in the Middle East,

Left: A quartet of P-40F Warhawks perform a classic fighter peel-off. The 'F' was identified by the lack of an intake above the engine, denoting the fitment of a Packard-built V-1650 Merlin engine. 1,311 of this model were completed, many with a lengthened rear fuselage.

A P-40E, 41-36504, based at Randolph Field. First of the P-40 Warhawks to serve with the USAAF in Europe in 1942, the type flew with a number of American squadrons in the Mediterranean theatre, but proved generally inferior to most other Allied fighters.

Curtiss P-40 Hawk family

Flown by Charles Older of the 3rd Squadron 'Hell's Angels' of the American Volunteer Group, this Hawk 81A-2 (P-8168) was based at Kunming, China, in the spring of 1942. Among its distinctive markings are 10 victory symbols below the windscreen.

Tomahawk Mk IB, AH806, of No. 400 (Canadian) Sqn based at Odiham, Hants, early in 1942. Generally outclassed as a fighter by this time, the aircraft was employed principally for army co-operation training in the UK.

first joining No. 112 (Fighter) Squadron at Sidi Heneish in October that year.

Bad show at Pearl

Production had continued at Buffalo, NY, with the P-40B (the P-40A designation was not used by US service aircraft, it being taken to cover the first export version). Some 131 were produced, introducing cockpit armour and an armament of four 7.62-mm (0.3-in) wing guns and two 12.7-mm (0.5-in) nose guns. When Japan struck on December 1941 there were 107 P-40s and P-40Bs present in the Philippines, but such was the measure of surprise achieved that only four managed to take off. Within four days the number of these fighters (flown by the 20th and 34th Pursuit Squadrons) had fallen to 22. The RAF Tomahawk Mk IIA corresponded to the P-40B (Hawk 81A-2) and the majority of the 110 aircraft despatched went direct to the Middle East. One hundred other Tomahawk Mk IIAs were diverted from RAF contracts to China, for service with the American Volunteer Group.

The next variant was the P-40C (Hawk 81A-3) which introduced self-sealing fuel tanks; only 193 were produced for the USAAC but this was the RAF's principal Tomahawk version, the Mk IIB. Out of a total of 945 produced under this designation, 21 were lost in transit at sea and 73 were delivered direct to the USSR. Those that reached the RAF entered service with Nos 2, 13, 26, 168, 171, 231, 239, 241, 268, 400, 414, 430 and 613 fighter, fighter-reconnaissance and Army Co-operation Squadrons in the UK, and with Nos 94, 112, 208, 250 and 260 Squadrons in the Middle East; they also served with Nos 2 and 4 Squadrons of the South African Air Force and No. 3 Squadron

Converted from the 10th production P-36A (30-18) to feature an 865-kW (1,160-hp) Allison V-1710-19 inline engine, the prototype XP-40 (Hawk 81) was first flown in October 1938. In its initial form, as shown here, the radiator was located under the rear fuselage.

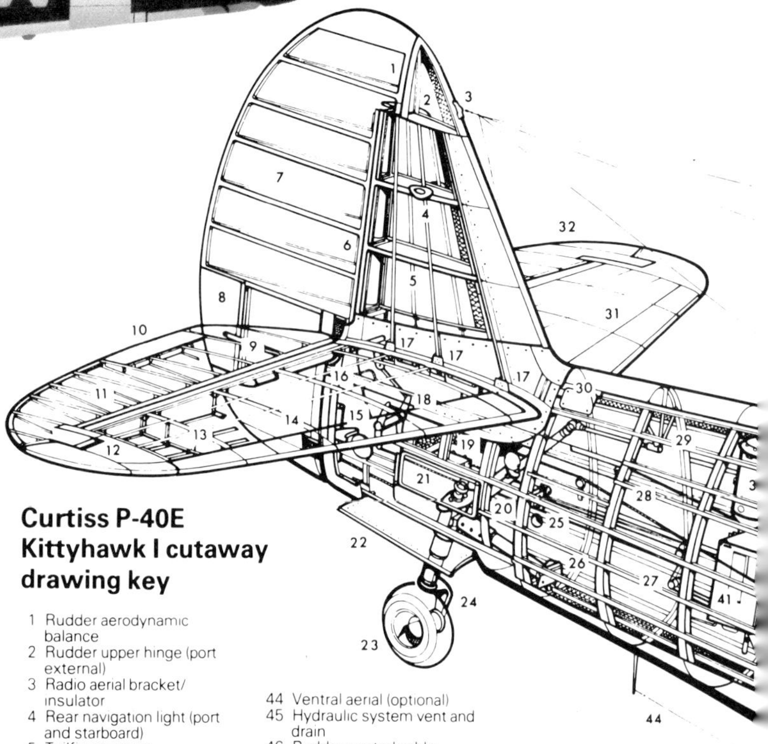

Curtiss P-40E Kittyhawk I cutaway drawing key

1 Rudder aerodynamic balance
2 Rudder upper hinge (port external)
3 Radio aerial bracket/insulator
4 Rear navigation light (port and starboard)
5 Tailfin structure
6 Rudder post/support tube
7 Rudder structure
8 Rudder trim tab
9 Rudder trim tab push-rod (starboard external)
10 Elevator tab
11 Elevator structure
12 Elevator aerodynamic balance
13 Tailplane structure
14 Rudder lower hinge
15 Rudder control horn
16 Tab actuator flexible drive shafts
17 Tailplane attachment lugs
18 Elevator control horn
19 Tab control rear sprocket housing/chain drive
20 Tailwheel retraction mechanism
21 Access panel
22 Tailwheel door
23 Retractable tailwheel
24 Tailwheel leg
25 Lifting point
26 Tailwheel lower attachment
27 Trim control cable turnbuckles
28 Elevator control cables
29 Tailwheel upper attachment
30 Access panel
31 Port tailplane
32 Port elevator
33 Radio aerials
34 Monocoque fuselage structure
35 Hydraulic reserve tank
36 Automatic recognition device
37 Aerial lead-in
38 Radio aerial mast
39 Hand starter crank stowage
40 Radio bay access door (port)
41 Radio receiver/transmitter
42 Support frame
43 Battery stowage
44 Ventral aerial (optional)
45 Hydraulic system vent and drain
46 Rudder control cable turnbuckle
47 Oxygen bottles
48 Radio equipment installation (optional)
49 Hydraulic tank
50 Hydraulic pump
51 Wingroot fillet
52 Streamline ventral cowl
53 Wing centreline splice
54 Fuselage fuel tank, capacity 51.5 Imp gal (234 litres)
55 Canopy track
56 Fuel lines
57 Rear-vision panels
58 Pilot's headrest
59 Rearward-sliding cockpit canopy
60 Rear-view mirror (external)
61 Bullet-proof windshield
62 Instrument panel coaming
63 Electric gunsight
64 Throttle control quadrant
65 Trim tab control wheels
66 Flap control lever
67 Pilot's seat
68 Elevator control cable horn
69 Seat support (wing upper surface)
70 Hydraulic pump handle
71 Control column
72 Rudder pedal/brake cylinder assembly
73 Bulkhead
74 Oil tank, capacity 10.8 Imp gal (49 litres)
75 Ring sight
76 Flap control push-rod rollers
77 Aileron control cables
78 Aileron cable drum
79 Aileron trim tab drive motor
80 Aileron trim tab
81 Port aileron
82 Port navigation light
83 Pitot head
84 Wing skinning
85 Ammunition loading panels
86 Bead sight
87 Coolant expansion tank, capacity 2.9 Imp gal (13 litres)
88 Carburettor intake
89 Engine bearer support attachment
90 Air vapour eliminator
91 Hydraulic emergency reserve tank
92 Junction box
93 Engine support tubes
94 Engine mounting vibration absorbers
95 Exhaust stacks
96 Cowling panel lines
97 Allison V-1710-39 engine
98 Carburettor intake fairing
99 Propeller reduction gear casing

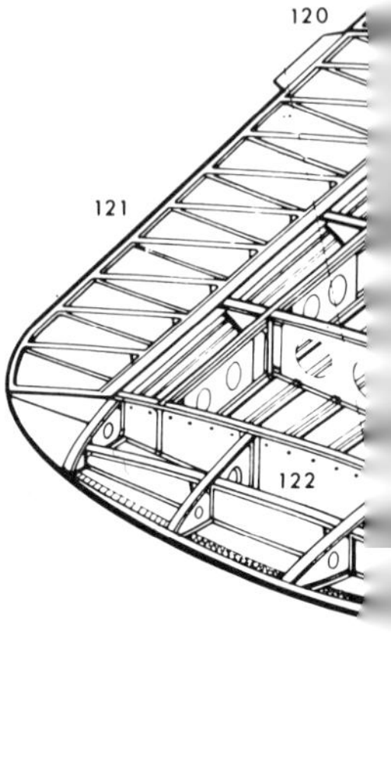

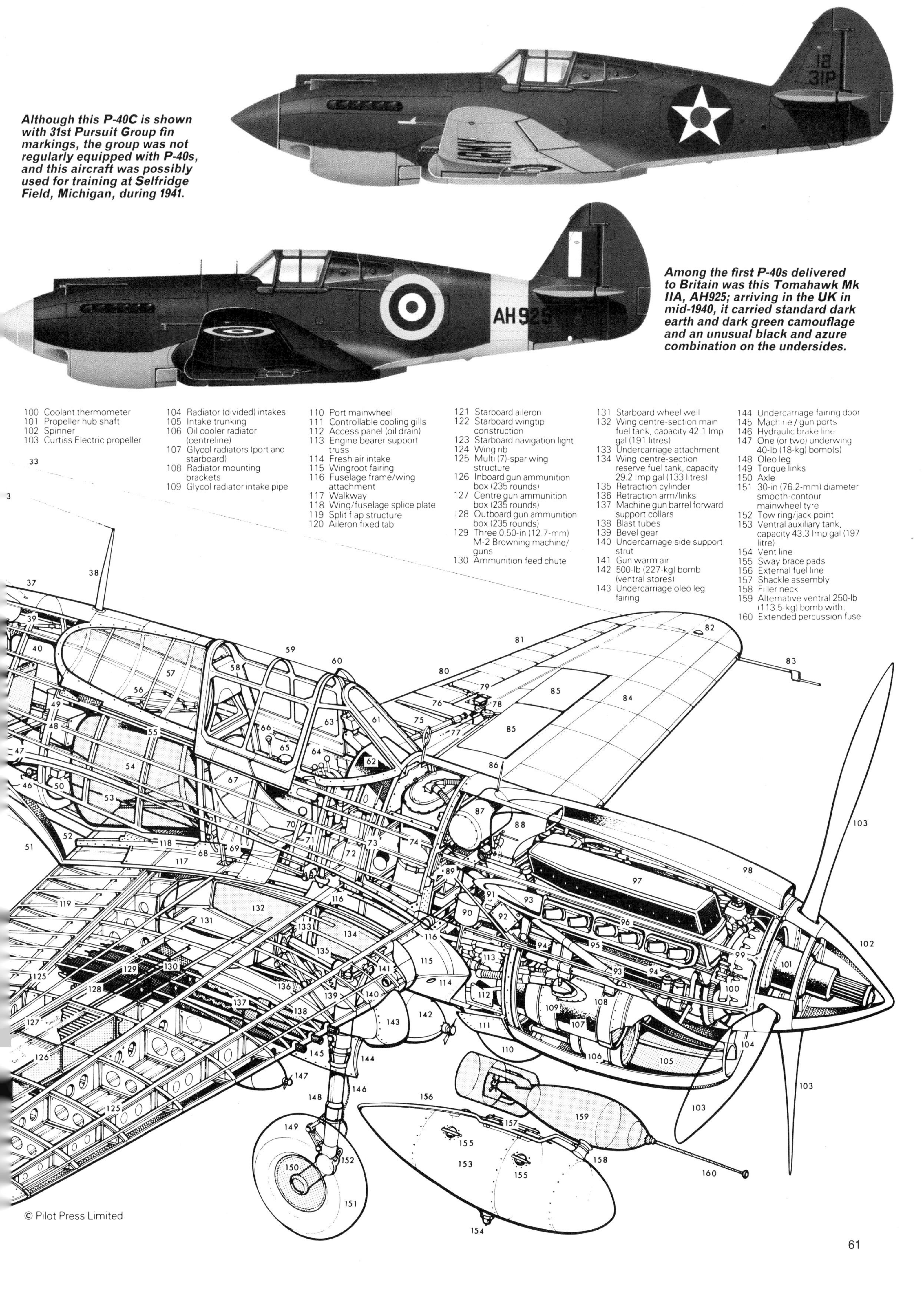

Although this P-40C is shown with 31st Pursuit Group fin markings, the group was not regularly equipped with P-40s, and this aircraft was possibly used for training at Selfridge Field, Michigan, during 1941.

Among the first P-40s delivered to Britain was this Tomahawk Mk IIA, AH925; arriving in the UK in mid-1940, it carried standard dark earth and dark green camouflage and an unusual black and azure combination on the undersides.

100 Coolant thermometer
101 Propeller hub shaft
102 Spinner
103 Curtiss Electric propeller
104 Radiator (divided) intakes
105 Intake trunking
106 Oil cooler radiator (centreline)
107 Glycol radiators (port and starboard)
108 Radiator mounting brackets
109 Glycol radiator intake pipe
110 Port mainwheel
111 Controllable cooling gills
112 Access panel (oil drain)
113 Engine bearer support truss
114 Fresh air intake
115 Wingroot fairing
116 Fuselage frame/wing attachment
117 Walkway
118 Wing/fuselage splice plate
119 Split flap structure
120 Aileron fixed tab
121 Starboard aileron
122 Starboard wingtip construction
123 Starboard navigation light
124 Wing rib
125 Multi (7)-spar wing structure
126 Inboard gun ammunition box (235 rounds)
127 Centre gun ammunition box (235 rounds)
128 Outboard gun ammunition box (235 rounds)
129 Three 0.50-in (12.7-mm) M-2 Browning machine/guns
130 Ammunition feed chute
131 Starboard wheel well
132 Wing centre-section main fuel tank, capacity 42.1 Imp gal (191 litres)
133 Undercarriage attachment
134 Wing centre-section reserve fuel tank, capacity 29.2 Imp gal (133 litres)
135 Retraction cylinder
136 Retraction arm/links
137 Machine gun barrel forward support collars
138 Blast tubes
139 Bevel gear
140 Undercarriage side support strut
141 Gun warm air
142 500-lb (227-kg) bomb (ventral stores)
143 Undercarriage oleo leg fairing
144 Undercarriage fairing door
145 Machine / gun ports
146 Hydraulic brake line
147 One (or two) underwing 40-lb (18-kg) bomb(s)
148 Oleo leg
149 Torque links
150 Axle
151 30-in (76.2-mm) diameter smooth-contour mainwheel tyre
152 Tow ring/jack point
153 Ventral auxiliary tank, capacity 43.3 Imp gal (197 litre)
154 Vent line
155 Sway brace pads
156 External fuel line
157 Shackle assembly
158 Filler neck
159 Alternative ventral 250-lb (113.5-kg) bomb with:
160 Extended percussion fuse

Curtiss P-40 variants

Curtiss XP-40 (Hawk 81): Allison V-1710-19; prototype converted from P-36A (30-18, re-numbered 38-010); all-up weight 3119 kg (6,870 lb)
Curtiss P-40 Warhawk (Hawk 81-A): Allison V-1710-33; 200 built in 1940 (39-156/-289; 40-292/-357); all-up weight 3277 kg (7,215 lb)
Curtiss Tomahawk Mk I (Hawk 81A-1): RAF version of P-40; 140 built (AH741-880)
Curtiss P-40A Warhawk: one USAAC example, converted from P-40 (40-326) as photo-reconnaissance aircraft in 1942
Curtiss P-40B Warhawk (Hawk 81A-2): Allison V-1710-33; introduced armour and increased armament; 131 built for USAAC (41-5205/-5304;41-13297/-13327); all-up weight 3450 kg (7,600 lb)
Curtiss Tomahawk Mk IIA (Hawk 81A-2): RAF version of P-40B; 210 built but 100 diverted to AVG (AH881-990)
Curtiss P-40C Warhawk (Hawk 81A-3): Allison V-1710-33; introduced self-sealing fuel tanks; 193 built for USAAC in 1941 (41-13328/-13520); all-up weight 3658 kg (8,058 lb)
Curtiss Tomahawk Mk IIB (Hawk 81A-3): RAF version of P-40C; 945 built (AH991-999, AK210-570, AM370-519, AN218-517); approximately 600 served with RAF, others lost at sea or transferred to other air forces; 15 retained in USA
Curtiss P-40D Warhawk (Hawk 87A-2): Allison V-1710-39 (F3R); deepened radiator; 12.7-mm (0.5-in) wing guns and store racks; 23 built for USAAC (40-359/-381); all-up weight 3677 kg (8,100 lb)
Curtiss Kittyhawk Mk I (Hawk 87A-2): Allison V-1710-39(F3R); RAF version of P-40D; 560 built (AK571-AL230); 24 to RCAF and 17 to Turkey
Curtiss P-40E Warhawk (Hawk 87A-3): Allison V-1710-39 (F3R); wing armament increased to six guns; 2,320 built for USAAF (40-358; 40-382/-681; 41-5305/-5744; 41-13521/-13599; 41-24776/-25195; 41-35874/-36953); all-up weight 4013 kg (8,840 lb)
Curtiss Kittyhawk Mk IA (Hawk 87A-3): RAF version of P-40E; 1,500 built, of which 911 served with RAF; of the remainder 171 lost at sea in transit to Russia or to Middle East; others diverted to Canada, Australia and New Zealand (ET100-EV699)
Curtiss XP-40F (Hawk 87D): single Merlin 28-powered prototype converted from production P-40D (40-360); all-up weight 4295 kg (9,460 lb)
Curtiss P-40F Warhawk: Packard-built Merlin-powered production; 1,311 built for USAAF (41-13600/-13695; 41-13697/-14599; 41-19733/-20044); all-up weight 4480 kg (9,870 lb)
Curtiss Kittyhawk Mks II and IIA: 330 aircraft converted for RAF from US P-40F (ex-batch 41-13697/-14599 to become FL219-448, FS400-499); 80 returned to USAAF, 7 lost at sea and 7 transferred to Free French
Curtiss P-40G Warhawk: 46 aircraft with RAF Tomahawk Mk I wings; 29 included in P-40 production above, plus 42-14261/-14274,-14277, -14278 and -14281 (new build)
Curtiss P-40H: cancelled designation
Curtiss P-40J: proposed version with turbocharged Allison, rendered superfluous by advent of Merlin installation; none built
Curtiss P-40K Warhawk: Allison V-1710-73; introduced small dorsal fairing; 1,300 built for USAAF (42-9730/-10429; 42-45722/-46321); all-up weight 4540 kg (10,000 lb)
Curtiss P-40L Warhawk: Packard-Merlin version with reduced fuel, armour and armament; 700 built for USAAF (42-10430/11129); all-up weight 4131 kg (9,100 lb)
Curtiss P-40M Warhawk: Allison V-1710-81; similar to P-40K with engine change; 600 built for USAAF (43-5403/-6002); 21 diverted to RAF (see Kittyhawk III below); all-up weight 3859 kg (8,500 lb)
Curtiss Kittyhawk Mk III: RAF version of P-40M; 616 delivered to Middle East including 21 P-40Ms (FL710-730) offset from US batch 43-5403/-6002; other aircraft were FL875-905, FR111-140, '210-361, '385-392, '412-521, '779-872, FS100-269)
Curtiss P-40N Warhawk (up to N-15 sub-series): Allison V-1710-81; lightened version; 1,977 built for USAAF in 1943-4 (42-104420/-106405); all-up weight 4018 kg (8,850 lb)
Curtiss P-40N Warhawk (N-20 to N-35): Allison V-1710-99; 3,023 built for USAAF in 1943-4 (42-106406/-106428, 43-22752/-24751, 44-7001-8000)
Curtiss P-40N Warhawk (N-40 sub-series): Allison V-1710-113; 1,000 ordered for USAAF but only 220 completed (44-47749/-47968)
Curtiss Kittyhawk Mk IV: RAF version of P-40N; 588 built (FR884-885, FS270-399, FT849-954, FX498-847; one aircraft, FX670 was ex-USAAF 43-23166); 7 lost at sea during delivery
Curtiss P-40R-1 and R-2 Warhawk: 300 P-40Fs and P-40Ls converted to Allison V-1710-81s in 1944 following shortage of Merlin spares; used as trainers
Curtiss XP-40Q: three experimental prototypes, 42-9987 (ex-P-40K) with Allison V-1710-121 and wing radiators; 42-45722 (ex-P-40K) and 43-24571 (ex-P-40L) with bubble canopies; 42-45722 later had wings clipped to become fastest P-40 (679 km/h/422 mph)
Curtiss TP-40N Warhawk: small number of P-40Es and P-40Ns converted to two-seat trainers

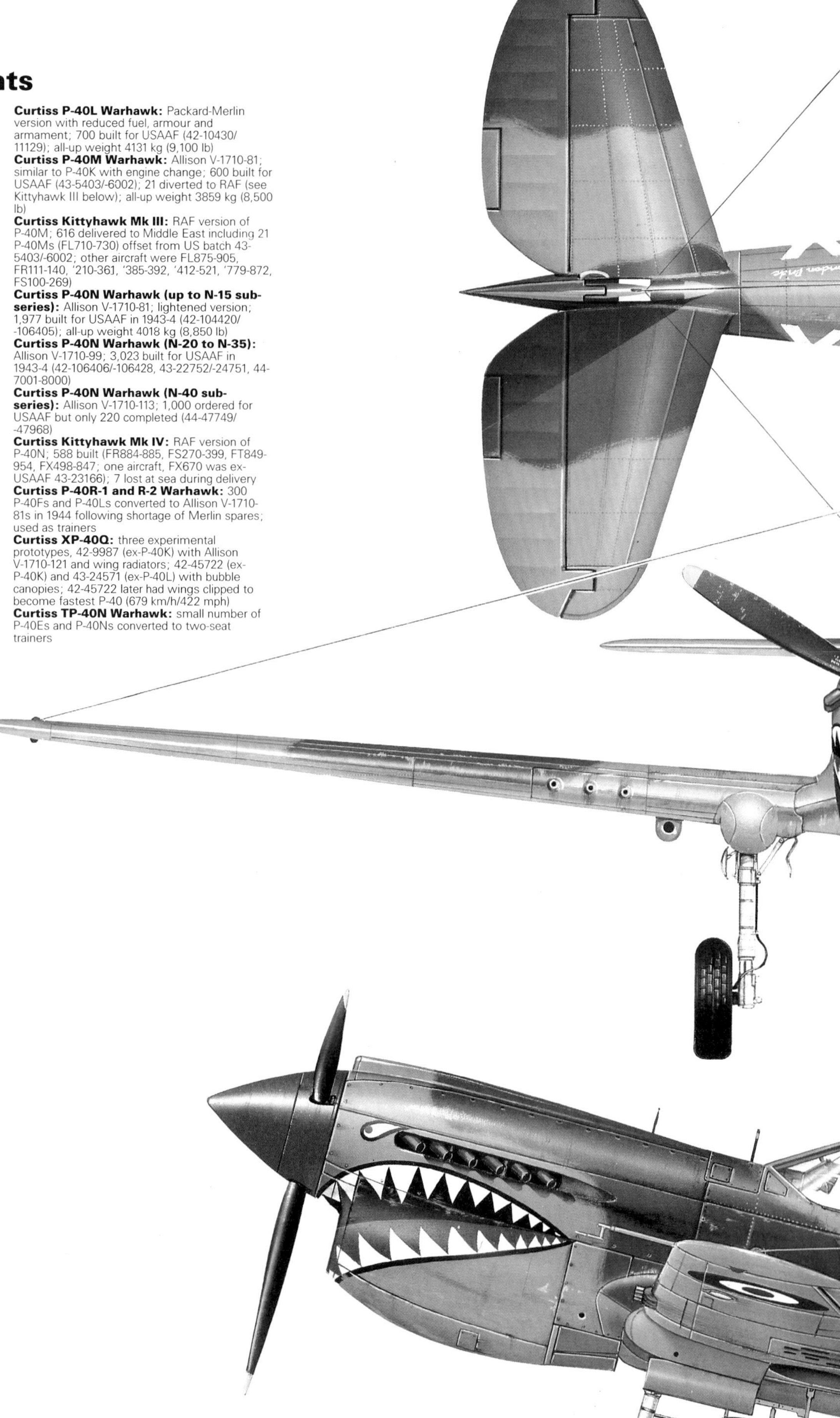

Specification
Curtiss P-40N-20 Warhawk
Type: single-seat interceptor and fighter-bomber
Powerplant: one 1015-kW (1,360-hp) Allison V-1710-81 inline piston engine
Performance: maximum speed 609 km/h (378 mph) at 3210 m (10,500 ft); climb to 4590 m (15,000 ft) in 6 minutes 42 seconds; service ceiling 11630 m (38,000 ft); normal range 386 km (240 miles)
Weights: empty 2724 kg (6,000 lb); maximum take-off 4018 kg (8,850 lb)
Dimensions: span 11.42 m (37 ft 4 in); length 10.2 m (33 ft 4 in); height 3.77 m (12 ft 4 in); wing area 21.95 m^2 (236 sq ft)
Armament: six 12.7-mm (0.5-in) machine-guns in wings and provision for one 227-kg (500-lb) bomb under fuselage

Resplendent in its sharkmouth markings, this Kittyhawk Mk I of No. 112 (Fighter) Sqn, RAF, is shown carrying a single 113-kg (250-lb) bomb under the fuselage, the most widely-used bomb carried by RAF fighters in North Africa early in 1942. At this time (January to April 1942) No. 112 Sqn was commanded by Squadron Leader Clive Caldwell, who later became the top-scoring Australian fighter pilot of the war, winning a DSO and two DFCs. He is on record as having stated that the Kittyhawk was not his favourite aircraft.

Kittyhawk Mk IA of the RAF, identifiable by the six wing guns and Allison engine (note exhaust stubs grouped in pairs). Although this photo was taken in Britain in April 1942, most RAF Kittyhawks served in the Middle East.

A P-40K of the 23rd Fighter Group (possibly an aircraft of the 74th Fighter Squadron) at Kweilin, China, early in 1944. Note the five victory emblems below the windscreen. The circular marking forward of the fuselage star was the pilot's personal emblem.

of the Royal Australian Air Force. With a maximum weight of 3658 kg (8,058 lb), compared with 3119 kg (6,870 lb) for the XP-40, the P-40C was the slowest of all the production variants, possessing a top speed of only 528 km/h (328 mph) at 4590 m (15,000 feet). When it arrived in North Africa late in 1941 it was found to be much inferior to the Messerschmitt Bf 109E and only marginally better than the Hawker Hurricane Mk I, and was therefore primarily used in the ground-attack role. When phased out of service from mid-1942 onwards, many ex-RAF Tomahawk Mk IIBs were supplied to the USSR, as well as to the Turkish air force and Royal Egyptian air force.

New nose, new name

The P-40D (Hawk 87A-2) brought a major redesign of the nose (hence the new company designation) with the introduction of the Allison V-1710-39 engine with external-spur reduction gear, permitting the nose to be shortened by 15.24 cm (6 in). The nose cross-section area was reduced, and the radiator moved forward and deepened; the main landing gear was shortened, the four wing guns were changed to 12.7-mm (0.5-in) calibre and the nose guns were deleted. Provision was also made for a rack capable of carrying a 227-kg (500-lb) bomb or 197-litre (52-US gal) drop tank under the fuselage. The P-40D had a top speed of 580 km/h (360 mph), but only 23 were produced for the USAAC. In the RAF, for which 560 were built, the new version was renamed Kittyhawk Mk I.

The first Kittyhawk Mk Is arrived in North Africa and joined the Tomahawks with No.112 Squadron in December 1941, subsequent deliveries being made to Nos 94, 250 and 260 Squadrons in the next four months, as well as to Nos 5 and 7 Squadrons of the SAAF, and No. 3 Squadron of the RAAF. Twenty-four aircraft from the RAF contract were diverted to the RCAF and 17 supplied to Turkey.

The P-40E (Hawk 87A-3) was the first Warhawk (as the whole P-40 series was named in American service) to be produced in large quantities after Pearl Harbor. It introduced an armament of six 12.7-mm (0.5-in) wing machine-guns, and accompanied the first American fighter squadrons to the UK in 1942, as well as those in the Middle East. With an all-up weight of 4013 kg (8,840 lb), it had a top speed of 570 km/h (354 mph), which was roughly the same as that of the Spitfire Mk VC with tropical filter. Production totalled 2,320 on American contracts plus 1,500 for the RAF as the Kittyhawk Mk IA; many of the latter were diverted direct to the RAAF, RNZAF and RCAF.

With dimensions approximately the same as the Allison V-1710, the Rolls-Royce Merlin, whose production had assumed enormous proportions by 1941, was selected for the P-40 and during that year a production P-40D (40-360) was experimentally fitted with a Merlin 28, resulting in the designation XP-40F (Hawk 87D); although the weight increased to 4295 kg (9,460 lb), the more powerful British engine raised maximum speed to 600 km/h (373 mph) at 5500 m (18,000 ft); this version was distinguishable by the absence of the carburettor air intake above the nose, the downdraught intake of the Allison being replaced by the updraught trunk of the Merlin; the revised ducting was developed on the third production aircraft (41-13602) as the YP-40F.

The first 260 aircraft employed the same fuselage as the P-40E, but the progressive increase in the forward keel area had introduced a progressive reduction in directional stability, so later P-40Fs featured a rear fuselage lengthened by 50.8 cm (20 in). Maximum weight of the production aircraft had crept up to 4480 kg (9,870 lb) and its top speed dropped to 586 km/h (364 mph).

Produced in parallel with the last P-40Fs was the P-40K with the marginally more powerful Allison V-1710-73 (988 kW/1,325 hp) which increased the top speed to 589 km/h (366 mph), thereby giving it an edge over the Bf109E in Europe and North Africa, and over the Mitsubishi A6M in the Far East. More power was added in the P-40M with the introduction of the V-1710-81 engine producing 1015 kW (1,360 hp). Some 1,300 P-40Ks (originally intended for Lend-Lease to China) and 600 P-40Ms were produced for the USAAF. RAF versions of the P-40F were the Kittyhawk Mks II and IIA, of which 330 were produced as an interim measure by converting USAAF aircraft, it being intended to transfer these back in due course to American squadrons; in the event, however, only 80 were returned to the USAAF. A total of 616 Kittyhawk Mk IIIs, equivalent to the P-40M, were delivered to the RAF.

P-40Fs of the USAAF preparing to take-off from an American aircraft-carrier in support of the 'Torch' landings in North Africa in November 1942. The Stars and Stripes markings on the fuselage were adopted during these operations to ensure recognition by French forces to whom the star insignia might prove unfamiliar.

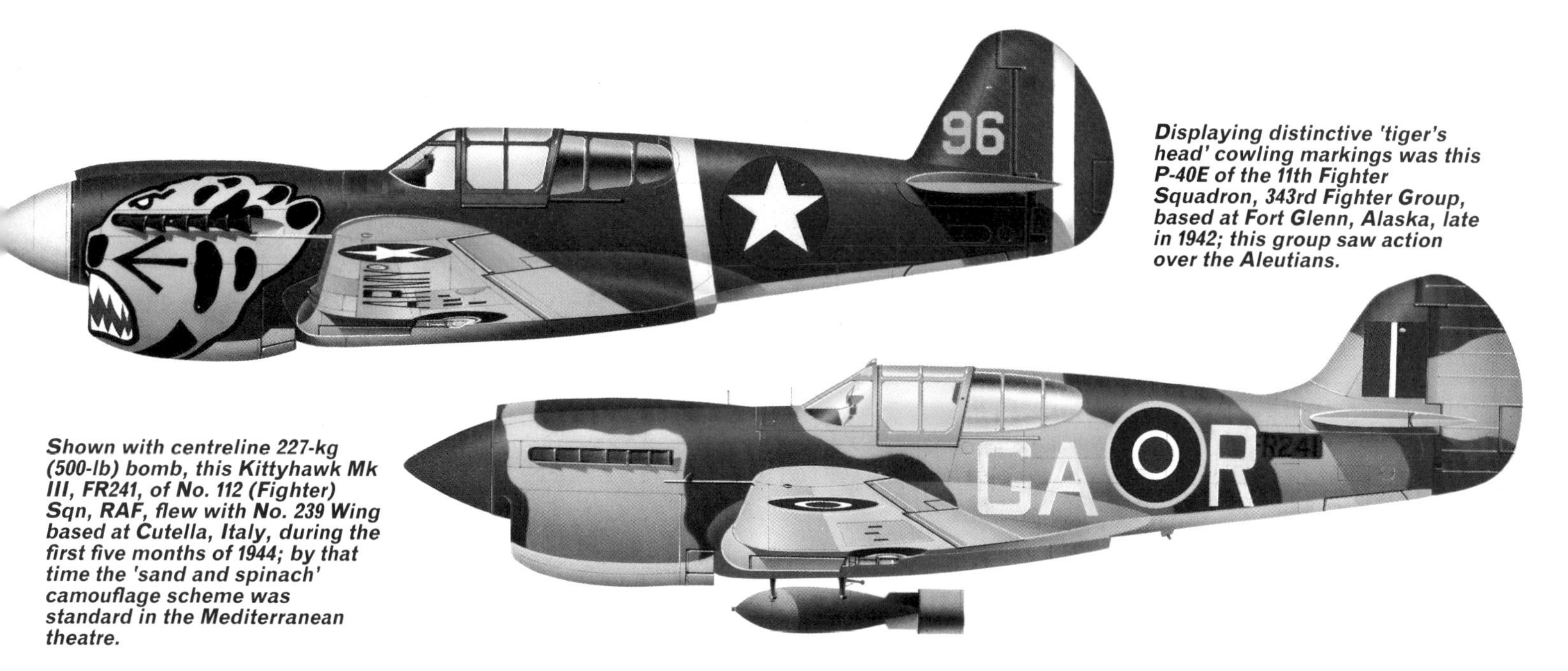

Displaying distinctive 'tiger's head' cowling markings was this P-40E of the 11th Fighter Squadron, 343rd Fighter Group, based at Fort Glenn, Alaska, late in 1942; this group saw action over the Aleutians.

Shown with centreline 227-kg (500-lb) bomb, this Kittyhawk Mk III, FR241, of No. 112 (Fighter) Sqn, RAF, flew with No. 239 Wing based at Cutella, Italy, during the first five months of 1944; by that time the 'sand and spinach' camouflage scheme was standard in the Mediterranean theatre.

A number of other interim versions had meanwhile been produced or planned. Some 45 P-40Gs had been built, combining the Kittyhawk fuselage with RAF Tomahawk wings and six 12.7-mm (0.5-in) wing guns; all were retained by the USAAF. The P-40J was intended to use a turbocharged Allison but was not built owing to the introduction of the Rolls-Royce Merlin. The Packard (Merlin) V-1650-1 was fitted in the P-40L, of which 700 were produced for the USAAF in 1943 (but none for the RAF), some of these aircraft having two guns, armour and some fuel removed to improve performance.

The definitive Warhawk was the P-40N, which entered production towards the end of 1943 and started delivery to the USAAF in March the following year. Reverting to the Allison engine, this was a lightweight version with the front fuselage fuel tank omitted. The early production blocks from -1 to -15, of which 1,977 were built, were armed with only four wing guns and weighed 4081 kg (8,850 lb) all-up. These were followed by 3,023 aircraft in the blocks -20 to -35 with V-1710-99 engines, with armament restored to six guns and provision to carry a 227-kg (500-lb) bomb on belly shackles. The final production version, in the -40 block, was powered by the V-1710-115 and had wing racks to carry two additional 227-kg (500-lb) bombs; 1,000 of this variant were ordered, but production of the Warhawk was terminated in September 1944 when only 220 had been completed. Some 588 were produced for the RAF, equivalent to the P-40N-20, as the Kittyhawk Mk IV.

Many versions, many theatres

In 1944, following the introduction of the Merlin in the P-51, there existed a heavy demand on spares for this engine and so 300 P-40Fs and P-40Ls were converted to take the V-1710-81, their designations being altered to P-40R-1 and R-2 respectively.

Three experimental XP-40Qs were produced with V-1710-121 engines and the radiators moved to the wings; the first, a converted P-40K (42-9987) with four-bladed propeller, was followed by another converted P-40K (42-45722) and a P-40N (43-24571) with clear-view 'bubble' canopies; 42-45722 later had its wings clipped to 10.79 m (35 ft 3 in) span and its radiator moved back to the nose position, and in this configuration it was the fastest of all Warhawks, with a top speed of 679 km/h (422 mph) at 6273 m (20,500 ft). Finally a small number of P-40Es and P-40Ns were converted to two-seat trainers under the designation TP-40N.

Warhawks of the USAAF served on almost all fronts during World War II with many Pursuit and Fighter Groups, among them the 8th and 49th Groups of the US 5th Air Force in the Far East between 1942 and 1944; the 15th and 18th Fighter Groups of the US 7th Air Force between 1941 and 1944; the 57th and 79th Fighter Groups of the US 9th Air Force in the Mediterranean theatre between 1942 and 1944; the 51st Pursuit Group with the US 10th Air Force in India and Burma between 1941 and 1944; and the 27th and 33rd Fighter Groups of the US 12th Air Force in the Mediterranean between 1942 and 1944. They also provided the backbone of the USAAF's fighter defences protecting the Panama Canal between 1941 and 1943, serving with the 16th, 32nd, 36th, 37th and 53rd Pursuit Groups.

While it might be suggested that the P-40 remained in service with the USAAF in secondary war theatres in order to allow delivery priorities to be bestowed upon more, advanced aircraft (such as the P-38, P-47 and P-51), in combat theatres, the prolonging of Warhawk production as late as 1944 – by which time its performance was thoroughly pedestrian among current fighters – has never been satisfactorily explained, especially having regard to the very large numbers built.

Be that as it may, many Tomahawks and Kittyhawks were also delivered against contracts for the RAF, RAAF, RCAF, RNZAF and SAAF; the relatively small number of squadrons so equipped is largely explained by the fact that a large proportion of the aircraft purchased by Britain were diverted to the USSR during 1942 and 1943 (2,091 of the 2,430 aircraft said to have been despatched arriving safely). During the last two years of the war the United States supplied 377 P-40s (mostly P-40Ns) to China, while in 1942 some P-40Es were delivered to Chile and 89 P-40Es went to Brazil the following year.

Among the last P-40Ns in operational service were those of No. 120 Squadron of the Netherlands Army Air Corps which took part in the sporadic campaign against the Indonesians during 1946-7.

Production of all P-40s totalled 16,802, including 4,787 on British contracts.

One theatre in which the P-40 starred was North Africa, where the RAF used its Kittyhawks to great effect. This Mk III wears the famous markings of No. 112 Sqn, and carries an air-to-ground load for harrying German forces. In air-to-air combat, the Kittyhawk proved a better match for the Bf 109F than the Hurricane.

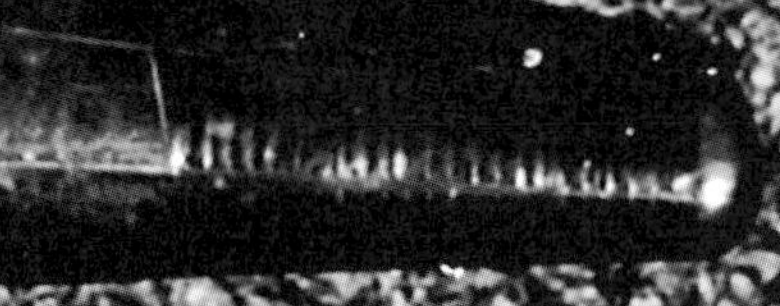

Northrop P-61 Black Widow

Although its long development delayed its entry into battle until the last year of World War II, the Black Widow nevertheless proved itself as a powerful and agile night fighter, despite the fact that there were few opponents for it to fight against. Designed from the outset for nocturnal battle, it was the biggest and heaviest fighter fielded by the Allies during the war.

If the RAF had had Black Widows in 1940 the story of the night *Blitz* would have been very different. In that particular conflict the giant Northrop night-fighter would have been able to destroy every aircraft onto which it was vectored. Unfortunately, it did not reach the squadrons until almost four years later, and by that time not only were hostile aircraft becoming scarce (both over Europe and in the Pacific) but they had far higher performance and were elusive enough to make victories much scarcer still. Nevertheless the P-61 deserves its place in history as the first aircraft ever designed (as distinct from being modified) for use as a night-fighter, using radar and all other electronic devices.

The US Army Air Corps had previously used primitive night-fighters, starting with the Curtiss PN-1 of 1921, and in 1940 was busy with a programme to convert A-20 bombers into P-70 night-fighters, keeping a close eye on the RAF's similar conversion into Havocs. The USAAC knew about the British development of AI (airborne interception) radar, and in fact 60 sets of this radar were shortly supplied for incorporation in the production P-70s even though the USA was strictly neutral. Even more significantly, the Tizard mission sent to the USA in August 1940 gave preliminary details of the most important single technical secret then possessed by the UK: the cavity magnetron. This totally new device was the key to radars operating on centimetric wavelengths (previous radars had wavelengths measured in metres) and enabled H^2S bombing radar, and also superior AI radars for fighters, to be created. The amazing disclosure was made on 28 September 1940, and on 18 October the USA decided to go ahead at top priority with a world-beating AI radar and a fighter to carry it.

The original XP-61 prototype (41-19509) was flown with a mock-up of the definitive dorsal gun barbette. Radar was replaced by ballast, and the whole aircraft bristled with details which were subsequently altered. It is seen at the Hawthorne plant at about the time of its first flight on 26 May 1942.

The radar was assigned to a large team headed by the Radiation Laboratory, a specially created subsidiary of the Massachusetts Institute of Technology (MIT). The work went ahead with a joint US/UK team, with astonishing rapidity. Two days ahead of the 'impossible' schedule, on 4 January 1941, the first microwave radar built in the USA was displaying a picture of the Boston skyline across the Charles River from an MIT roof. It had one of the vital British (GEC) magnetrons, a Westinghouse pulser, Sperry power-driven dish aerial, fixed receiver aerial, Bell Telephone Laboratories receiver (with IF unit by RCA) and General Electric oscilloscope display. It first flew in a Douglas B-18A on 10 March and eventually matured as the production SCR-720, which was also used in many British night-fighters as AI.Mk X.

Night operations

While the challenging radar needed the resources of all the chief companies in the emergent US electronics industry, the aircraft to carry it, which was launched three days later in a letter of 21 October 1940, was assigned to Northrop Aircraft, of Hawthorne (Los Angeles) in California. Northrop lacked nothing in skill and dedication, but had never had a major production programme, nor anything in such an exceptionally difficult field. In October 1940 the US Army Air Corps mission to the UK, headed by General Emmons, had just returned to Washington. Among a host of recommendations it urged development of a purpose-designed night-fighter, and the arrival of the British magnetron was a large bonus. With the benefit of hindsight, while SCR-720 was unquestionably a war weapon of the very first importance, which the RAF was glad to use in post-war night-fighters into the 1950s, the 'clean sheet of paper' night-fighter arrived late and was no better than a modification of (for example) the Douglas A-26 Invader for the same purpose. Indeed, the considered opinion of many experts, not only in the RAF but also in the USAF, was that it offered little that the compromised lash-up night-fighter versions of the Bristol Beaufighter and de Havilland Mosquito had not been doing since 1941. The author, who flew the British aircraft and rode as passenger in Black Widows, considers the P-61 a first-class aircraft whose only fault was the burden it placed on everyone concerned with maintaining and flying it.

It was not meant to be like that. John K. Northrop expected to get into production inside a year. His right-hand man on design was Walt Cerny, who came with him to present the outline NS-8A proposal to Wright Field on 5 November 1940. Aerodynamics were assigned to a small group under Dr William Sears, who came on the payroll in 1942. From the start the US Army insisted on a crew of three, ex-

The 19th production P-61C on routine flight test in the closing weeks of the war. This model had many new features, notably including turbocharged R-2800-73 engines, the inlets to the General Electric CH-5 turbos being visible on each side of the cowlings. Most obvious of all were the new airbrakes, here seen fully open.

Near the end of the P-61B production run, by which time the dorsal barbette had been reinstated, the alternating blocks of single aircraft suddenly gave way to a block of 90 P-61B-15s, and aircraft 42-39728 was from this block. Every 'Widow' had to be flight tested with a full combat crew to operate the various systems and controls.

ceptional all-round view and armament including a power-driven turret or turrets. The original scheme comprised a central nacelle with twin-boom tail, and three crew in a row: pilot, radar/gunner above and behind and thus able to use a gunsight directly ahead as could the pilot, and a gunner in the rear of the nacelle to cover the aft hemisphere. As in the US Navy Grumman F7F, which had the same tremendous power of two R-2800 engines, four 20-mm cannon were to be in the inboard wing or in the outer panels. In addition there was to be a dorsal turret with four 12.7-mm (0.5-in) guns and a ventral turret with two more such guns.

In those days, even with telephones, Wright Field was a long way from Los Angeles. At the mock-up review board, on 2 April 1941, no fewer than 76 engineering changes were called for, the most serious being relocation of the fixed cannon to the underfloor area of the nacelle, the ventral barbette being omitted. Countless other factors conspired to delay the programme, which had been designated XP-61 in December 1940, including argument over the engine installation, structural materials, flight controls and tankage; and Northrop's priority task of building 400 Vengeance dive-bombers for the RAF and US Army did not help either. Despite this the original contract of 11 January 1941, amounting to $1,167,000 for design, development and two prototypes, was augmented in September 1941 by an order for 150 production P-61s, followed on 12 February 1942 by 410 more! This was a backlog of over $26 million, about 26 times anything Northrop had known before, and still the first prototype was incomplete.

Eventually the unpainted XP-61 (41-19509) was completed in early May 1942, and flown by Vance Breese with generally excellent results. It was certainly an odd-looking machine, enormous for a fighter with a wing of 61.53 m^2 (662.36 sq ft) area, even bigger than the wing of today's F-15, and with a crew area considerably more spacious than most medium bombers despite the mass of controls

In 1946 Northrop built 36 dedicated reconnaissance aircraft designated F-15A Reporters. These were subsequently re-designated RF-61Cs in 1948 and served with the USAF until 1952. This photograph shows the XF-15A, a prototype conversion of a P-61A.

Northrop P-61 Black Widow cutaway drawing key

1 Starboard navigation light
2 Starboard formation light
3 Aileron hinge fairing
4 Conventional aileron
5 Aileron tab
6 Full span flaps
7 Retraction aileron (operable as spoiler)
8 Wing skinning
9 De-icer boot
10 Intercooler controllable shutters
11 Intercooler and supercharger induction
12 Fuel filler cap
13 Starboard outer wing fuel tank
14 Nacelle fairing
15 Cooling gills
16 Pratt & Whitney R-2800-65 engine
17 Nacelle ring
18 Starboard outer auxiliary tank
19 Four-bladed Curtiss Electric propeller
20 Propeller cuffs
21 Propeller boss
22 Heater air induction
23 Front spar
24 Plexiglas canopy
25 Cannon access bulkhead cut-out
26 Front gunner's compartment
27 Sighting station
28 Bullet resistant windshield
29 Inter-cockpit/ compartment armour (shaded)
30 Pilot's canopy
31 Pilot's seat
32 Control column
33 Gunsight (fixed cannon)
34 Bullet resistant windshield
35 Fuselage structural joint (armour plate deleted for clarity)
36 Radar modulator
37 Di-electric nose cone
38 SCR-720 radar scanner
39 Gun camera (gunsight aiming point)
40 Mast
41 Pitot head
42 Radar equipment steel support tube
43 Bulkhead (centre joint)
44 Rudder pedals
45 Drag strut
46 Torque link
47 Towing eye
48 Nosewheel
49 Cantilever steel strut
50 Mudguard (often deleted)
51 Taxi lamp
52 Air-oil shock strut (shimmy damper on forward face)
53 Nosewheel door
54 Cockpit floor
55 Radar aerials
56 Gunner compartment floor (stepped)
57 Forward gunner's seat-swivel mechanism
58 Cannon ports
59 Heater air induction
60 Cannon ammunition magazines
61 Ammunition feed chute
62 20-mm cannon in ventral compartment
63 Magazine forward armour plate
64 Front-spar fuselage cut-out
65 Magazine rear armour plate
66 Rear-spar fuselage cut-out
67 Dorsal turret support/drive motor
68 Front spar carry-through
69 Turret support forward armour plate
70 Flush-riveted aluminium alloy skin
71 Gun mantlet (four 0.50-in
72 General Electric remote-control power turret
73 Turret drive ring
74 Rear spar carry-through
75 Turret support rear armour plate

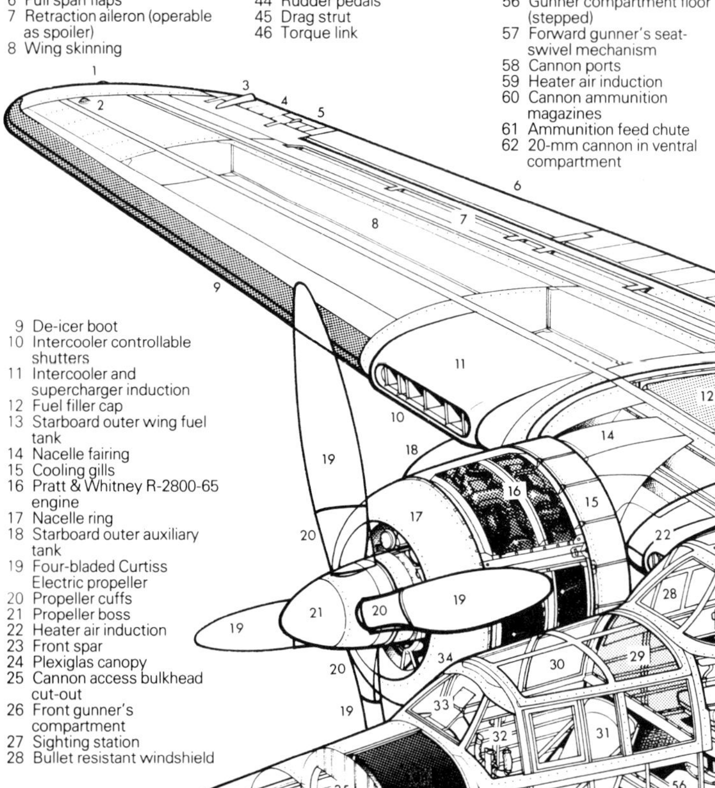

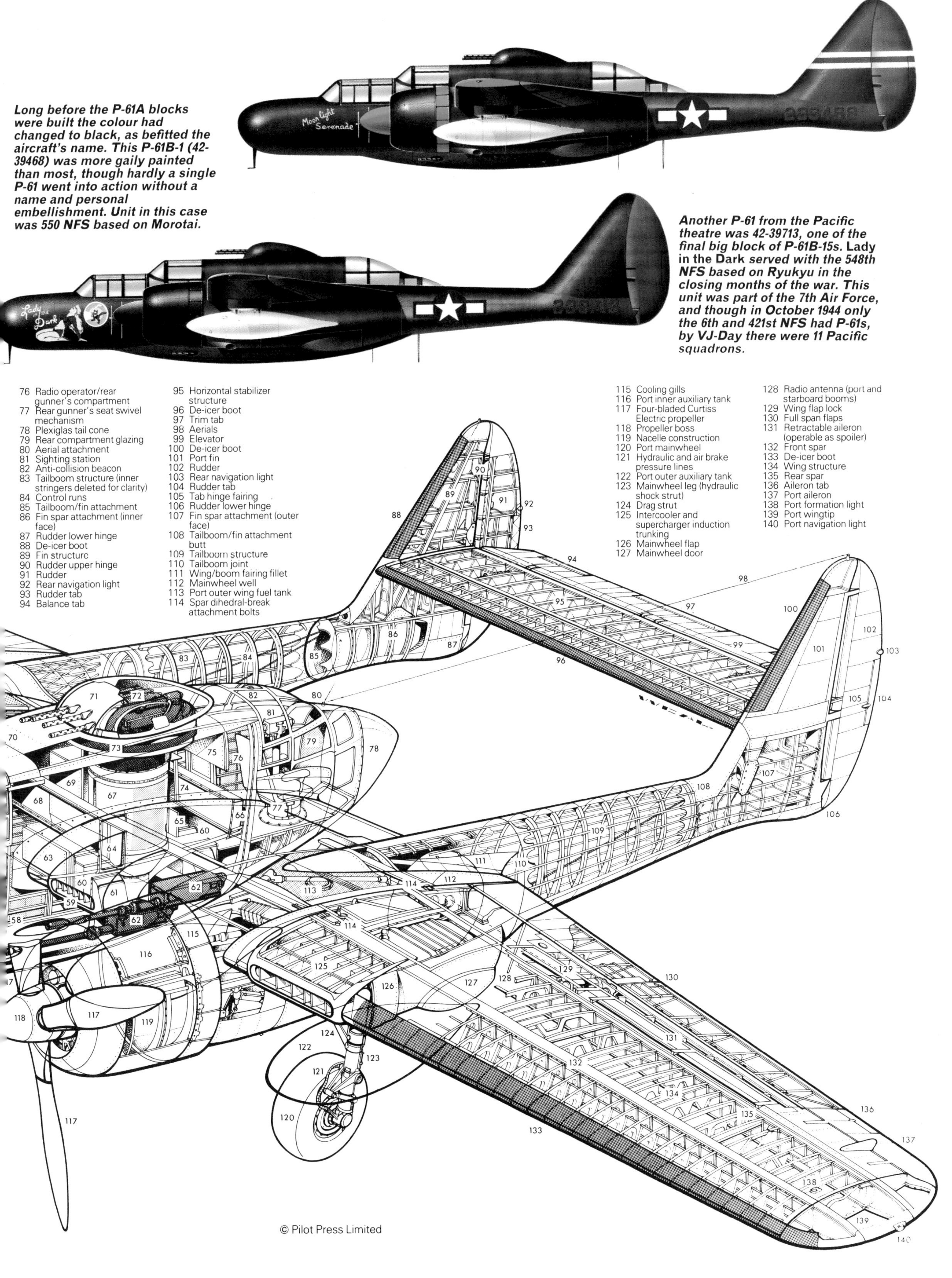

Long before the P-61A blocks were built the colour had changed to black, as befitted the aircraft's name. This P-61B-1 (42-39468) was more gaily painted than most, though hardly a single P-61 went into action without a name and personal embellishment. Unit in this case was 550 NFS based on Morotai.

Another P-61 from the Pacific theatre was 42-39713, one of the final big block of P-61B-15s. Lady in the Dark served with the 548th NFS based on Ryukyu in the closing months of the war. This unit was part of the 7th Air Force, and though in October 1944 only the 6th and 421st NFS had P-61s, by VJ-Day there were 11 Pacific squadrons.

Northrop P-61 Black Widow

Specification
Northrop P-61B-1-NO
Type: three-seat night-fighter
Powerplant: two 1491-kW (2,000-hp) Pratt & Whitney R-2800-65 Double Wasp 18-cylinder radials
Performance: maximum speed (1678-kW/2,250-hp war emergency power) 589 km/h (366 mph) at 6096 m (20,000 ft); initial climb (military power 1491-kW/2,000-hp) 637 m (2,090 ft) per minute; range (long-range cruise power) 2172 km (1,350 miles) at 368 km/h (229 mph)
Weights: empty 10637 kg (23,450 lb); maximum overload 16420 kg (36,200 lb)
Dimensions: span 20.11 m (66 ft 0¾ in); length 15.11 m (49 ft 7 in); height 4.47 m (14 ft 8 in); wing area 61.53 m^2 (662.36 sq ft)
Armament: four 20-mm (0.78-in) M2 cannon each with 200 rounds; dorsal barbette with four 12.7-mm (0.5-in) Colt-Browning machine-guns each with 560 rounds; four external pylons each rated at up to 726 kg (1,600 lb) and able to carry bombs or other stores of up to this weight

Northrop P-61 variants

XP-61: two prototypes, with R-2800-10 engines (41-19509/10)
YP-61: service-test aircraft (13), with Dash-10 engines (41-18876-88)
P-61A: production aircraft (200), from 38th without dorsal turret (often restored later); from 46th with water-injection Dash-65 engine (42-5485/5634 and -39348/39397)
P-61B: production aircraft (450), with Dash-65 engines; most with turret and four pylons, various equipment fits (42-39398/39757 and 43-8231/8320)
P-61C: production aircraft, with Dash-73 engines and CH-5 turbochargers, wet emergency rating 2089 kW (2,800 hp), Curtiss Electric paddle-blade hollow steel propellers, 692 km/h (430 mph) at high altitude (476 cancelled at VJ-Day and only 41, 43-8321/8361, delivered)
XP-61D: P-61As 42-5559 and 42-5587 re-engined with Dash-77 turbocharged engines
XP-61E: P-61Bs 42-39549 and 42-39557 rebuilt with slim nacelle, four 12.7-mm (0.5-in) guns in nose in place of radar, pilot and navigator under bubble hood (then largest piece of moulded Plexiglas ever attempted), 4382 litres (1,158 US gal) of internal fuel; first became XF-15
XP-61F: P-61C 43-8338 to be modified as P-61E but never completed
P-61G: production weather-reconnaissance aircraft modified from P-61Bs in 1945 (various numbers)
XF-15 Reporter: first XP-61E rebuilt as unarmed reconnaissance aircraft with six cameras in modified nose
XF-15A: P-61C (43-8335) modified with same nacelle as F-15 (visually distinguished from F-15 by large turbocharger ducts under engines)
F-15A Reporter: production aircraft (originally 175, only 36 actually built), based on part-complete P-61C airframes (45-59300/35)
F2T-1N: surplus P-61As (12) used as night-fighter trainers by US Marine Corps (Bu. Nos 52750/61)

and switchgear. The second XP-61 (19510) followed on 18 November 1942, painted from the start in the glossy black dope which helped give the fighter its name. Altogether it was a very fine machine, though there were enough major problems to prevent the initiation of full production. The original fuel system, with a 1023-litre (270-US gal) flexible cell between the wing spars in the engine nacelles, was augmented by two further 455-litre (120-US gal) tanks and provision for 1173-litre (310-US gal) drop tanks on underwing pylons (these were not introduced until well into production). The rectangular tailplane and elevators were redesigned aerodynamically to improve pitch control, the welded-magnesium tail booms were replaced by conventional flush-rivetted light alloy, and the Zap flaps (pioneered by Northrop with an OS2U Kingfisher in May 1941) had to be replaced by double-slotted flaps which were a practical production job. Even then flap flutter caused major difficulties (and frightening vertical acceleration readings of +9g/−6g, which says much for the strength of the wing). The flaps were extremely powerful. Northrop had long understood better than most designers that lift coefficient is very important, and the P-61 had flaps over almost the whole span. The conventional ailerons were very small, but roll control was backed up when needed by four sections of differential spoiler on each wing. This enabled the P-61 to be amazingly agile considering its size and weight. It would have stood little chance in daylight against Fw 190s, but at night it easily outmanoeuvred every twin it met.

The radar finally got into the second prototype in late April 1943, at Wright Field, by which time the 13 service-test YP-61s (numbered sequentially earlier than the prototypes at 41-18876/18888) were visible on the line. These all flew in August and September, and though they incorporated reinforced skin over the nose gear and many other areas to withstand the firing of the cannon, it was found that an operative dorsal turret could, when slewed to the beam position, cause severe tail buffet. Accordingly the turret was fitted to only the first 37 production P-61As (numbers from 42-5485); moreover, the structure was stiffened and often had only the outboard guns fitted. From the 38th the turret was omitted, and it is remarkable that the gain in speed was a mere 4.8 km/h (3 mph). Later at least 10, and possibly many more, of the remaining 163 P-61As had the turret installed after the buffet trouble had been eradicated.

Teething problems

It seemed that every day there were at least a dozen new problems, and this if anything got worse after the start of service deliveries in March 1944 to the 348th NFS of the 481st NFG, which sweltered in Florida training future Black Widow crews. The troubles were due almost entirely to the fact that there was so much

This superb illustration shows one of the most famous P-61s of the Pacific theatre. Built as P-61B-1-NO, no. 42-39403, it was almost unique in having the dorsal gun barbette fitted; it did not come back into production until the P-61B-15 block, the first 200 (except for this aircraft and 42-39419) being turretless like the later P-61As. Other features of the B-model include a slightly longer nose, Curtiss Electric propellers with broader and more efficient blades, and four external pylons (here occupied by tanks) instead of two.

403

Northrop P-61 Black Widow

Husslin Hussey ***was a P-61A-5, the seventh of this block, naturally devoid of the dorsal barbette and shown with invasion stripes after seeing action with the 422nd NFS at RAF Hurn (detached from Scorton) in July 1944. Part of the 9th AF, No. 422 had all three of the European theatre P-61 'aces': Axtell, Smith and Ernst.***

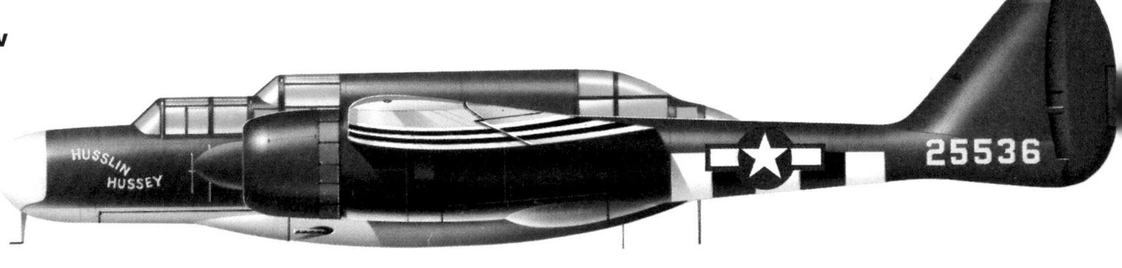

to go wrong; for example there were 229 design changes in the cannon installation alone between early 1942 and spring 1944. Once crews had got over the shock of the size of the 'Widow' they were pleased at the way it could be flung round the sky, the only prohibited manoeuvres being stalls, spins, flick rolls and sustained inverted flight. Other unpopular features were the fact the 3.71 m (12 ft 2 in) Curtiss Electric four-blade propellers were in line with the pilot, and the absence (at first) of any way for a trapped force-landed crew to be released from outside.

From June 1944 the floodgates were opened and aircraft came through at about three a day to the ETO (European Theater of Operations) and CPA (Central Pacific Area). The first P-61 'kill' was scored in the latter area on 6 July, when the 6th NFS bagged a Mitsubishi G4M 'Betty'. In the UK the first units were the 422nd and 425th NFS, which arrived in May and continued what they had done before: endless, slogging training in classrooms. On 6 June (D-Day) the 425th watched endless streams of Douglas C-47s pulling Airspeed Horsa and Waco CG-4 gliders to France from their base at Charmy Down; then in the full light of day they went back to their own war effort in the classroom. On 28 June things got worse: IX Fighter Command had decided the Mosquito could outfight the big 'Widow'. Lieutenant Colonel Oris B. Johnson of the 422nd and Major Leon G. Lewis of the 425th gathered their best crews and arranged a showdown fly-off at Hurn. The beefy P-61 held its own, and by July both units were in business with 16 'Widows', a North American AT-6 Texan and a Cessna UC-78 Bobcat, even though to save time and fuel they had been relocated 322 km (200 miles) to the north at RAF Scorton!

It says much for the power and strength of the P-61 that in its first ETO actions it succeeded in catching and shooting down nine flying bombs, one of them from a mere 30 m (100 ft) dead astern which almost took the 'Widow' with it. From August the 422nd and 425th NFSs got into real action in deep intruder missions, bagging not only large numbers of locomotives, supply convoys and even the odd bridge but also Bf 109s, Bf 110s, Me 410s, Fw 190s, Do 217s and various unidentified types. In Italy the 12th Air Force got the 414th converted from the trusty Beaufighter by January 1945 and got five kills, but the 415th, 416th and 417th NFSs did not convert until March, by which time the show was over. In the Pacific units were luckier, the 418th and 421st NFSs seeing a lot of action from mid-1944, and in China the 426th and 427th NFSs converted in late 1944 and were used mainly on ground-attack with rocket tubes.

From July 1944 deliveries were of the P-61B version, which had not only the R-2800-65 engine with a 1679-kW (2,250-hp) wet rating (this had been introduced on the 46th P-61A) but also the four-gun dorsal turret (of an improved type from the P-61B-20 onwards) and, from the B-10 block, four wing pylons each stressed for a tank or a 726-kg (1,600-lb) bomb. Other variants are listed separately. Certainly the best-looking of the whole family were the XP-61E and F-15A, because these had slim nacelles with graceful teardrop canopies. The F-15A Reporter reconnaissance aircraft turned the '3' figures of the 'Widow' into '4' figures: 708 km/h (440 mph), 12495 m (41,000 ft) and 6437 km (4,000 miles), all extremely impressive for a 1945 aircraft. As for the P-61, 674 were built by VJ-Day and 706 altogether, and the P-61C did not pass from the scene until the 68th and 339th NFSs (347th FG in the Pacific) finally re-equipped in 1950.

The 23rd production P-61A is seen here in an original wartime colour photograph on flight test in the Los Angeles area. At this time the dorsal barbette was still fitted, and the standard colour scheme was olive drab, with the radome unpainted (the dielectric material was off-white). The serial number was red.

Opposite: Two P-61Bs make their way to attack Japanese targets in the Marianas Islands in January 1945. No fewer than 10 squadrons of 'Black Widows' operated in this theatre as the standard Army Air Force night-fighter, employing their newly-restored four-gun dorsal turret.

Lockheed P-38 Lightning

Unfairly overshadowed by its single-engined compatriots, the P-47 and P-51, Lockheed's Lightning was a formidable long-range fighter, proving hard-hitting, manoeuvrable and highly effective in all of the many theatres in which it served.

Fighter, bomber, night-fighter, reconnaissance aircraft, air ambulance, torpedo-bomber and even glider tug: there seemed no limit to the adaptability of the Lockheed P-38, one of the brilliant trio of 'pursuit' fighters produced by the USA during World War II, and the only one to remain in series production throughout the entire period of American participation in the war.

Originally conceived to meet a 1937 requirement for a high-altitude fighter capable of 580 km/h (360 mph) at 6095 m (20,000 ft), and a full-throttle endurance of one hour at this altitude, the Lockheed design team under H. L. Hibbard (undertaking its first military essay) embarked on a radical twin-engined, twin-boom design, there being no engine available to meet the performance demands in a single-engine layout. After examination of other alternatives, it was found that the twin-boom configuration bestowed numerous advantages, such as accommodation of engines, main landing gear, superchargers and radiators, as well as providing the benefits of endplate effect on the tailplane with twin vertical surfaces. Although the nose was thus left free for armament without synchronisation, the foreshortened central nacelle always proved difficult to adapt for additional equipment. The original gross weight of 6713 kg (14,800 lb) was higher than that of most contemporary American light bombers.

The Lockheed Model 22 design was accepted by the USAAC on 23 June 1937 and a single XP-38 prototype ordered. This was flown by Lieutenant B. S. Kelsey at March Field on 27 January 1939. Two weeks later the aircraft was flown across the continent in 7 hours 2 minutes with two refuelling stops, but was destroyed when it undershot on landing at Mitchell Field.

A batch of 13 YP-38 pre-production test aircraft had already been ordered, and the first of these was flown on 16 September 1940, powered by 858-kW (1,150-hp) Allison V-1710-27/29 engines with spur reduction gear driving outward-rotating propellers in place of the prototype's 716-kW (960-hp) V-1710-11/15 engines with epicyclic gear driving inward-rotating propellers. Armament provision was also changed from one 23-mm Madsen cannon and four 12.7-mm (0.5-in) Browning machine-guns to one 37-mm Oldsmobile cannon, two 12.7-mm (0.5-in) machine-guns and two 7.62-mm (0.3-in) machine-guns.

Delivery of the YP-38s was completed from Burbank, California, in March 1941. But long before, in September 1939, an initial production order for 66 P-38s had been signed, followed quickly by another for 607. The P-38 reverted to the armament of the XP-38 and, with the addition of some armour round the cockpit, grossed up to 6958 kg (15,340 lb), with a top speed of 636 km/h (395 mph) at 6035 m (19,800 ft). Deliveries of the first 30 aircraft were completed in mid-1941, but these aircraft were largely confined to training duties. One P-38 was modified as the XP-38A with an experimental pressure cabin, but the P-38B and P-38C projects remained unbuilt.

First flown by Lieutenant B. S. Kelsey at March Field on 27 January 1939, the prototype XP-38 (37-457) promised to be an outstanding fighter from the outset, and its high-speed trans-continental dash (despite its landing accident) made immediate headlines.

European feedback

The first fully combat-standard version was the P-38D, which incorporated many features recommended in reports of air fighting in Europe, the first deliveries to the USAAC starting in August 1941 with the 27th Pursuit Squadron, 1st Pursuit Group, at Selfridge Field, Michigan. This version, of which 36 were produced, featured self-sealing fuel tanks and introduced increased tailplane incidence which led to improved elevator control and reduced buffeting at low speeds; a retractable landing light and low-pressure pilot's oxygen system were also introduced. At the time of Pearl Harbor the USAAC had on inventory a total of 47 P-38s and P-38Ds.

As production at Burbank switched to the P-38E (of which 210 were built) in November 1941, three P-38s were experimentally modified as RP-38s to include a second cockpit in the port tail boom (the supercharger gear being removed) to test pilot experience of asymmetric flight, although the reason for this interest remains unknown. The P-38E dispensed with the 37-mm gun, instead featuring a 20-mm Hispano with increased ammunition capacity; later sub-variants introduced Curtiss Electric propellers with solid dural blades in place of Hamilton Standard Hydromatic propellers with hollow steel blades, revised electrical and hydraulic systems and SCR-274N radio. P-38Es served with a total of 12 squadrons of the USAAF during 1942 and 1943, the majority of them in the Southwest Pacific theatre and in the Aleutians.

Meanwhile, the Royal Air Force had expressed interest in the P-38 (now named the Lightning, the name Atlanta – at one time favoured – having been discarded), a British Purchasing Mission having signed a cash purchase order for 667 aircraft in March 1940. Records of 1941 show that it was intended to equip Nos 46, 69, 89,

Sharkmouth P-38F-5 of the 374th Fighter Group, commanded by Lieutenant Colonel M. McNeese, on detachment to the 13th Air Force, Guadalcanal, February 1943. This Group comprised the 67th, 68th and 70th Fighter Squadrons and was engaged in escort duties during attacks on Japanese bases on New Georgia, the Russell Islands and Bougainville.

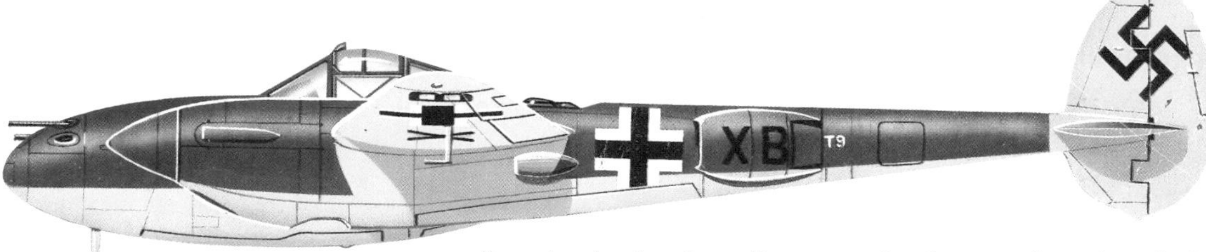

Captured and repaired after a forced landing in enemy-occupied territory, this P-38E of Sonderkommando Rosarius was flown for demonstration purposes for Luftwaffe units during 1943 and 1944. By then, however, the improved P-38F was in service with the USAAF.

137 and 263 Squadrons with this long-range fighter but, as a result of an American ban on the export of superchargers to Europe at that stage of the war, the British version was powered by unsupercharged Allison V-1710-C15R engines (with right-hand rotation only) and proved to possess relatively sluggish performance (top speed 570 km/h/354 mph at 6400 m/21,000 ft). A small number of Lightning Mk Is was shipped to the UK early in 1942 and flew at Boscombe Down and Farnborough, where pilots recommended that further deliveries be suspended. Accordingly, about 130 of the first 143 Lightning Mk Is were repossessed by the USAAF for use as trainers (known as P-322s) or fully modified as P-38F-13s or -15s. The remainder of the British order (Lightning Mk IIs) was completed with V-1710-F2R engines but, following the USA's entry into the war, all were repossessed by the USAAF and most were modified at a Dallas plant to become P-38G-15s.

In March 1942 the USAAF received the first deliveries of a reconnaissance version, the F-4 (converted from P-38Es), in which all armament had been replaced by four K-17 cameras; a drift sight and autopilot were also introduced as standard. Some 99 F-4s were converted, first joining the 5th and 7th Photographic Squadrons in the USA.

The P-38F joined the Burbank line early in 1942 with 988-kW (1,325-hp) V-1710-49/53 engines which maintained the top speed at 636 km/h (395 mph) at 7620 m (25,000 ft) at an all-up weight increased to 8165 kg (18,000 lb). The additional weight was the result of introducing underwing bomb racks for two 454-kg (1,000-lb) bombs, a smoke-laying installation or long-range drop tanks. The last bestowed a maximum range of 2816 km (1,750 miles), a useful performance attribute for warfare in the Pacific theatre.

The P-38F-5-LO introduced A-12 oxygen equipment, the F-13-LO was the repossessed Lightning Mk I with instrument display to BS.2338, and the P-38F-15-LO featured provision for a combat flap setting of 8° that allowed tighter turning at combat speeds by increasing the lift coefficient. At least one P-38F-13 was test flown with a pair of 559-mm (22-in) torpedoes on the underwing racks. The P-38F was the first version to undergo modification as a two-seater, a small number having the radio removed and a second seat installed on the wing main spar; no controls were fitted in this cockpit and the variant was intended only to provide air experience for pilots who were unaccustomed to a nosewheel landing gear, and in any case would have been extremely cramped and uncomfortable. A total of 527 P-38Fs was produced, this number including 20 reconnaissance F-4As which, apart from the later engines, was similar to the F-4.

First kill

P-38F-1-LOs with SCR-522 and SCR-535 radio were the first American fighters to be flown to the UK across the Atlantic, aircraft of the 1st and 14th Fighter Groups (accompanied by Boeing B-17s as navigator/escort ships) flying from the USA to Goxhill and Atcham respectively in July and August 1942 before being assigned to the 12th Air Force in North Africa later in that year. Another group flew to North Africa by way of the South Atlantic. The first German aircraft to be shot down by a P-38 had, however, long before been claimed by the pilot of a P-38E of an Iceland-based group, who had disposed of a Focke-Wulf Fw 200 Condor within hours of the USA's declaration of war.

The P-38G was little changed from the F-series. It featured 988-kW (1,325-hp) V-1710-51/55 engines, boost-governed to deliver no more than 858 kW (1,150 hp) at 8230 m (27,000 ft) owing to inadequate radiator area; it also reverted to the SCR-274N radio. The P-38G-3-LO had B-13 superchargers and the P-38G-15 was the repossessed RAF Lightning Mk II. Of the 1,082 P-38Gs built, 181 were converted to F-5A reconnaissance aircraft and 200 to F-5Bs (similar to the F-5As but with intercoolers). Whereas the earlier F-4s equipped 20 reconnaissance squadrons between 1942 and 1945 (including the 18th Combat Mapping Squadron, the 111th Tactical Reconnaissance Squadron and the 154th Weather Reconnaissance Squadron), the F-5 sub-variants reached 33 squadrons, remaining on some after the war.

P-38Gs joined 27 USAAF squadrons in the Pacific theatre during

Drop tank-carrying P-38G pictured in 1943. This version featured the so-called manoeuvring flap, previously introduced in the late sub-variants of the F-series, and served in large numbers in Europe and the Mediterranean theatre.

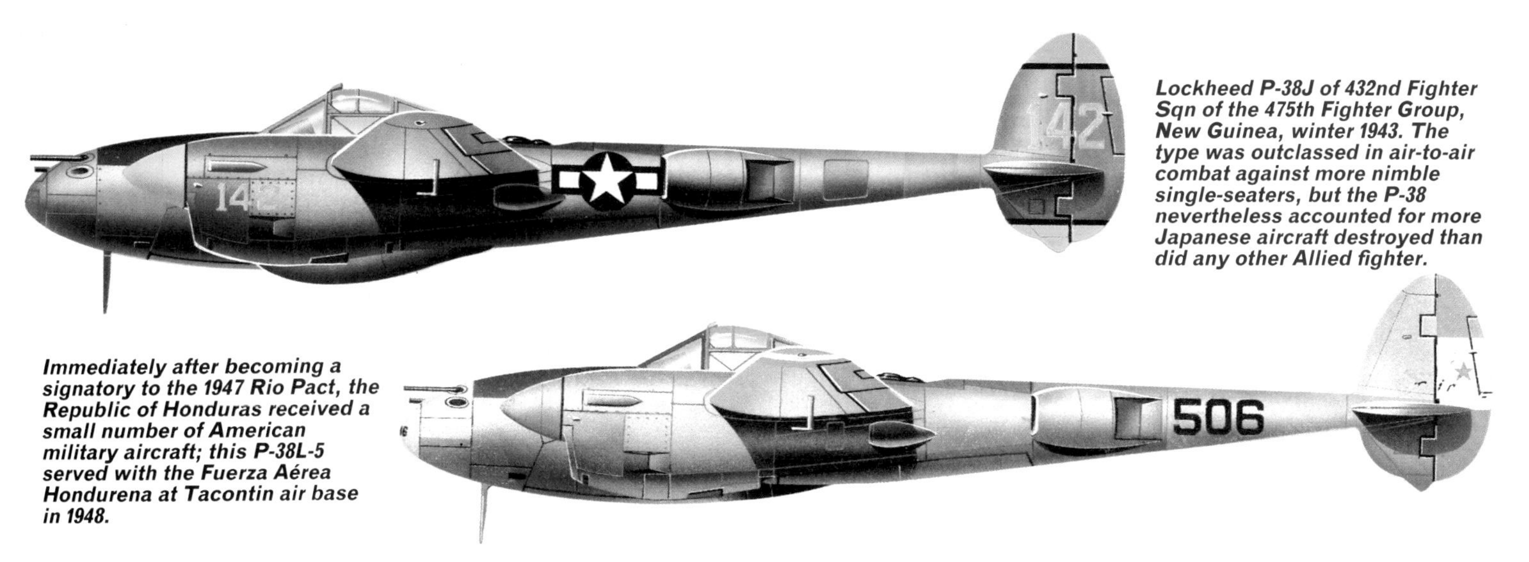

Lockheed P-38J of 432nd Fighter Sqn of the 475th Fighter Group, New Guinea, winter 1943. The type was outclassed in air-to-air combat against more nimble single-seaters, but the P-38 nevertheless accounted for more Japanese aircraft destroyed than did any other Allied fighter.

Immediately after becoming a signatory to the 1947 Rio Pact, the Republic of Honduras received a small number of American military aircraft; this P-38L-5 served with the Fuerza Aérea Hondurena at Tacontin air base in 1948.

Final wartime production version was the P-38L, of which Lockheed produced 3,810 and Vultee 113. It was similar to the J-series but was powered by 1,600-hp V-1710-111/113 engines and was equipped to mount rocket projectiles under the wings.

1943, and it was the drop tank-equipped aircraft of a detachment from the 339th Fighter Squadron, 347th Fighter Group, based on Guadalcanal, that intercepted and destroyed the Japanese aircraft carrying Admiral Isoroku Yamamoto 885 km (550 miles) from their base. The P-38 pilot who claimed this victory was Lieutenant Thomas G. Lanphier, who later flew with Lockheed as a test pilot.

Increased all-up weight to 8709 kg (19,200 lb) and 1063-kW (1,425-hp) V-1710-89/91 engines identified the P-38H, of which Lockheed built 601 and which entered service in May 1943, reaching the European theatre the following month. The increased weight resulted from restressing the underwing pylons to carry bombs or other stores of up to a total of 1452 kg (3,200 lb). Later sub-variants introduced automatically-operating oil cooler flaps in an effort to cure persistent overheating troubles, while the P-38H-5-LO featured the General Electric B-33 supercharger which provided high boost at altitude. Maximum speed of the P-38H-5 was 673 km/h (418 mph).

Converted from the P-38L, the photo-reconnaissance F-5G carried a combination of forward-facing and vertical cameras in the cockpit nacelle; it saw service in Europe and the Far East during the last year of the war.

Meanwhile the P-38 was in constant action in Europe and the Mediterranean theatre, earning the German soubriquet *der gabelschwanz Teufel* (the fork-tail devil). Despite the obvious benefit of the combat flap, the P-38 did not prove entirely suitable for combat with the single-engined fighters of the Luftwaffe. This was learned at some cost during the first bomber-escort flights to Berlin from bases in England. Nevertheless, the reconnaissance F-5s of the 12th Photographic Reconnaissance Squadron, 3rd Photographic Group, based at La Marsa, Tunisia, succeeded in mapping some 80 per cent of the Italian mainland before the invasion of that country. There were 128 conversions of P-38Hs to F-5C reconnaissance standard.

The first externally-obvious alteration to the P-38 was made in the P-38J series, which entered combat service in August 1943. Powered by 1063-kW (1,425-hp) V-1710-89/91 engines (like the previous version), this series introduced 'chin' fairings under the nose to enclose the intercooler intakes sandwiched between the oil radiator intakes. On the P-38J-5-LO the space previously occupied by the intercoolers in the wing leading edges now accommodated two additional 208-litre (55-US gal) fuel tanks, thereby increasing the total internal fuel capacity to 1552 litres (410 US gal). When carrying two 1363-litre (360-US gal) drop tanks, the P-38J had a range of 3701 km (2,300 miles) with a 10-minute combat allowance, thereby permitting long-distance penetration flights to the heart of Europe.

Shortcomings in the fighter-versus-fighter combat role proved largely academic with the build-up of P-47 and P-51 squadrons in Europe, and henceforth the P-38 tended increasingly to be com-

Complete with nose-mounted Norden bomb-sight and bombadier's station in a transparent nose, this 'droop snoot' P-38L conversion served with the USAAF in Europe in the closing months of World War II.

Lockheed P-38 Lightning variants

(Except where stated, all aircraft were built at Lockheed-Burbank)

XP-38: single prototype, 37-457; two 716-kW (960-hp) Allison V-1710-11/15 engines; first flight 27 January 1939 (Lockheed Model 22)
YP-38: 13 pre-production aircraft, 39-689 to -701; two 858-kW (1,150-hp) V-1710-27/29 engines; first flight 16 September 1940 (Lockheed Model 122)
P-38: 30 aircraft, 40-744 to -773; V-1710-27/29 engines; 37-mm gun; three two-seat conversions to RP-38 (Lockheed Model 222)
XP-38A: one aircraft, modified from 40-762, with pressurised cockpit (Lockheed Model 622)
P-38: 36 aircraft, 40-774 to -809; increased tailplane incidence and self-sealing tanks (Lockheed Model 222)
P-38E: 210 aircraft, 41-1983 to -2102; V-1710-27/29 engines; 20-mm gun (Lockheed Model 222)
Lightning Mk I: 143 aircraft built for RAF, AE978-AF220; small number to UK, remainder repossessed by USAAF (within 43-2035 to -2184) after modification to P-38F-13 (built as Lockheed Model 322-61, repossessed as P-332s)
Lightning Mk II: 524 aircraft built for RAF, AF-221-AF744, but none delivered; repossessed by USAAF (as 43-2185 to -2558) after modification to P-38F-15 or G-15 (built as Lockheed Model 322-60)
P-38F: 527 aircraft (including repossessed P-322s), 41-2293 to -2392, 41-7484 to -7680, 42-12567 to -12666, 43-2035 to -2184; 988-kW (1,325-hp) V-1710-49/53 engines; underwing store racks; P-38F-15 introduced 'combat flap'; some two-seat trainers (Lockheed Model 222)
P-38G: 1,082 aircraft (including repossessed P-322s), 42-12667 to -12866, 42-12870 to -13557, 43-2185 to -2558; minor equipment changes (Lockheed Model 222)
P-38H: 600 aircraft, 42-13559, 42-66502 to -67101; increased underwing load; 1063-kW (1,425-hp) V-1710-89/91 engines and improved superchargers (Lockheed Model 222)
P-38J: 2,970 aircraft, 42-12867 to -12869, 42-13560 to -13566, 42-67102 to -68191, 42-103979 to -104428, 43-28248 to -29047, 44-23059 to -23768; introduced 'chin' radiators and two 1362-litre (360-US gal) drop tanks (Lockheed Model 422)
P-38K: one aircraft, 42-13558, with V-1710-75/77 engines and large propellers
P-38L: 3,810 aircraft, 44-23769 to -27258, 44-53008 to -53327 built at Lockheed-Burbank, plus 113 aircraft, 43-50226 to -50338, built at Consolidated Vultee, Nashville; 1194-kW (1,600-hp) V-1710-111/113 engines; introduced wing rocket-launchers
TP-38L: two-seat trainer conversion of small number of P-38Ls
P-38M: two-seat radar-equipped night-fighter converted from P-38L
F-4: 99 reconnaissance conversions of P-38E with four K-17 cameras
F-4A: 20 reconnaissance conversions of P-38E, as above but later engines
F-5A: 181 reconnaissance conversions of P-38G
F-5B: 200 reconnaissance conversions of P-38G, as above but with intercoolers
F-5C: 128 reconnaissance conversions of P-38H
XF-5D: one F-5A rebuilt as two-seat reconnaissance fighter
F-5E: 705 reconnaissance conversions of P-38J and P-38L
F-5F and F-5G: variations of F-5E with alternative camera and arrangements
XP-49: single prototype, 40-3055 (Lockheed Model 522) with Continental engines, increased armament and pressurised cockpit
XP-58 'Chain Lightning': single prototype, 41-2670, built as enlarged development of P-38 with Allison V-3420 engines and 692-km/h (430-mph) top speed

mitted to ground-attack tasks in this theatre. In the Pacific and Far East, however, the P-38 continued to give unsurpassed service as a long-range fighter, Lightning pilots being credited with the destruction of more Japanese aircraft than those of any other fighter. America's highest-scoring pilot, Major Richard Bong, who flew with the 9th Fighter Squadron, 49th Fighter Group, and the 39th Fighter Squadron, 35th Fighter Group, and later as gunnery officer with V Fighter Command, achieved his entire score of 40 enemy aircraft destroyed while flying P-38s (he also later flew as a Lockheed test pilot but was killed in a P-80). Runner-up in the Far East was another P-38 pilot, Major Thomas Buchanan McGuire, who destroyed 38 Japanese aircraft while with the 9th and 431st Fighter Squadrons. Both pilots won the Medal of Honor.

High-speed changes

Maximum speed of the P-38J was 666 km/h (414 mph) at 7620 m (25,000 ft) without external stores, and combat experience showed that the aircraft could be dived at speeds of around 885 km/h (550 mph), although this was accompanied by a strong pitch-down moment. To overcome this the P-38J-25-LO introduced a small electrically actuated flap under each wing; at the same time hydraulically boosted control systems were incorporated to alleviate aileron-reversal – one of the earliest instances of power-assisted controls in an operational aircraft. One P-38J was modified to become the P-38K, powered by V-1710-75/77 engines driving larger-diameter propellers.

In 1944 production of the P-38J gave place to the P-38L, numerically the most important of all Lightnings. Lockheed completed 3,810 at Burbank and a Vultee plant at Nashville, Tennessee, produced a further 113, but contract cover for 1,887 other P-38Ls was cancelled on VJ Day in 1945.

The P-38L, powered by 1194-kW (1,600-hp) V-1710-111/113 engines and with a maximum all-up weight of 9798 kg (21,600 lb), was the first Lightning to be armed with underwing rocket projectiles, 10 127-mm (5-in) weapons being mounted on 'tree' tiers outboard of the engine nacelles.

By the end of 1944 P-38s had reached 101 squadrons, the majority of earlier versions having made way for P-38Js and P-38Ls. Of these, 34 squadrons were serving in the West Pacific and Southeast

Lockheed P-38J Lightning cutaway drawing key

1 Starboard navigation light
2 Wingtip trailing edge strake
3 Landing light (underwing) location
4 Starboard aileron
5 Aileron control rod/ quadrant
6 Wing outer spar
7 Aileron tab drum
8 Aileron tab control pulleys
9 Aileron tab control rod
10 Aileron trim tab
11 Fixed tab
12 Tab cable access
13 Flap extension/retraction cables
14 Control pulleys
15 Flap outer carriage
16 Fowler-type flap (extended)
17 Control access panel
18 Wing spar transition
19 Outer section leading-edge fuel tanks (P-38J-5 and subsequent) capacity 46 Imp gal (208 litres) each
35 Machine gun blast tubes
36 Four 0.5-in (12.7-mm) machine guns
37 Cannon flexible hose hydraulic charger
38 Chatellerault-feed cannon magazine (150 rounds)
39 Machine gun firing solenoid
40 Cannon ammunition feed chute
41 Nose armament cowling clips
42 Case ejection chute (port lower machine gun)
43 Ammunition box and feed chute (port lower machine gun)
44 Case ejection chute (port upper machine gun)
45 Ammunition box and feed chute (port upper machine gun)
46 Radio antenna
47 Ejection chute exit (shrouded when item 52 attached)
48 Nosewheel door
49 Nosewheel shimmy damper assembly and reservoir
50 Torque links
51 Towing eye
52 Type M10 triple-tube 4.5-in (11.4-cm) rocket-launcher
53 Rearward-retracting nosewheel
54 Alloy spokes cover plate
55 Fork
56 Rocket-launcher forward attachment (to 63)
57 Nosewheel lower drag struts
58 Nosewheel oleo leg
59 Nosewheel pin access
60 Side struts and fulcrum
61 Actuating cylinder
62 Upper drag strut
63 Rocket-launcher forward attachment bracket
64 Rudder pedal assembly
65 Engine controls quadrant
66 Instrument panel

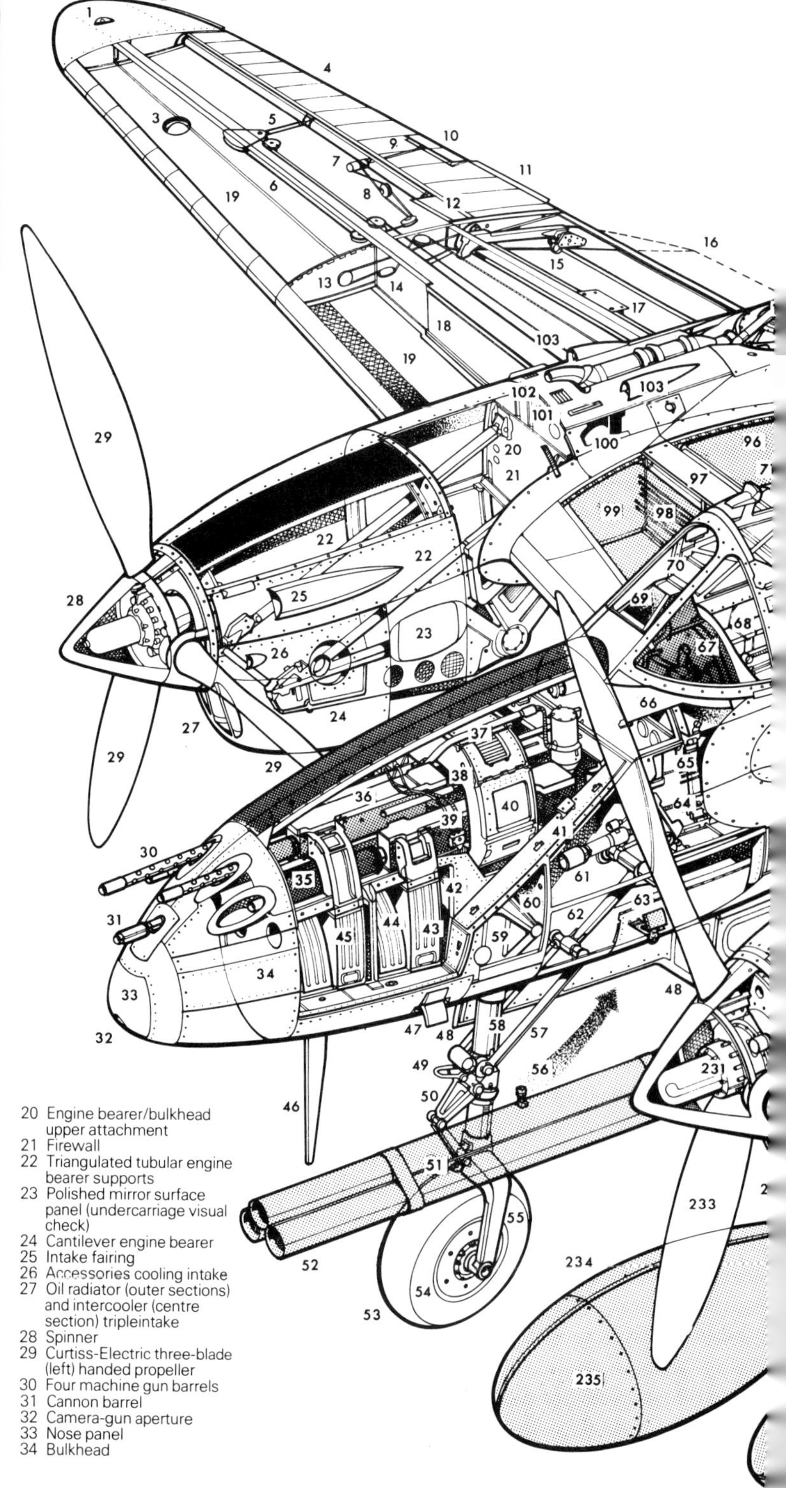

20 Engine bearer/bulkhead upper attachment
21 Firewall
22 Triangulated tubular engine bearer supports
23 Polished mirror surface panel (undercarriage visual check)
24 Cantilever engine bearer
25 Intake fairing
26 Accessories cooling intake
27 Oil radiator (outer sections) and intercooler (centre section) tripleintake
28 Spinner
29 Curtiss-Electric three-blade (left) handed propeller
30 Four machine gun barrels
31 Cannon barrel
32 Camera-gun aperture
33 Nose panel
34 Bulkhead

While still retaining a foothold on the mainland in 1945, the Nationalist air force of China acquired a number of modern American aircraft (most of them from USAAF stocks in the theatre), representative of which was this F-5B-1 (44-24082).

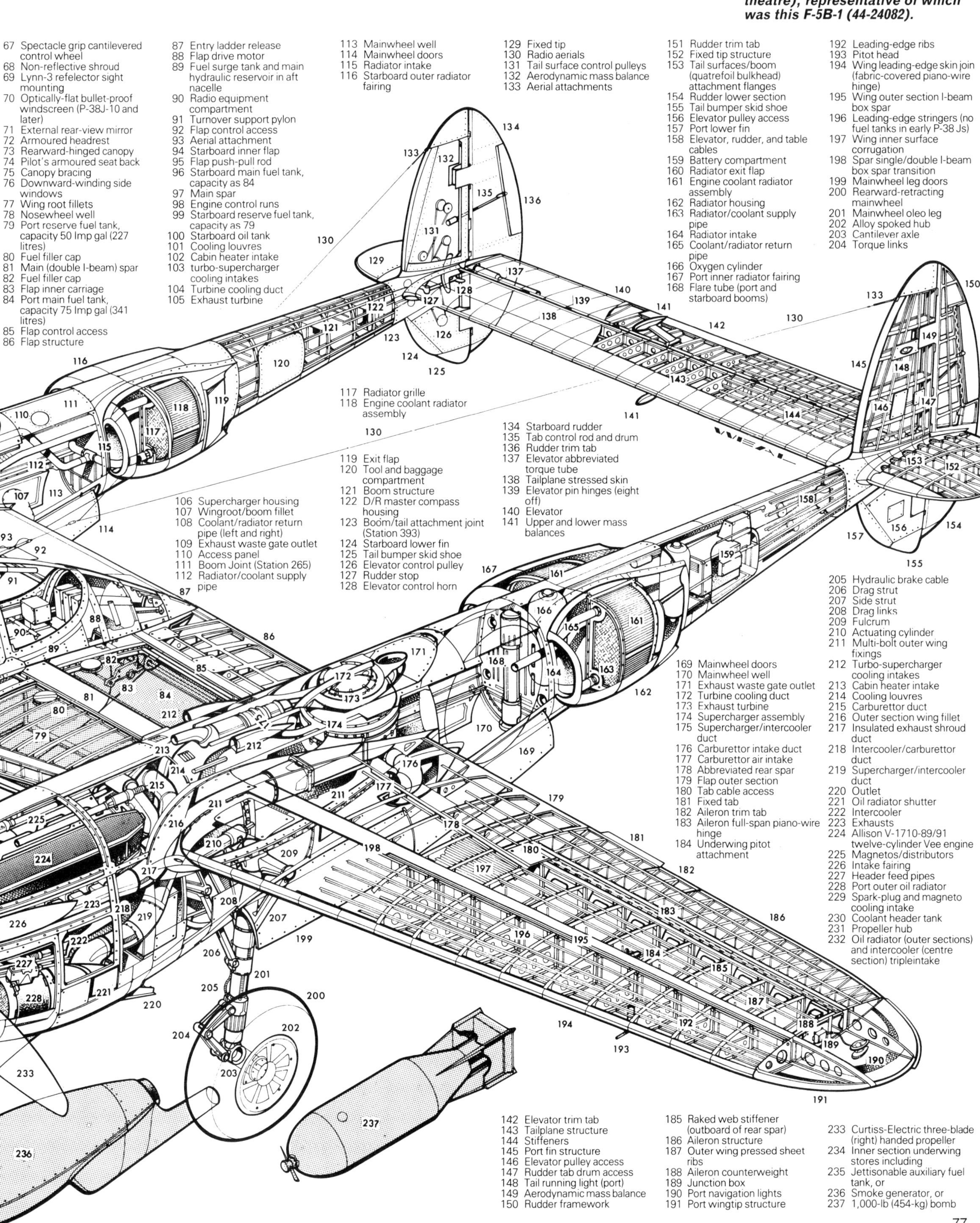

67 Spectacle grip cantilevered control wheel
68 Non-reflective shroud
69 Lynn-3 refelector sight mounting
70 Optically-flat bullet-proof windscreen (P-38J-10 and later)
71 External rear-view mirror
72 Armoured headrest
73 Rearward-hinged canopy
74 Pilot's armoured seat back
75 Canopy bracing
76 Downward-winding side windows
77 Wing root fillets
78 Nosewheel well
79 Port reserve fuel tank, capacity 50 Imp gal (227 litres)
80 Fuel filler cap
81 Main (double I-beam) spar
82 Fuel filler cap
83 Flap inner carriage
84 Port main fuel tank, capacity 75 Imp gal (341 litres)
85 Flap control access
86 Flap structure
87 Entry ladder release
88 Flap drive motor
89 Fuel surge tank and main hydraulic reservoir in aft nacelle
90 Radio equipment compartment
91 Turnover support pylon
92 Flap control access
93 Aerial attachment
94 Starboard inner flap
95 Flap push-pull rod
96 Starboard main fuel tank, capacity as 84
97 Main spar
98 Engine control runs
99 Starboard reserve fuel tank, capacity as 79
100 Starboard oil tank
101 Cooling louvres
102 Cabin heater intake
103 turbo-supercharger cooling intakes
104 Turbine cooling duct
105 Exhaust turbine
106 Supercharger housing
107 Wingroot/boom fillet
108 Coolant/radiator return pipe (left and right)
109 Exhaust waste gate outlet
110 Access panel
111 Boom Joint (Station 265)
112 Radiator/coolant supply pipe
113 Mainwheel well
114 Mainwheel doors
115 Radiator intake
116 Starboard outer radiator fairing
117 Radiator grille
118 Engine coolant radiator assembly
119 Exit flap
120 Tool and baggage compartment
121 Boom structure
122 D/R master compass housing
123 Boom/tail attachment joint (Station 393)
124 Starboard lower fin
125 Tail bumper skid shoe
126 Elevator control pulley
127 Rudder stop
128 Elevator control horn
129 Fixed tip
130 Radio aerials
131 Tail surface control pulleys
132 Aerodynamic mass balance
133 Aerial attachments
134 Starboard rudder
135 Tab control rod and drum
136 Rudder trim tab
137 Elevator abbreviated torque tube
138 Tailplane stressed skin
139 Elevator pin hinges (eight off)
140 Elevator
141 Upper and lower mass balances
142 Elevator trim tab
143 Tailplane structure
144 Stiffeners
145 Port fin structure
146 Elevator pulley access
147 Rudder tab drum access
148 Tail running light (port)
149 Aerodynamic mass balance
150 Rudder framework
151 Rudder trim tab
152 Fixed tip structure
153 Tail surfaces/boom (quatrefoil bulkhead) attachment flanges
154 Rudder lower section
155 Tail bumper skid shoe
156 Elevator pulley access
157 Port lower fin
158 Elevator, rudder, and table cables
159 Battery compartment
160 Radiator exit flap
161 Engine coolant radiator assembly
162 Radiator housing
163 Radiator/coolant supply pipe
164 Radiator intake
165 Coolant/radiator return pipe
166 Oxygen cylinder
167 Port inner radiator fairing
168 Flare tube (port and starboard booms)
169 Mainwheel doors
170 Mainwheel well
171 Exhaust waste gate outlet
172 Turbine cooling duct
173 Exhaust turbine
174 Supercharger assembly
175 Supercharger/intercooler duct
176 Carburettor intake duct
177 Carburettor air intake
178 Abbreviated rear spar
179 Flap outer section
180 Tab cable access
181 Fixed tab
182 Aileron trim tab
183 Aileron full-span piano-wire hinge
184 Underwing pitot attachment
185 Raked web stiffener (outboard of rear spar)
186 Aileron structure
187 Outer wing pressed sheet ribs
188 Aileron counterweight
189 Junction box
190 Port navigation lights
191 Port wingtip structure
192 Leading-edge ribs
193 Pitot head
194 Wing leading-edge skin join (fabric-covered piano-wire hinge)
195 Wing outer section I-beam box spar
196 Leading-edge stringers (no fuel tanks in early P-38 Js)
197 Wing inner surface corrugation
198 Spar single/double I-beam box spar transition
199 Mainwheel leg doors
200 Rearward-retracting mainwheel
201 Mainwheel oleo leg
202 Alloy spoked hub
203 Cantilever axle
204 Torque links
205 Hydraulic brake cable
206 Drag strut
207 Side strut
208 Drag links
209 Fulcrum
210 Actuating cylinder
211 Multi-bolt outer wing fixings
212 Turbo-supercharger cooling intakes
213 Cabin heater intake
214 Cooling louvres
215 Carburettor duct
216 Outer section wing fillet
217 Insulated exhaust shroud duct
218 Intercooler/carburettor duct
219 Supercharger/intercooler duct
220 Outlet
221 Oil radiator shutter
222 Intercooler
223 Exhausts
224 Allison V-1710-89/91 twelve-cylinder Vee engine
225 Magnetos/distributors
226 Intake fairing
227 Header feed pipes
228 Port outer oil radiator
229 Spark-plug and magneto cooling intake
230 Coolant header tank
231 Propeller hub
232 Oil radiator (outer sections) and intercooler (centre section) tripleintake
233 Curtiss-Electric three-blade (right) handed propeller
234 Inner section underwing stores including
235 Jettisonable auxiliary fuel tank, or
236 Smoke generator, or
237 1,000-lb (454-kg) bomb

Lockheed P-38 Lightning

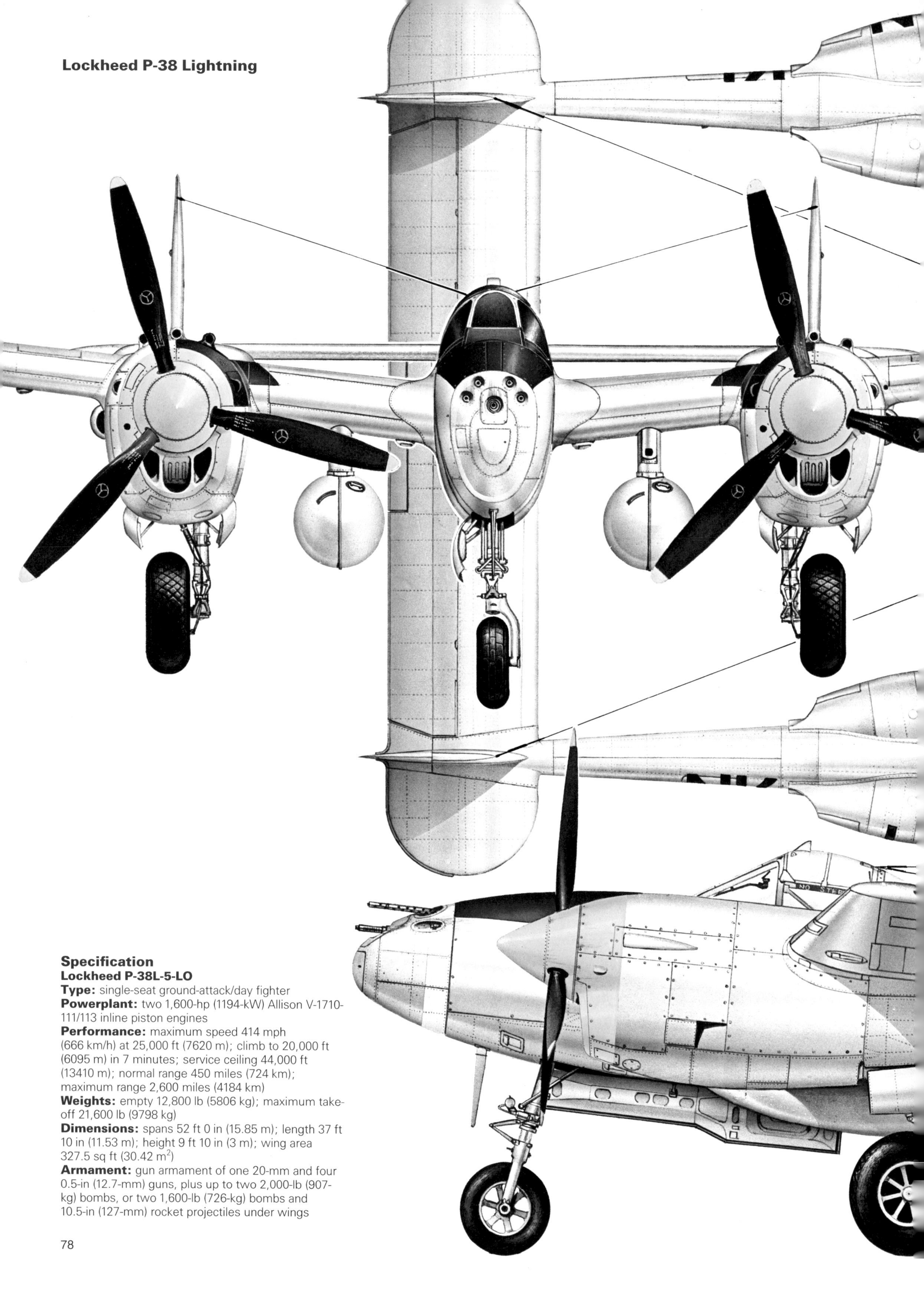

Specification
Lockheed P-38L-5-LO
Type: single-seat ground-attack/day fighter
Powerplant: two 1,600-hp (1194-kW) Allison V-1710-111/113 inline piston engines
Performance: maximum speed 414 mph (666 km/h) at 25,000 ft (7620 m); climb to 20,000 ft (6095 m) in 7 minutes; service ceiling 44,000 ft (13410 m); normal range 450 miles (724 km); maximum range 2,600 miles (4184 km)
Weights: empty 12,800 lb (5806 kg); maximum take-off 21,600 lb (9798 kg)
Dimensions: spans 52 ft 0 in (15.85 m); length 37 ft 10 in (11.53 m); height 9 ft 10 in (3 m); wing area 327.5 sq ft (30.42 m^2)
Armament: gun armament of one 20-mm and four 0.5-in (12.7-mm) guns, plus up to two 2,000-lb (907-kg) bombs, or two 1,600-lb (726-kg) bombs and 10.5-in (127-mm) rocket projectiles under wings

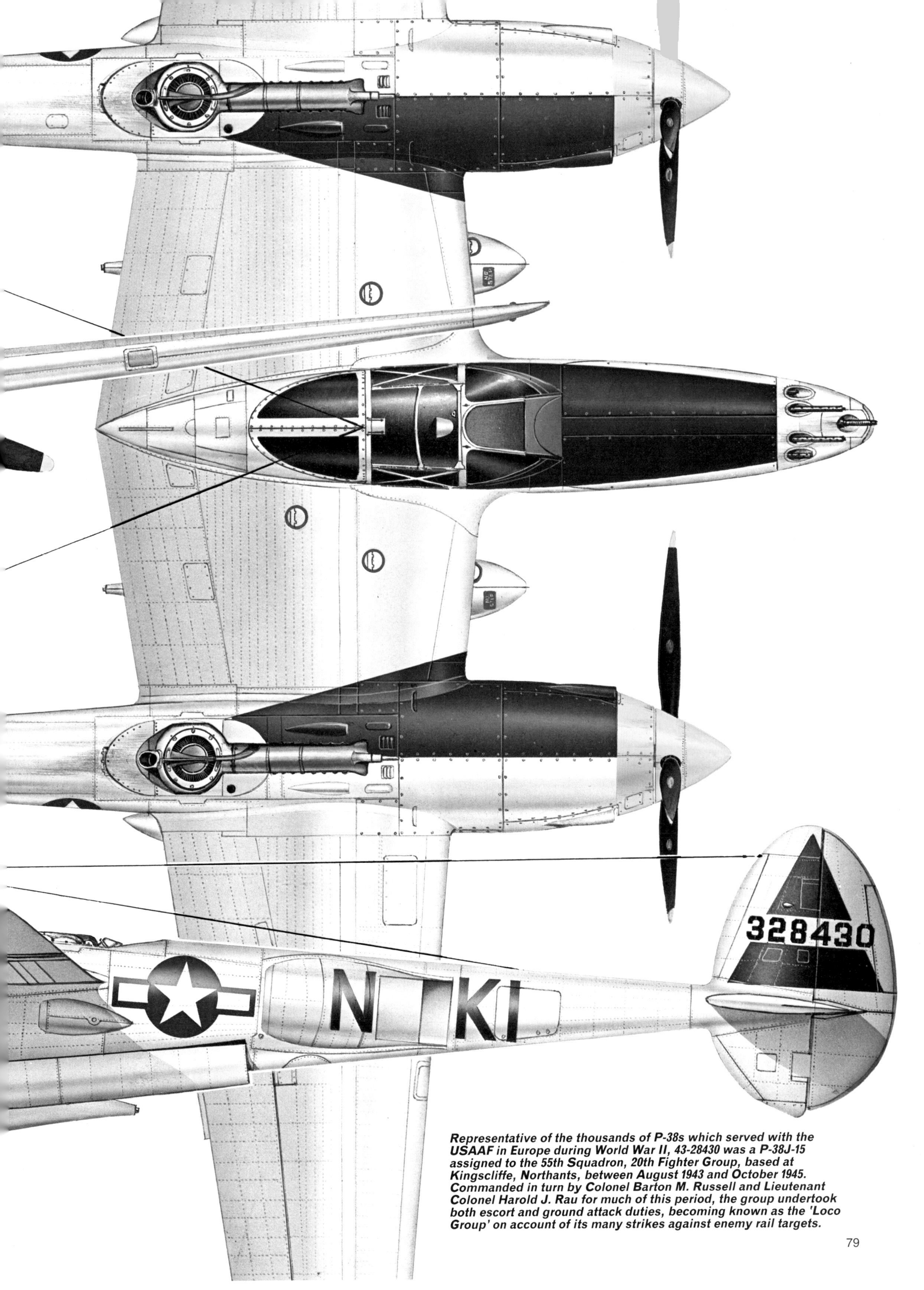

Representative of the thousands of P-38s which served with the USAAF in Europe during World War II, 43-28430 was a P-38J-15 assigned to the 55th Squadron, 20th Fighter Group, based at Kingscliffe, Northants, between August 1943 and October 1945. Commanded in turn by Colonel Barton M. Russell and Lieutenant Colonel Harold J. Rau for much of this period, the group undertook both escort and ground attack duties, becoming known as the 'Loco Group' on account of its many strikes against enemy rail targets.

Portugal acquired its first P-38 when two USAAF aircraft diverted to Lisbon while en route from England to North Africa in 1944. The second aircraft flew off, but '300' was impressed into service by the Portuguese to serve alongside a whole squadron of Bell P-39 Airacobras which had arrived under similar inauspicious circumstances.

Although the Aeronautica Militaire Italiana possessed a number of wartime aircraft in 1946 (among them this P-38L of the 4° Stormo based at Capodichino), the Peace Treaty of September 1947 severely restricted Italy's postwar military strength and the older aircraft were soon grounded by lack of spares.

Asia, 16 in the Southwest Pacific, 12 in the North Pacific and the Aleutian Islands, and 24 in Europe and the Mediterranean; the remainder were in the USA and Panama Canal Zone. Among the reconnaissance versions, F-5 sub-variants (see development list) were serving with 44 photographic and tactical reconnaissance squadrons throughout the Pacific, and in Burma, India, China, Australia, Puerto Rico, Panama, Italy, France, England and North Africa, some units such as the 21st Photo Reconnaissance Squadron in India retaining their F-5s until the end of the war.

In Europe, as the emphasis shifted from use of the P-38 as a fighter in 1944, Lightning squadrons came to be used more and more in the tactical bombing role, and a tactic was evolved by which large formations of Lightnings released their bombloads (by now increased to two 907-kg/2,000-lb bombs) simultaneously with the lead aircraft's release. These leading aircraft were two-seat adaptations of the P-38J and P-38L in which a bombardier, complete with Norden bomb sight, was located in a transparent nose (all gun armament having been removed). Following the success of these so-called 'droop-snoot' P-38s, the next expedient was to replace the visual bomb-aiming position by 'Mickey' or BTO (bombing-through-overcast) radar; use of these P-38 Pathfinders enabled targets to be attacked despite being obscured by cloud. Neither of these P-38 versions was much used outside Europe.

Two-seat night-fighter

On the other hand the P-38M, produced too late for the war in Europe, saw limited service during the final weeks of the war in the Pacific. This was a two-seat night-fighter in which a radar operator was squeezed into a raised rear cockpit and a radar pod was mounted beneath the nose. About 80 such aircraft were prepared as conversions of P-38Ls, and served with V Fighter Command's 421st and 457th Night-Fighter Squadrons on Luzon, XIII Fighter Command's 419th and 550th Night-Fighter Squadrons at Mindanao and Leyte respectively, and with the 10th Bomb Wing's 418th Night-Fighter Squadron at Okinawa from July 1945 onwards. Another two-seat conversion of the P-38L was the TP-38L-LO trainer, of which a few were produced in 1945.

Adaptability of the P-38 was allowed full rein during the last year of the war. Cargo and personnel pods were developed which could be mounted on the underwing store pylons, enabling P-38 units to remain self-supporting by moving ground personnel and spares forward to new bases with the pilots and aircraft. Casualty evacuation was performed in the same manner, using modified drop tanks with transparent nose sections, each of which could carry two stretcher cases. Another P-38J was flown with a retractable ski landing gear to prepare for possible use in the Aleutians, while others were tested as glider tugs, the P-38 proving capable of towing three fully-laden light assault gliders into the air.

Although the P-38 largely disappeared from front-line squadron use in 1946, and was officially declared surplus to military requirements in 1949, mention should be made of two P-38 developments.

The XP-49 flew in November 1942 with 1007-kW (1,350-hp) Continental XIV-1430-13/15 engines, a pressure cabin and an armament of two 20-mm and four 12.7-mm (0.5-in) guns; it was employed in high-altitude research. The XP-58 (dubbed the 'Chain Lightning') was in effect an enlarged P-38 with an all-up weight of 19505 kg (43,000 lb); with 2240-kW (3,000-hp) Allison V-3420-11 engines, and a four-gun turret plus an interchangeable nose armament of a 75-mm or two 20-mm and four 12.7-mm (0.5-in) guns; it had a top speed of 702 km/h (436 mph) at 7620 m (25,000 ft); it was flown in June 1944 but, with the P-38 then assuming the role of ground-attack fighter, no requirement was seen for this very large fighter.

Total production of all variants derived from the Model 22 was 9,924.

Developed just in time to give service against Japan in 1945, the P-38M two-seat, radar-equipped night fighter was modified from the L-series. As may be imagined, the occupant of the rear cockpit was decidedly cramped.

B-25 Mitchell

With one of the finest fighting records of any American bomber, the North American B-25 perpetuated the name of General 'Billy' Mitchell, and carried the war to Japan's homeland at a time when the USA's situation in the Pacific appeared desperate. The type then went from strength to strength in many other theatres.

In an environment of thinly concealed disinterest in rapidly deteriorating world affairs during the mid-1930s, the US Army Air Corps possessed neither the political influence nor financial appropriations to undertake the scale of re-equipment or expansion being pursued in Europe. The turning point arrived on 28 September 1938 with a White House meeting at which President Roosevelt demanded massive expansion of the US Army Air Corps, prompting General Arnold to express a belief that his service had finally achieved its 'Magna Carta'.

At that time a US Army Air Corps requirement existed for a medium bomber, a design for which North American Aviation Inc. at Inglewood, California, had already started work at private expense. This NA-40 design was a twin-engine, three-seat shoulder-wing aircraft with tricycle landing gear, designed for two 821-kW (1,100-hp) Pratt & Whitney R-1830-56C3G radials. By chance this prototype was first flown by Paul Balfour in January 1939, the same month that the USAAC announced a competition for medium bomber designs to be submitted by 5 July that year. With engines changed to 1007-kW (1,350-hp) Wright GR-2600-A71s, the prototype (now the NA-40B) was delivered for tests at Wright Field in March.

The NA-40B was destroyed in an accident after only two weeks at Wright Field, but had already so impressed USAAC pilots that North American was instructed to continue development, specifying a number of changes. A wider fuselage allowed the bombload to be doubled; the wing was moved to mid-fuselage position and the top line of the cockpit was redrawn to be flush with the upper line of the fuselage; the crew was increased from three to five and the armament increased to three 7.62-mm (0.3-in) guns in nose, dorsal and ventral positions, and one 12.7-mm (0.5-in) gun in the extreme tail. The new design was not completed until September 1939, but already North American had (on 10 August) received an $11,771,000 contract for 184 production aircraft.

Flight test programme

The first aircraft was a static test airframe, completed in July 1940, and the first flight by a production B-25 took place on 19 August with 1268-kW (1,700-hp) R-2600-9s at a gross weight of 12388 kg (27,310 lb), an increase of more than 3538 kg (7,800 lb) compared with the original NA-40 prototype. Early flight tests with the first B-25 disclosed a marked lack of directional stability, a shortcoming that was quickly and effectively cured by almost eliminating the dihedral of the wings outboard of the engines, a change that gave the B-25 its characteristic gull wing. Only the first nine B-25s (40-2165 to 40-2173) were completed with the straight dihedral wing, followed by 15 with the modified wing, no differentiation being made in the basic designation.

Early wartime combat experience in Europe had demonstrated the need for protection from gunfire, and 1941 saw the widespread modification of many American aircraft to benefit from this rather obvious lesson. The next B-25s on the Inglewood production line were 40 B-25As (NA-62A) with armour protecting the pilots and with self-sealing fuel tanks. First service deliveries were made in the

Originally produced by North American at Inglewood as a B-25C, this aircraft was converted to mount the M-4 75-mm field gun and two 50-calibre guns in the nose as a B-25G. Production aircraft, with a crew of four, dispensed with the ventral turret.

This was the only RAF Mitchell Mk I (FK161) to be delivered to the UK, the remainder going to the Middle East; it was evaluated at the Aeroplane and Armament Experimental Establishment, Boscombe Down. Subsequent Mitchell Mk IIs and IIIs served with RAF Bomber Command and the 2nd Tactical Air Force in Britain and northern Europe.

spring of 1941 to the 17th Bombardment Group (Medium), commanded by Lieutenant Colonel (later Brigadier General) Walter R. Peck, whose component squadrons (the 34th, 37th and 95th) were based at Lexington County Airport, South Carolina. At the end of that year the group moved to the west coast of the USA for coastal anti-shipping patrols after the Japanese attack at Pearl Harbor, and one of its B-25As sank a Japanese submarine on 24 December.

Meanwhile the original 1939 production contract was completed in 1941 with the production of 120 B-25Bs (although one aircraft, 40-2243, crashed and was written off before delivery). This version featured electrically operated Bendix dorsal and ventral turrets, each with a pair of 12.7-mm (0.5-in) machine-guns; the tail gun was deleted, however, and the gross weight increased to 12909 kg (28,460 lb). With considerably accelerated production already planned for further improved versions, the American government was able to supply 23 B-25Bs to the UK under Lend-Lease. However, only one such aircraft (termed the Mitchell Mk I in the Royal Air Force) arrived in the United Kingdom, the remainder being shipped to North Africa. Inadequate maintenance facilities existed to introduce them into service with an operational unit and late in 1942 they were moved to India where they eventually joined No.681 Squadron at Dum Dum in January 1943, and later flew reconnaissance sorties over Burma and Siam. A small number of other B-25Bs were shipped to the North Russian ports as deck cargo in the early PQ convoys.

US diversions

About 40 B-25Bs were scheduled for delivery to the Dutch in the Netherland East Indies, but as a result of the rapidly deteriorating situation facing the Americans in the South West Pacific, all were diverted to the 13th and 19th Squadrons of the 3rd Bombardment Group, USAAF, at Brisbane, Australia, commanded by Robert F. Strickland (who rose from first lieutenant to full colonel in only nine months, in 1942). Other aircraft were delivered to the 17th Bombardment Group (Medium), replacing the earlier B-25As.

It was in April 1942 that the B-25 leapt into the headlines with one

Prominently marked with stripes, this target-towing TB-25N-25 is shown at Seattle in July 1956. The 'O' prefix before the USAF number on the tail denoted that the aircraft was 'old', i.e. built more than 10 years ago; it was converted from a B-25J, 44-29672.

Rarely pictured were the B-25s delivered to the US Navy under PBJ designations. Shown here is a PBJ-1D (basically equivalent to late sub-variants of the B-25D), of which 152 were supplied, with nose radar, waist guns, dorsal turret and a single gun in the tail. Colour was midnight blue.

North American B-25J Mitchell cutaway drawing key

1 Flexible 0.50-in (12.7-mm) machine-gun
2 Fixed nose machine-gun
3 Bomb sight
4 Nose compartment glazing
5 Bomb fusing and release switch panel
6 Bombardier's instrument panel
7 Cabin heater blower
8 Nose undercarriage leg strut
9 Nosewheel
10 Undercarriage torque scissors
11 Aerial mast
12 Heating air ducting
13 Bombardier's seat
14 Nose compartment emergency escape hatch
15 Armoured cockpit bulkhead
16 Windscreen panels
17 Instrument panel shroud
18 Pilot's gunsight
19 Windscreen de-misting air ducting
20 Instrument panel
21 Rudder pedals
22 Control column
23 Cockpit armoured skin plating
24 Crawlway to nose compartment
25 D/F loop aerial
26 Ventral aerial cable
27 Extending ladder
28 Forward entry hatch
29 Machine-gun blister fairing
30 0.50-in (12.7-mm) fixed machine-guns
31 Ammunition boxes
32 Ammunition feed chutes
33 Fire extinguisher
34 Pilot's seat
35 Safety harness
36 Co-pilot/navigator's seat
37 Seat back armour plating
38 Cockpit roof ditching hatch
39 Starboard fixed gun ammunition boxes
40 Radio racks
41 Turret foot pedals
42 Ammunition boxes
43 Hydraulic reservoir
44 Turret mounting ring
45 Front/centre fuselage joint frame

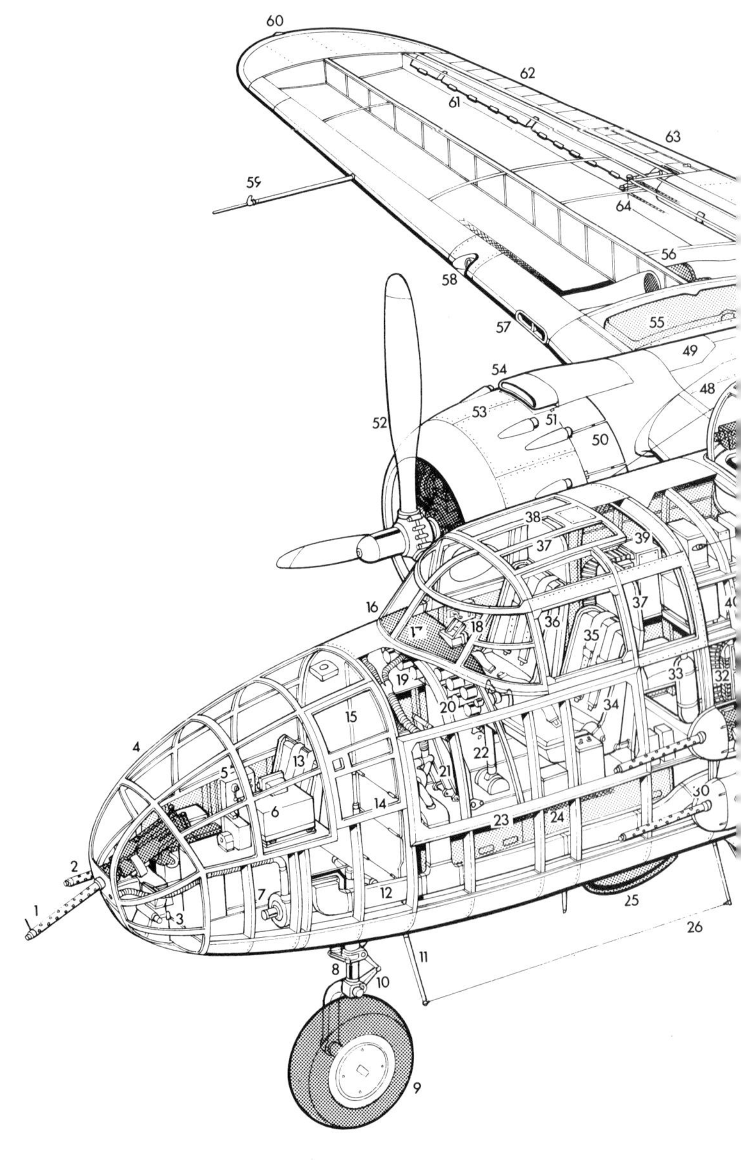

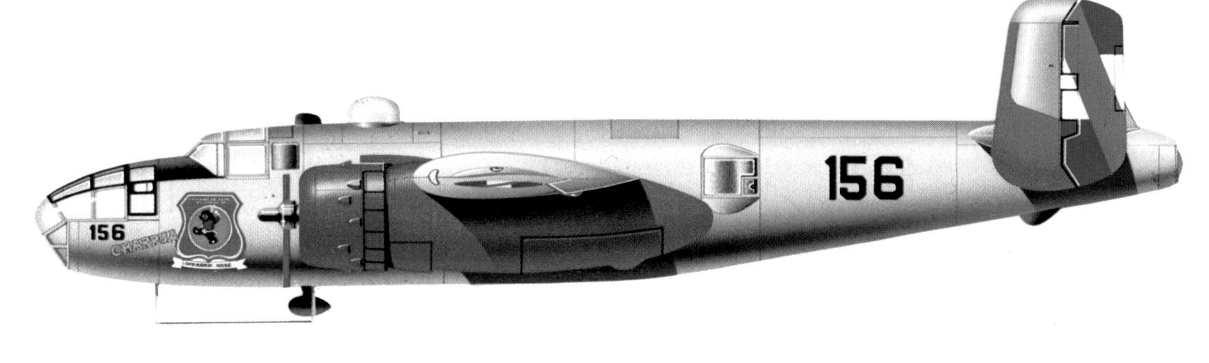

Among the large number of foreign air forces which received war-surplus B-25s was that of Uruguay, whose Aéronautica Militar (later Fuerza Aérea Uruguaya) continued to fly B-25J bombers for some 15 years after the war.

of the war's most daring epics, when 16 B-25Bs made an extraordinary attack on the Japanese mainland. Using aircraft from the 17th Group, modified to carry 4319 litres (1,141 US gal) of fuel compared with the standard 2627 litres (694 US gal), these B-25Bs were crewed by volunteers led by Lieutenant Colonel James H. Doolittle, one of America's greatest airmen who as long ago as 1925 had won a Schneider Trophy race, and who later in the war commanded the 8th, 12th and 15th US Air Forces. The B-25's ventral turrets and

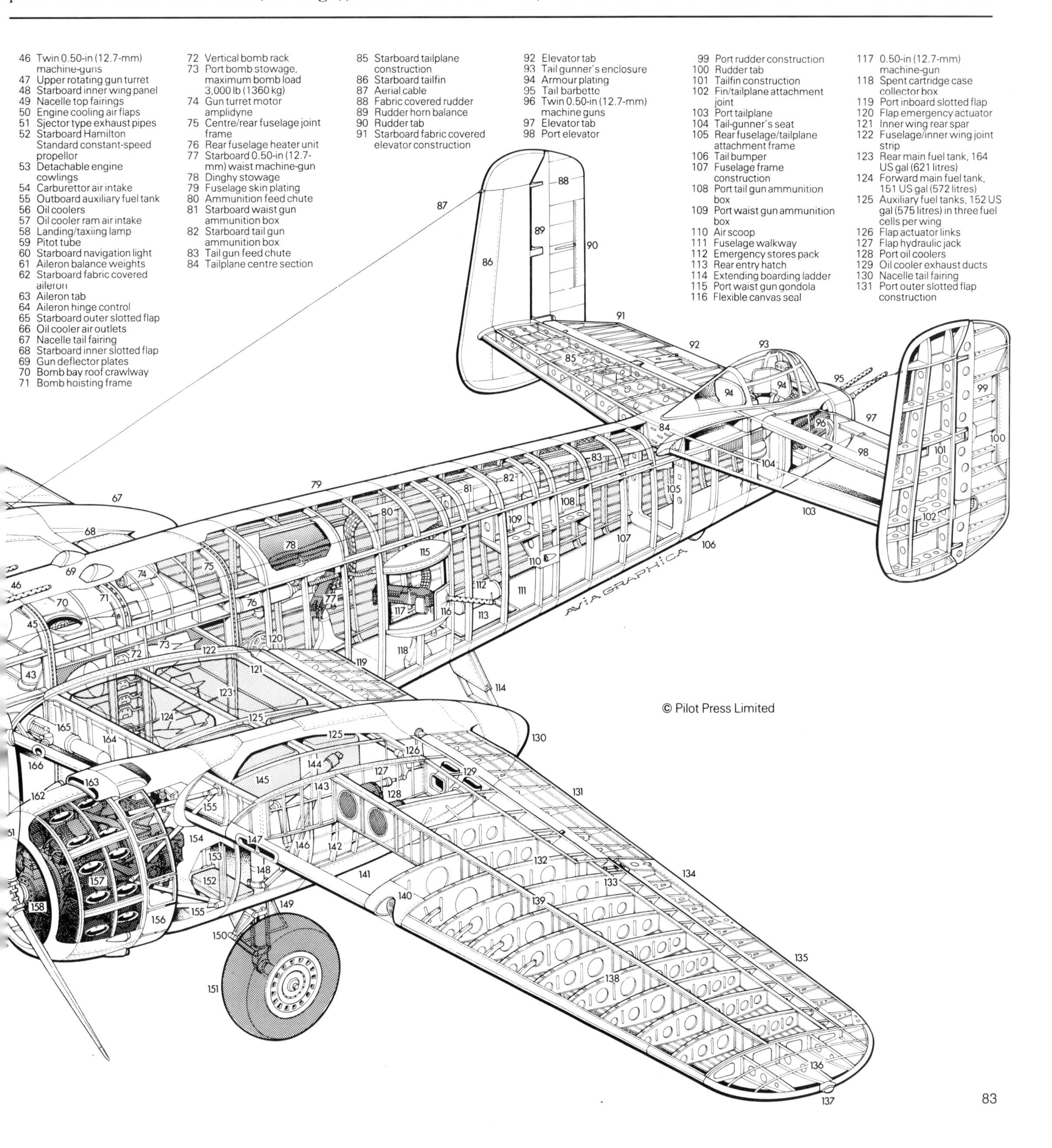

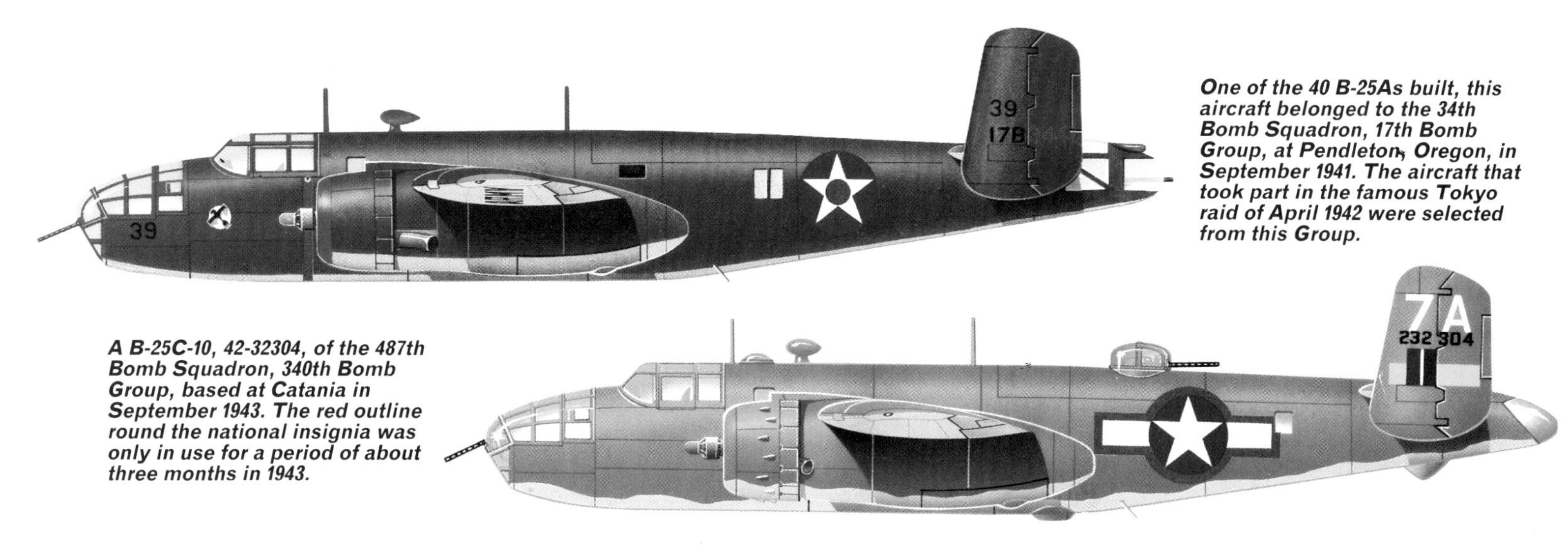

One of the 40 B-25As built, this aircraft belonged to the 34th Bomb Squadron, 17th Bomb Group, at Pendleton, Oregon, in September 1941. The aircraft that took part in the famous Tokyo raid of April 1942 were selected from this Group.

A B-25C-10, 42-32304, of the 487th Bomb Squadron, 340th Bomb Group, based at Catania in September 1943. The red outline round the national insignia was only in use for a period of about three months in 1943.

Norden bombsights were removed and two wooden 'guns' fitted in the tail for deception purposes, yet the gross weight rose to 14062 kg (31,000 lb). Carried to within 1290 km (800 miles) of the Japanese mainland aboard the carrier USS *Hornet*, Doolittle led his aircraft in low level attacks on targets in Tokyo, Kobe, Yokohama and Nagoya on 18 April. All the raiders either crashed or force-landed, the majority of crews being repatriated by the Russians or Chinese. Doolittle was awarded the Medal of Honor on his return from this token but inspiring attack at a time when America's forces were still reeling from the Japanese onslaught after Pearl Harbor. At that time the B-25 was the heaviest aircraft ever to have been launched from the deck of a carrier.

Detail improvements

Extensive detail redesign identified the B-25C, of which deliveries started just before the end of 1941, 1,619 being produced at the parent plant at Inglewood and 2,290 (designated B-25D) at a second North American factory at Dallas, Texas. The aircraft were powered by 1268-kW (1,700-hp) R-2600-13s and were equipped with autopilots; external racks on the fuselage could increase the fuel capacity to 4164 litres (1,100 US gal), while this and a bomb-bay fuel tank carrying 2214 litres (585 US gal) took the maximum gross weight to 18960 kg (41,800 lb). Maximum bombload of 2359 kg (5,200 lb) comprised 1452 kg (3,200 lb) internally plus eight 113-kg (250-lb) bombs on wing racks. B-25Cs and B-25Ds occasionally carried a 907-kg (2,000-lb) torpedo externally for shipping attacks. Maximum speed of this version was 457 km/h (284 mph) at 4570 m (15,000 ft).

A total of 455 B-25Cs and 40 B-25Ds was supplied to the UK, serving with Nos 98, 180, 226, 305, 320 and 342 Squadrons of the RAF based in the UK under the designation Mitchell Mk II. Some 182 B-25Cs were supplied to the Soviet Union (although eight were lost at sea in transit), as well as 688 B-25Ds. Others were delivered to Canada, mainly for use as trainers.

The next production version was the B-25G, developed from the XB-25G prototype which had been taken from the B-25C production line and modified to mount a standard US Army 75-mm field gun in the nose. The production B-25G, of which 405 were produced, carried an M4 75-mm gun with 21 6.81-kg (15-lb) shells, and was developed for anti-shipping strikes in the Pacific theatre. Loaded by the navigator/bombardier by hand, the big gun could seldom fire more than four shots in a single attack. The four-crew B-25G was not regarded as successful, but a great improvement was found in the B-25H, of which 1,000 were produced with the lighter T13E1 75-mm gun and a crew of five. With four 12.7-mm (0.5-in) guns in the extreme nose, four more in blister packs on the sides of the nose, two in each of the dorsal and tail positions and two in the fuselage waist, plus a bombload of 1361 kg (3,000 lb) and up to eight 12.7-cm (5-in) underwing rockets, the B-25H was indeed a formidable aircraft and was highly successful in operations against the Japanese.

The main and by far the most widely-used version of the B-25 was the B-25J variant, of which 4,318 (as B-25J-NCs) were built at a new factory at Kansas City, Kansas. This reverted to a six-man crew and a glazed nose, without 75-mm gun but retained the four 'blister' guns, and the dorsal turret was moved forward to a position immediately aft of the pilots' cockpit; power was provided by two R-2600-29 radials.

Among the groups to fly the B-25J were the 3rd, 38th, 41st, 42nd and 345th Bombardment Groups (Medium) in the Pacific theatre; the 12th, 310th, 321st and 340th Bombardment Groups (Medium) in the Mediterranean theatre; the 341st Bombardment Group

One of the first nine B-25s, showing the original wing with constant dihedral, a configuration that was accompanied by inadequate directional stability. This was the first version to enter the Air Corps' inventory and differed from the original company prototype in having its cabin roof flush with the upper fuselage line.

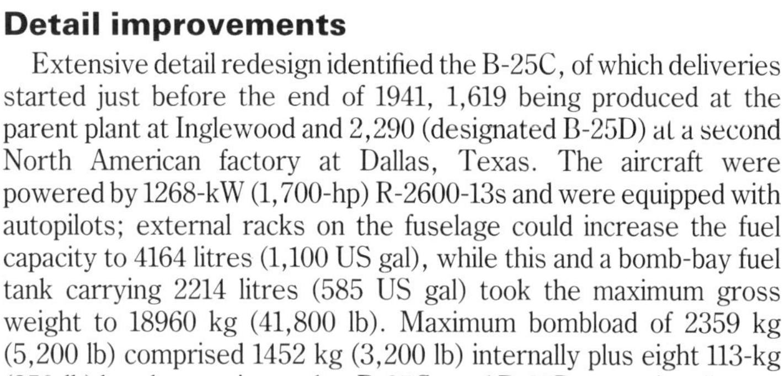

One of Colonel James Doolittle's B-25Bs taking off from the deck of USS Hornet (CVA-8) for the famous raid on Tokyo on 18 April 1942. Heavily laden with fuel to a gross weight of 14061 kg (31,000 lb), these aircraft were probably the heaviest that had ever taken off from a carrier.

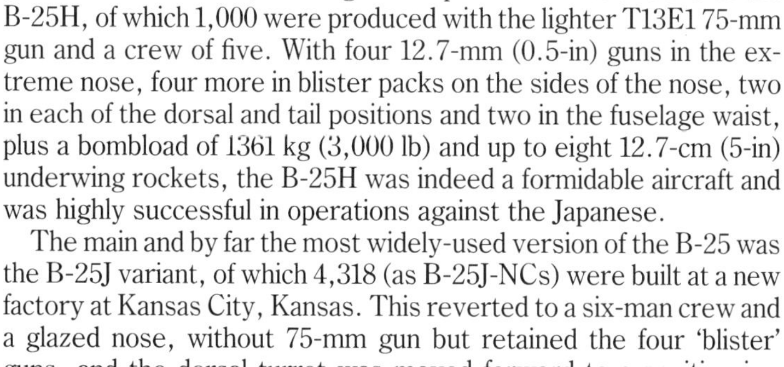

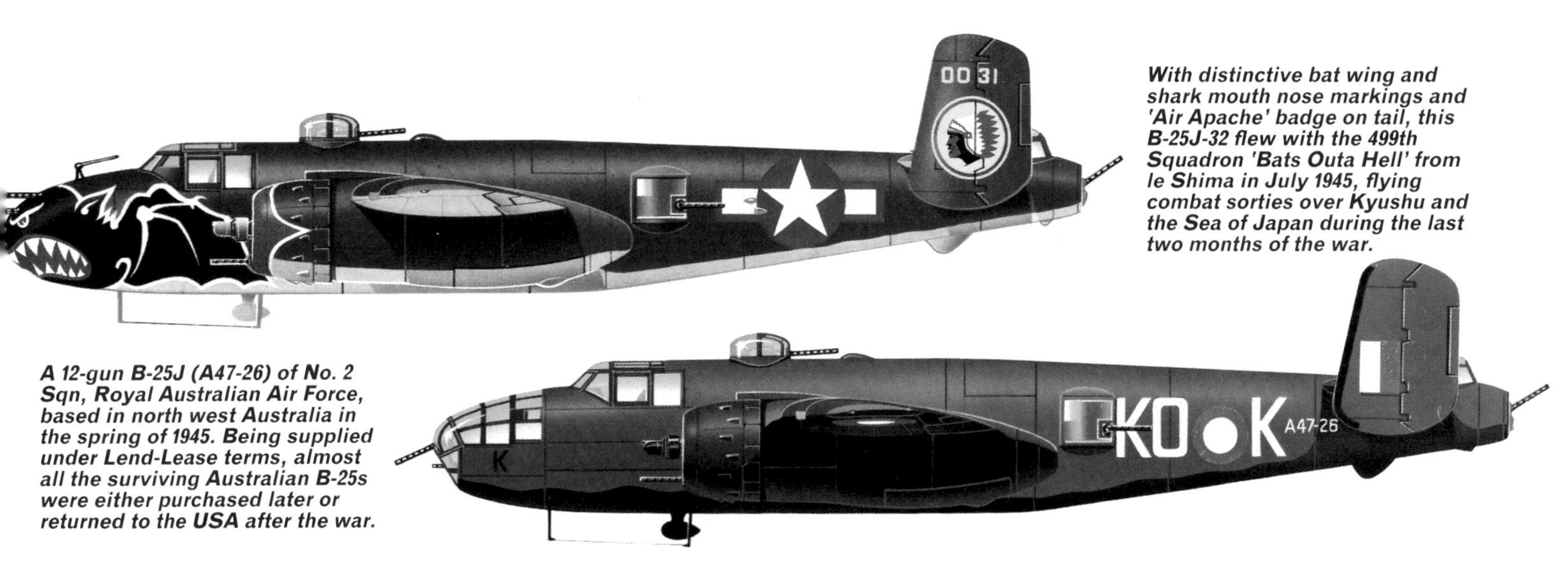

With distinctive bat wing and shark mouth nose markings and 'Air Apache' badge on tail, this B-25J-32 flew with the 499th Squadron 'Bats Outa Hell' from Ie Shima in July 1945, flying combat sorties over Kyushu and the Sea of Japan during the last two months of the war.

A 12-gun B-25J (A47-26) of No. 2 Sqn, Royal Australian Air Force, based in north west Australia in the spring of 1945. Being supplied under Lend-Lease terms, almost all the surviving Australian B-25s were either purchased later or returned to the USA after the war.

(Medium) in South East Asia, and the 13th, 17th, 25th and 309th Bombardment Groups (Medium) in the USA. Further Medals of Honor were awarded to B-25 pilots, including a posthumous award to Major Raymond H. Wilkins, commanding the 8th Bomb Squadron, 3rd Bomb Group, who sank two Japanese ships during an attack on Simpson Harbour, New Britain, on 2 November 1943, but, having been crippled by flak, deliberately attracted fire from a destroyer while his squadron withdrew before he himself crashed. In an attack on a heavily defended airfield in New Guinea on 18 August 1943 Major Ralph Cheli was awarded a Medal of Honor for leading the 405th Squadron, 38th Bomb Group, and despite a severely damaged aircraft, continuing to head the attack rather than disrupt his formation before crashing into the sea.

Change of armament

In 1944 an analysis of B-25 operations in the Far East disclosed that most attacks were being carried out at low level and that the bombardier was seldom needed. His station was accordingly deleted and a 'solid' nose re-introduced, first as a field modification and later in the production line. In place of the two hand-held machine-guns previously fitted, a battery of eight 12.7-mm (0.5-in) guns was mounted, bringing to a total of 18 the number of guns carried by later B-25Js.

295 B-25Js were purchased by the UK, but 20 of these were transferred back to the USAAF in North Africa; in the RAF this version was termed the Mitchell Mk III, and served almost exclusively with the UK-based squadrons already listed. Despite the large number of B-25s built, the USAAF inventory at no time exceeded 2,500, the balance being composed of large numbers supplied to other friendly air forces during the last year of the war and shortly afterwards (of which further details are summarised in the accompanying type development list).

The B-25 was also widely used by the USAAF as a reconnaissance aircraft, early B-25s (mostly Bs) being given rudimentary camera installations in the field and issued to the 89th Reconnaissance Squadron in December 1941; others followed to the 5th Photographic Reconnaissance Group in the Mediterranean early in 1943 and the 26th Observation Group in the USA. A dedicated photographic-reconnaissance version, the F-10, with a fan of three cameras for trimetrogen photography in a 'chin' fairing, was not developed until 1943; all guns were removed and fuel tanks were installed in the bomb bay.

During the latter half of the war 60 B-25Cs, B-25Ds, B-25Gs and B-25Js were stripped of all operational equipment and converted for use as trainers, being given designations in the AT (later TB) categories. After the war this conversion continued with the B-25J until more than 600 had been delivered to the USAF. Some of these went on to become TB-25Ks, TB-25Ls, TB-25Ms and TB-25Ns. Others were converted to become utility and staff transports with CB, VB and ZB designations, some serving with Strategic Air Command for communications duties from 1946 onwards. The last USAF unit to fly the B-25 in service was based at Reese Air Force Base, whose TB-25L and TB-25N pilot trainers were eventually declared obsolete in January 1959.

Finally, the third largest operator of the B-25 (after the USAAF and RAF) was the US Navy, following the policy decision reached in July 1942 to allow the US Navy to take a share of land-based bomber production. Deliveries started in January 1943; of the first 50 PBJ-1Cs (equivalent to the B-25C) delivered, the US Marine Corps Bombing Squadron VMB-413 was the first to receive 20. These were followed by 152 PBJ-1Ds, one PBJ-1G, 248 PBJ-1Hs and 255 PBJ-1Js (US Navy equivalents to the B-25D, B-25G, B-25H and B-25J respectively).

North American B-25Cs and B-25Ds of the 340th Bomb Group flying over Tunisia in the spring of 1943. For some months most B-25s of the USAAF serving in the Mediterranean carried RAF-style fin flashes to assist identification of unfamiliar American aircraft.

One of 870 B-25s supplied to the Soviet Union during the war, a B-25J-25 (44-30052). Though some early B-25Cs and B-25Ds were shipped to Russia in the North Cape convoys in 1942-3, the majority were flown direct on the Alaska-Siberia route.

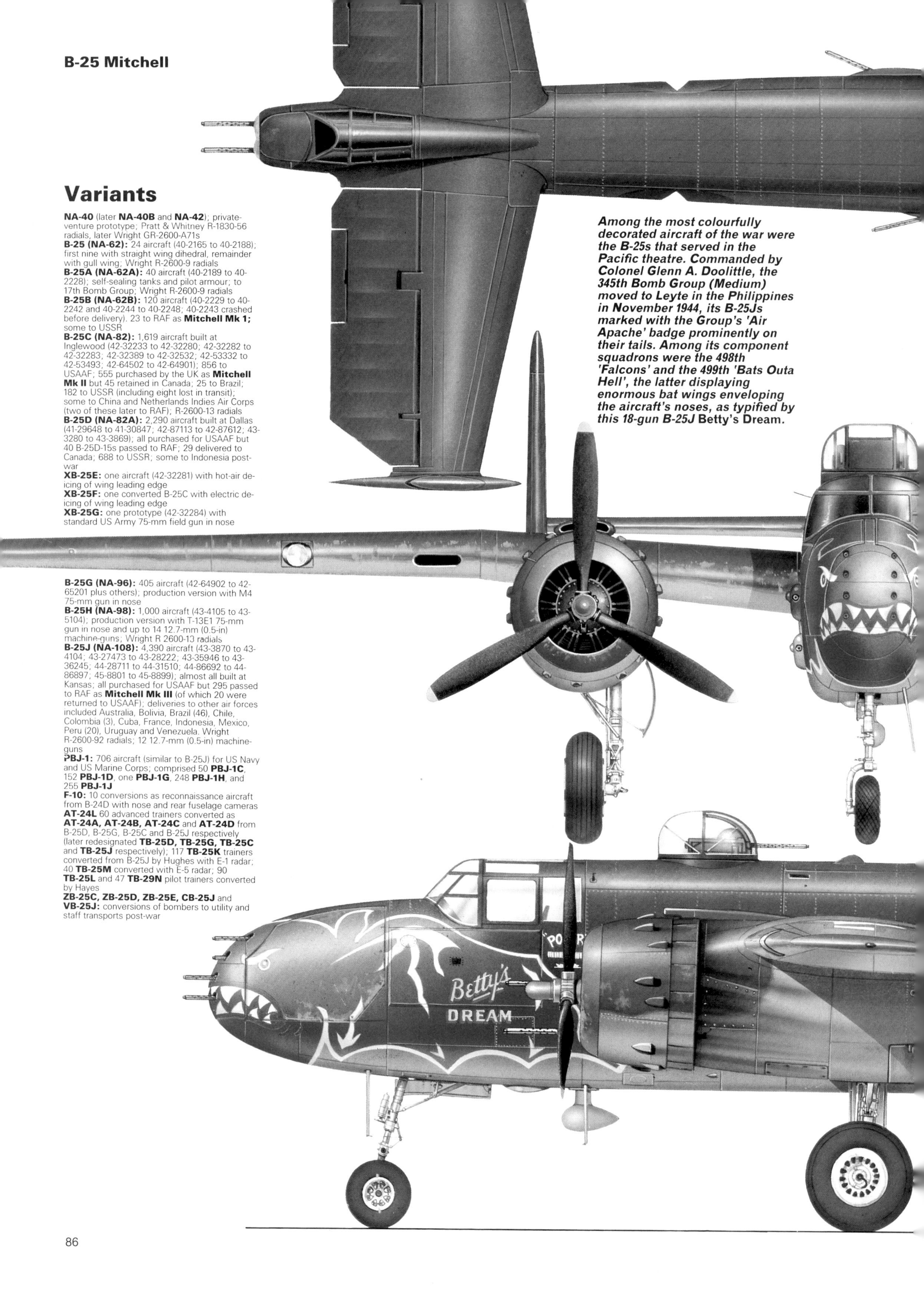

Variants

NA-40 (later **NA-40B** and **NA-42**); private-venture prototype; Pratt & Whitney R-1830-56 radials, later Wright GR-2600-A71s
B-25 (NA-62): 24 aircraft (40-2165 to 40-2188); first nine with straight wing dihedral, remainder with gull wing; Wright R-2600-9 radials
B-25A (NA-62A): 40 aircraft (40-2189 to 40-2228); self-sealing tanks and pilot armour; to 17th Bomb Group; Wright R-2600-9 radials
B-25B (NA-62B): 120 aircraft (40-2229 to 40-2242 and 40-2244 to 40-2248; 40-2243 crashed before delivery). 23 to RAF as **Mitchell Mk 1;** some to USSR
B-25C (NA-82): 1,619 aircraft built at Inglewood (42-32233 to 42-32280; 42-32282 to 42-32283; 42-32389 to 42-32532; 42-53332 to 42-53493; 42-64502 to 42-64901); 856 to USAAF; 555 purchased by the UK as **Mitchell Mk II** but 45 retained in Canada; 25 to Brazil; 182 to USSR (including eight lost in transit); some to China and Netherlands Indies Air Corps (two of these later to RAF); R-2600-13 radials
B-25D (NA-82A): 2,290 aircraft built at Dallas (41-29648 to 41-30847; 42-87113 to 42-87612; 43-3280 to 43-3869); all purchased for USAAF but 40 B-25D-15s passed to RAF; 29 delivered to Canada; 688 to USSR; some to Indonesia post-war
XB-25E: one aircraft (42-32281) with hot-air de-icing of wing leading edge
XB-25F: one converted B-25C with electric de-icing of wing leading edge
XB-25G: one prototype (42-32284) with standard US Army 75-mm field gun in nose
B-25G (NA-96): 405 aircraft (42-64902 to 42-65201 plus others); production version with M4 75-mm gun in nose
B-25H (NA-98): 1,000 aircraft (43-4105 to 43-5104); production version with T-13E1 75-mm gun in nose and up to 14 12.7-mm (0.5-in) machine-guns; Wright R 2600-13 radials
B-25J (NA-108): 4,390 aircraft (43-3870 to 43-4104; 43-27473 to 43-28222; 43-35946 to 43-36245; 44-28711 to 44-31510; 44-86692 to 44-86897; 45-8801 to 45-8899); almost all built at Kansas; all purchased for USAAF but 295 passed to RAF as **Mitchell Mk III** (of which 20 were returned to USAAF); deliveries to other air forces included Australia, Bolivia, Brazil (46), Chile, Colombia (3), Cuba, France, Indonesia, Mexico, Peru (20), Uruguay and Venezuela. Wright R-2600-92 radials; 12 12.7-mm (0.5-in) machine-guns
PBJ-1: 706 aircraft (similar to B-25J) for US Navy and US Marine Corps; comprised 50 **PBJ-1C**, 152 **PBJ-1D**, one **PBJ-1G**, 248 **PBJ-1H**, and 255 **PBJ-1J**
F-10: 10 conversions as reconnaissance aircraft from B-24D with nose and rear fuselage cameras
AT-24L 60 advanced trainers converted as **AT-24A, AT-24B, AT-24C** and **AT-24D** from B-25D, B-25G, B-25C and B-25J respectively (later redesignated **TB-25D, TB-25G, TB-25C** and **TB-25J** respectively); 117 **TB-25K** trainers converted from B-25J by Hughes with E-1 radar; 40 **TB-25M** converted with E-5 radar; 90 **TB-25L** and 47 **TB-29N** pilot trainers converted by Hayes
ZB-25C, ZB-25D, ZB-25E, CB-25J and **VB-25J:** conversions of bombers to utility and staff transports post-war

Among the most colourfully decorated aircraft of the war were the B-25s that served in the Pacific theatre. Commanded by Colonel Glenn A. Doolittle, the 345th Bomb Group (Medium) moved to Leyte in the Philippines in November 1944, its B-25Js marked with the Group's 'Air Apache' badge prominently on their tails. Among its component squadrons were the 498th 'Falcons' and the 499th 'Bats Outa Hell', the latter displaying enormous bat wings enveloping the aircraft's noses, as typified by this 18-gun B-25J **Betty's Dream.**

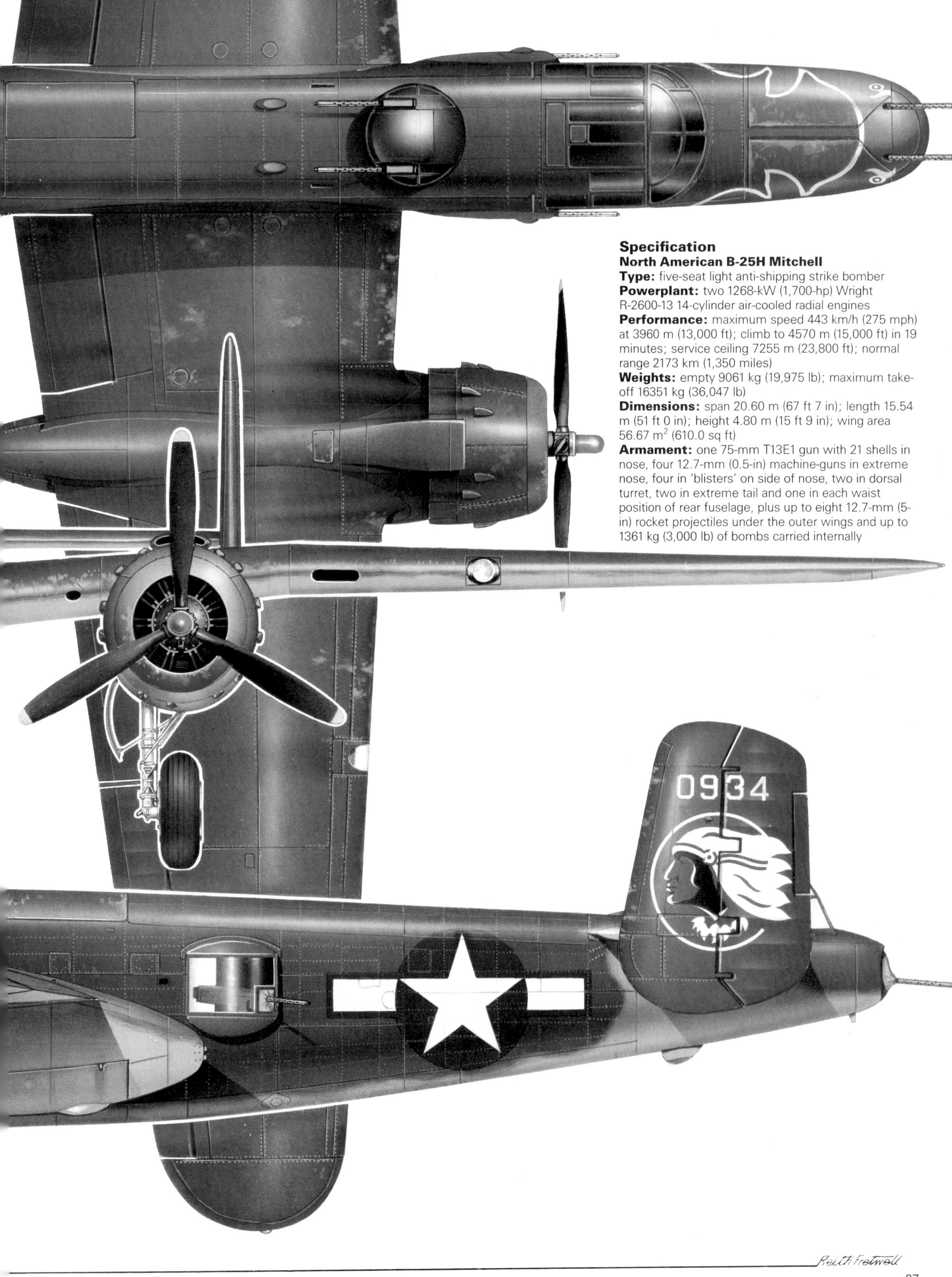

Specification
North American B-25H Mitchell
Type: five-seat light anti-shipping strike bomber
Powerplant: two 1268-kW (1,700-hp) Wright R-2600-13 14-cylinder air-cooled radial engines
Performance: maximum speed 443 km/h (275 mph) at 3960 m (13,000 ft); climb to 4570 m (15,000 ft) in 19 minutes; service ceiling 7255 m (23,800 ft); normal range 2173 km (1,350 miles)
Weights: empty 9061 kg (19,975 lb); maximum take-off 16351 kg (36,047 lb)
Dimensions: span 20.60 m (67 ft 7 in); length 15.54 m (51 ft 0 in); height 4.80 m (15 ft 9 in); wing area 56.67 m^2 (610.0 sq ft)
Armament: one 75-mm T13E1 gun with 21 shells in nose, four 12.7-mm (0.5-in) machine-guns in extreme nose, four in 'blisters' on side of nose, two in dorsal turret, two in extreme tail and one in each waist position of rear fuselage, plus up to eight 12.7-mm (5-in) rocket projectiles under the outer wings and up to 1361 kg (3,000 lb) of bombs carried internally

Douglas SBD Dauntless

The Battle of Midway was the turning point of the war in the Pacific and set the seal on Japan's fate. Architect of this victory was the reliable, if unspectacular, Douglas Dauntless, which gave the American carriers the striking power they so desperately needed.

The Douglas SBD Dauntless dive-bomber turned the tide of war at the Battle of Midway on 4 June 1942. To the men involved, the size of their success may not have been immediately evident: their aircraft had a low power-to-weight ratio, burdening it with only fair climbing and manoeuvring characteristics; and their arming systems malfunctioned, at times pitching their centreline-mounted 227-kg (500-lb) bombs uselessly into the sea. Launched from Admiral Chester Nimitz's carrier groups to seek out those of Admiral Isoroku Yamamoto, they were running out of fuel, running out of daylight, and stretched to the limits of range and endurance when they came upon the enemy fleet and attacked. Lieutenant Commander C. Wade McClusky, Commander Max Leslie and the other Dauntless fliers from squadrons VS-5 and VB-3 on USS *Yorktown*, VS-6 and VB-6 on USS *Enterprise*, and VS-8 and VB-8 on USS *Hornet* lost 40 of their 128 dive-bombers swarming down from the late-afternoon sun to strike the *Kaga, Akagi, Hiryu* and *Soryu*, but when they sent all four Japanese carriers to the bottom of the sea they reversed the trend of the Pacific conflict. Few other aircraft types, perhaps none but the Supermarine Spitfire and Hawker Hurricane, can lay claim to having so altered history as the Dauntless dive-bomber, 5,936 of which were produced before the end of World War II.

The Dauntless owes its origins to the low-wing, two-seat tandem Northrop BT-1 dive-bomber of 1938, and to the superb design work of Jack Northrop and of the mild-tempered but brilliant Edward H. Heinemann. When the El Segundo, California, manufacturer became a division of Douglas Aircraft with Jack Northrop's January 1938 departure, a development of the BT-1, known as the XBT-2, was being tested but seemed to offer only limited potential. Heinemann's design team reworked the sole XBT-2 (BuAer No. 0627), powering it with the 746-kW (1,000-hp) Wright XR-1830-32 engine which would become the world-famous Cyclone, driving a three-bladed propeller. The tail of the aircraft was redesigned following extensive wind tunnel tests, and the XBT-2 was redesigned XSBD-1. Accepted by the US Navy in February 1939, while parallel work was under way on the Curtiss SB2C Helldiver, the SBD was to become the standard by which all other carrierborne dive-bombers ('scout bombers' in the jargon of the time) would be judged.

On 8 April 1939, Douglas received an order for 57 SBD-1 and 87 SBD-2 airplanes. The SBD-1, with the definitive fin and rudder shape for the Dauntless type, was armed with two forward-firing 7.62-mm (0.3-in) guns in the engine cowling and a single 7.62-mm (0.3-in) gun for the radio operator/gunner, who sat with his back to the pilot. Not yet fully cleared for carrier operations, the SBD-1 was earmarked instead for the US Marine Corps and was delivered between April 1939 and June 1940. The SBD-2 model, which differed in having self-sealing rubber-lined metal fuel tanks and two additional 246-litre (65-US gal) tanks in the outer wing panels, went to US Navy squadrons between November 1940 and May 1941.

The fall of France, punctuated by the scream of descending Stukas, impressed the Washington authorities with the value of the dive-bomber (although the US Congress's Truman Committee in 1941 recommended against procuring such aircraft) and a further 174 Dauntlesses were ordered as the SBD-3. The SBD-3 variant had a second 7.62-mm (0.3-in) gun for the rear crewmen, improved armour and electrical system, and bladder-type self-sealing fuel tanks. By now the familiar Dauntless shape was established: the not ungraceful machine had a maximum speed of 406 km/h (252 mph) in level flight, going up to 444 km/h (276 mph) in a dive, a range of 1971 km (1,225 miles) with or 2205 km (1,370 miles) without a bombload, and a service ceiling of 8260 m (27,100 ft).

US Marine Corps Dauntlesses were destroyed on the ground during the 7 December 1941 attack on Pearl Harbor. During the Battle of Coral Sea on 7 May 1942, the airwaves were cluttered with radio transmissions and anxious crewmen aboard the USS *Lexington* and *Yorktown* could not tell how the battle was going until a clear voice blasted through: 'Scratch one flat-top! Dixon to carrier. Scratch one flat-top!' Lieutenant Commander Robert E. Dixon, commander of Bombing Two (VB-2), was reporting the sinking of the Japanese carrier *Shoho* with 545 of her crew after a 30-minute battle at the cost of only three US aircraft, a triumph for the SBD-2 and SBD-3 models of the Dauntless, to be exceeded only during the pivotal Midway battle a few weeks later.

In the US Army Air Forces, where it was officially given the name Banshee but still called Dauntless, this aircraft type seemed un-

SBD-1 Dauntless (BuAer No. 1597), the second machine in the initial production run, shows the unexciting markings worn by US Marine Corps aircraft before America's entry into World War II. Fuselage coding '2-MB-1' identifies this craft as belonging to the 2nd Marine Aircraft Wing, apparently at Quantico, Virginia, in about August 1940.

An early production Douglas SBD-3 sporting an overall light grey colour scheme. Sarcastically nicknamed 'Speedy Three', this workhorse was at the forefront of operations in the Pacific until 1942.

glamorous from the beginning. In January 1941, the USAAF had placed an order for 78 A-24s similar to the US Navy's SBD-3 but for the deletion of carrier landing equipment. In addition, 90 SBD-3s from a US Navy contract were modified to land-based standard and delivered to the USAAF as the SBD-3A (A for Army). Eventually, the USAAF ordered 100 A-24As identical to the SBD-4, and 615 A-24Bs equivalent to the SBD-5 but manufactured at the Douglas plant in Tulsa, Oklahoma.

Although A-24s served with the 27th Bombardment Group at New Guinea and with the 531st Fighter Bomber Squadron at Makin, USAAF pilots found themselves unable to outmanoeuvre aggressive Japanese fighters. Where the rear-seat gunner had been highly effective in the US Navy machine (one US Navy crew actually shot down seven Mitsubishi Zeros in two days) he was less potent aboard the A-24. Casualties were so high that the A-24 was quickly withdrawn from front-line service. Since US Navy pilots at Coral Sea and Midway had demonstrated the ability to handle themselves against the Zero, the US Army's less satisfactory performance with the Dauntless is usually attributed to the inexperience and lesser *esprit de corps* of its flight crews.

Carrier air group

A carrier air group aboard a typical US Navy carrier usually comprised two squadrons of fighters (Grumman F4F Wildcats, or later F6F Hellcats), one of torpedo-bombers (Douglas TBD Devastators, later Grumman TBF Avengers) and two Dauntless squadrons, one in the bombing role and one for the scout mission. These were designated VB and VS squadrons respectively. The scouting mission had been conceived before it was clear that American carriers would have the protection of radar, which they enjoyed from the outset of the conflict while Japanese carriers did not. In practice, there was little distinction and scouting pilots trained and prepared for dive-bombing missions just as their colleagues in the VB squadrons did.

The next model of the Dauntless was the SBD-4, delivered between October 1942 and April 1943. The SBD-4 had improved radio navigation aids, an electric fuel pump, and an improved Hamilton Standard Hydromatic constant speed, full-feathering propeller. A total of 780 was built before production at El Segundo shifted to the SBD-5, powered by an improved R-1820-60 engine delivering 895 kW (1,200 hp); 2,965 examples of this variant were produced between February 1943 and April 1944, one of which became the XSBD-6 with installation of a 1007-kW (1,350-hp) Wright R-1820-66, the 'ultimate' Cyclone. Some 450 SBD-6s were built.

By late in the war, the Dauntless was supplanted in the dive-bomber role by the more advanced Curtiss Sc2C Helldiver, though this troublesome aircraft never won the recognition accorded the Douglas project. The Dauntless was relegated to less glamorous anti-submarime patrol and close air support duties. The SBD also served with no less than 20 US Marine Corps squadrons. Many hundreds of SBDs were retrofitted with Westinghouse ASB radar.

Several ex-USAAF Douglas A-24s were operated by the Mexican air force as late as 1959. Illustrated is an A-24B, which found its way on to the Mexican civil register in 1957.

Identifiable by the deletion of the deck landing hook, the land-based USAAF Douglas A-24s were delivered from the US Navy production line of El Segundo between June and October 1941. Further orders were to follow.

Douglas SBD-3 Dauntless cutaway drawing key

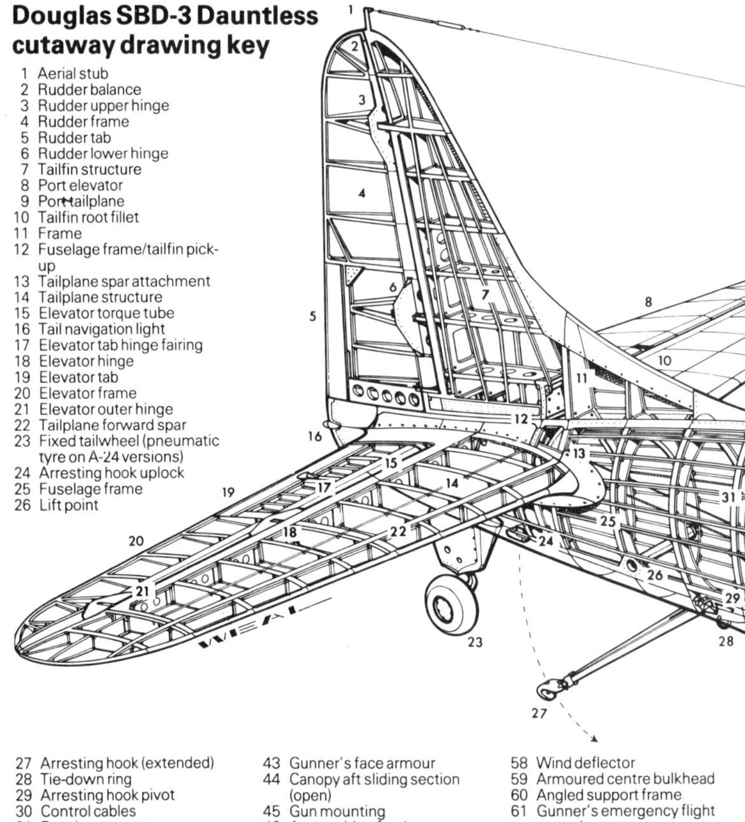

1 Aerial stub
2 Rudder balance
3 Rudder upper hinge
4 Rudder frame
5 Rudder tab
6 Rudder lower hinge
7 Tailfin structure
8 Port elevator
9 Port tailplane
10 Tailfin root fillet
11 Frame
12 Fuselage frame/tailfin pick-up
13 Tailplane spar attachment
14 Tailplane structure
15 Elevator torque tube
16 Tail navigation light
17 Elevator tab hinge fairing
18 Elevator hinge
19 Elevator tab
20 Elevator frame
21 Elevator outer hinge
22 Tailplane forward spar
23 Fixed tailwheel (pneumatic tyre on A-24 versions)
24 Arresting hook uplock
25 Fuselage frame
26 Lift point
27 Arresting hook (extended)
28 Tie-down ring
29 Arresting hook pivot
30 Control cables
31 Fuselage structure
32 Bulkhead
33 Section light
34 Radio bay
35 Radio bay access door
36 Wingroot fairing frame
37 Stringers
38 Life-raft cylindrical stowage (access door port side)
39 Dorsal armament stowage
40 Hinged doors
41 Aerial
42 Twin 0.30-in (7.62-mm) Browning machine-guns
43 Gunner's face armour
44 Canopy aft sliding section (open)
45 Gun mounting
46 Ammunition feed
47 Canopy aft sliding section (closed)
48 Ammunition box
49 Oxygen cylinder
50 Oxygen rebreather
51 Oxygen spare cylinder
52 Entry hand/foothold
53 Aft cockpit floor
54 Radio controls
55 Gunner's position
56 Gun mounting
57 Canopy fixed centre section
58 Wind deflector
59 Armoured centre bulkhead
60 Angled support frame
61 Gunner's emergency flight controls
62 Control direct linkage
63 Hydraulics controls
64 Entry hand/foothold
65 Oxygen rebreather
66 Map case
67 Pilot's seat and harness
68 Back armour
69 Catapult headrest
70 Canopy forward sliding section
71 Compass
72 Perforated dive flap
73 Aerial mast

A-24 Dauntless, serial number 42-54543, of France's Goupe de Chasse-Bombardement 1/18 'Vendée', located at Vannes in about November 1944. The ex-USAAF Dauntlesses flown by Free French pilots performed a variety of roles but, like their New Zealand counterparts, were introduced too late in the war to be especially effective as front-line dive-bombers.

74 Aileron tab
75 Port aileron
76 Aileron tab control linkage
77 Port formation light
78 Port navigation light
79 Pitot head
80 Fixed wing slots
81 Wing skinning
82 Underwing ASB radar antenna (retrofit)
83 Port outer wing fuel tank (55 US gal/208 litre capacity)
84 Aileron control rod
85 Telescopic sight
86 Windscreen
87 Armoured inner panel
88 Instrument panel shroud
89 Two 0.50-in (12.7-mm) machine-guns
90 Control column
91 Switch panel
92 Instrument panel
93 Case ejection chute
94 Ammunition box
95 Engine bearer upper attachment
96 Armoured deflection plate
97 Machine-gun barrel shrouds
98 Engine bearers
99 Oil tank
100 Exhaust slot
101 Oil cooler
102 Cooling gills
103 Exhaust manifold
104 Engine cowling ring
105 Machine-gun troughs
106 Carburettor air intake duct
107 Wright R-1820-52 Cyclone radial engine
108 Three-blade propeller
109 Spinner
110 Propeller hub
111 Port mainwheel
112 Oil cooler intake
113 Exhaust outlet
114 Engine bearers
115 Bomb displacement crutch (in-flight position)
116 Hydraulics vent
117 Case ejection chute outlet
118 Engine bearer lower attachment
119 Starboard mainwheel well
120 Wingroot walkway
121 Starboard/inner wing fuel tank (75 US gal/284 litre capacity)
122 Centre-section dive flap (lower)
123 Wing outer section attachment plate fairing
124 Starboard outer wing fuel tank (55 US gal/208 litre capacity)
125 Mainwheel leg pivot
126 Mainwheel leg door actuation
127 Wing nose ribs
128 Multi-spar wing structure
129 Wing ribs
130 Stiffeners
131 Perforated dive flaps
132 Aileron inner hinge
133 Starboard aileron frame
134 Aileron outer hinge
135 Starboard navigation light
136 Starboard formation light
137 Wingtip structure
138 Fixed wing slots
139 Wing leading-edge
140 Underwing radar antenna (retrofit)
141 Underwing stores pylon
142 100-lb (45.4-kg) bomb
143 Mainwheel leg door
144 Starboard mainwheel
145 Mainwheel axle
146 Mainwheel leg
147 Bomb displacement crutch
148 500-lb (226.8-kg) bomb
149 Aluminium drop tank (58 US gal/219.5 litre capacity
150 Underwing shackles/fuel line

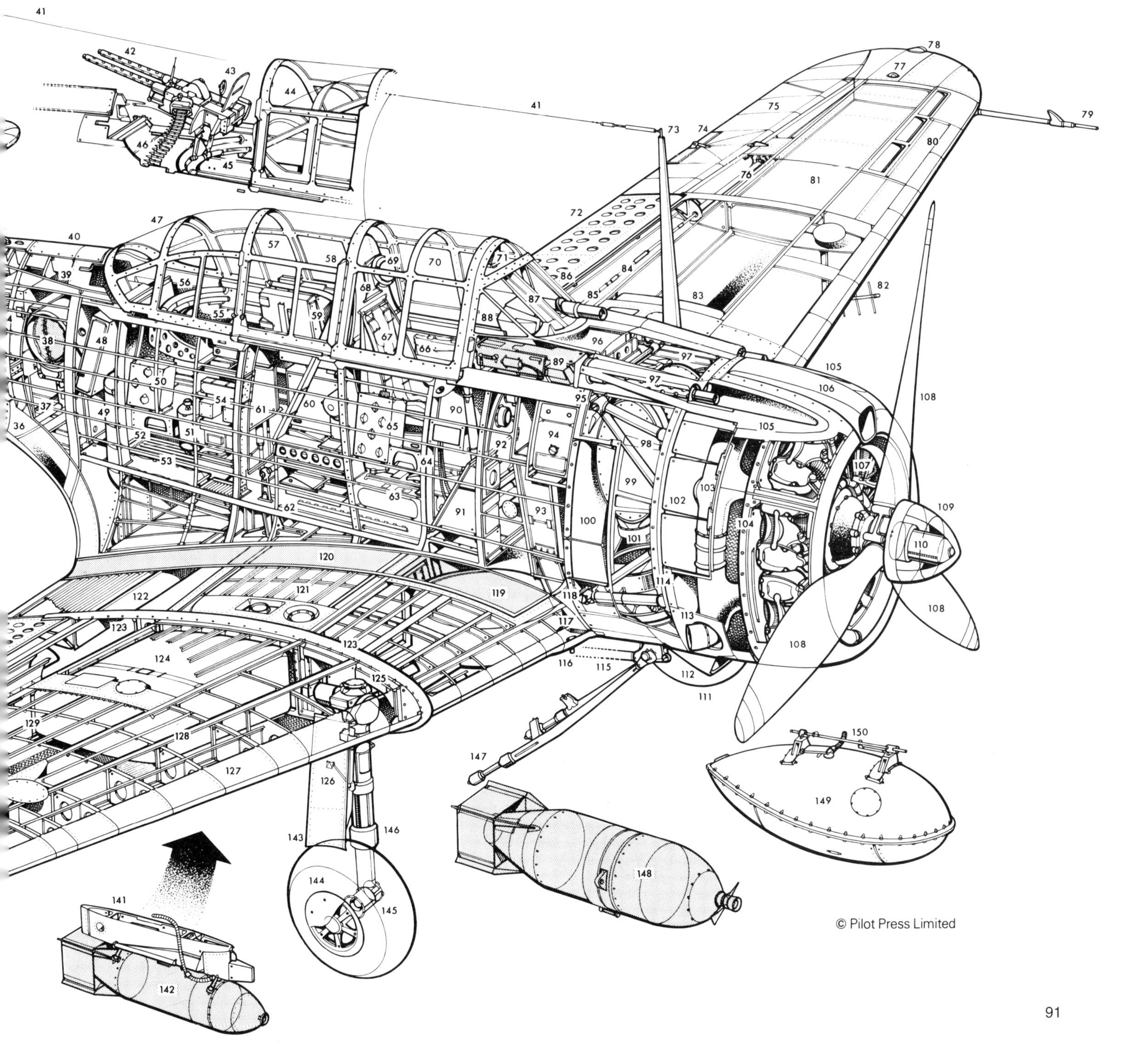

Douglas SBD Dauntless

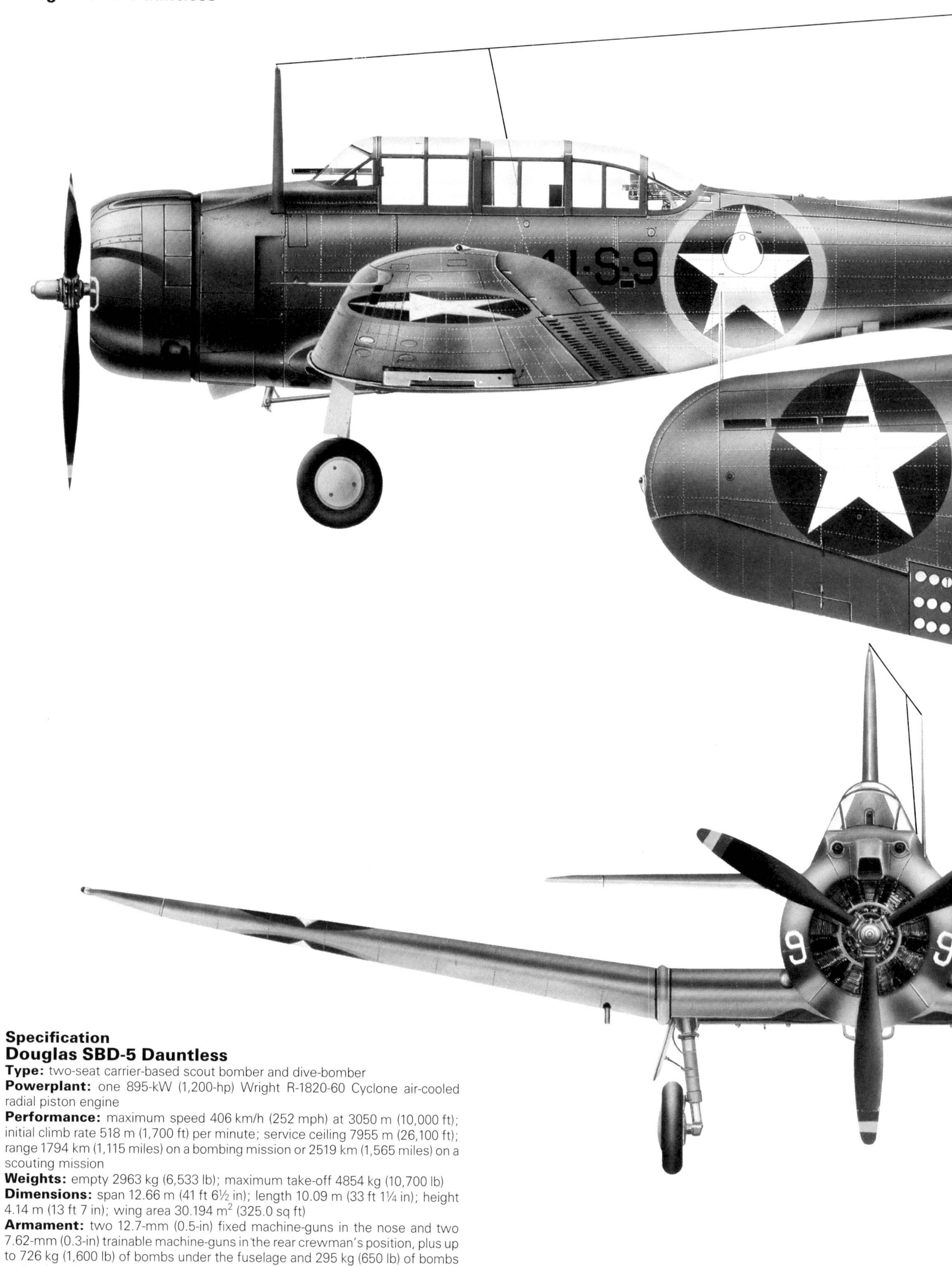

Specification
Douglas SBD-5 Dauntless

Type: two-seat carrier-based scout bomber and dive-bomber
Powerplant: one 895-kW (1,200-hp) Wright R-1820-60 Cyclone air-cooled radial piston engine
Performance: maximum speed 406 km/h (252 mph) at 3050 m (10,000 ft); initial climb rate 518 m (1,700 ft) per minute; service ceiling 7955 m (26,100 ft); range 1794 km (1,115 miles) on a bombing mission or 2519 km (1,565 miles) on a scouting mission
Weights: empty 2963 kg (6,533 lb); maximum take-off 4854 kg (10,700 lb)
Dimensions: span 12.66 m (41 ft 6½ in); length 10.09 m (33 ft 1¼ in); height 4.14 m (13 ft 7 in); wing area 30.194 m^2 (325.0 sq ft)
Armament: two 12.7-mm (0.5-in) fixed machine-guns in the nose and two 7.62-mm (0.3-in) trainable machine-guns in the rear crewman's position, plus up to 726 kg (1,600 lb) of bombs under the fuselage and 295 kg (650 lb) of bombs under the wings

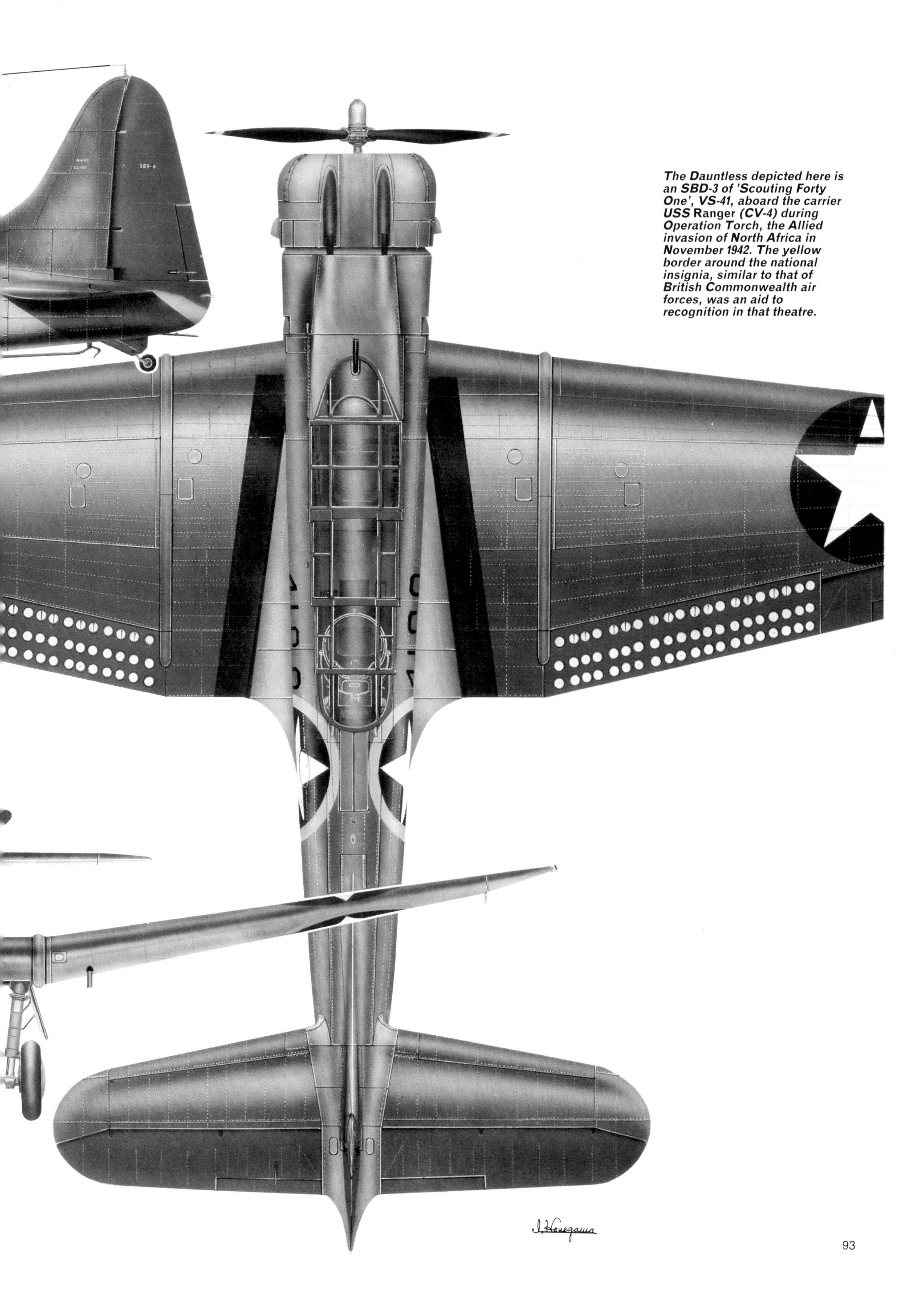

The Dauntless depicted here is an SBD-3 of 'Scouting Forty One', VS-41, aboard the carrier USS Ranger (CV-4) during Operation Torch, the Allied invasion of North Africa in November 1942. The yellow border around the national insignia, similar to that of British Commonwealth air forces, was an aid to recognition in that theatre.

Airbrakes extended, this Dauntless is in classic dive-bomber pose. Early SBDs could carry a 545-kg (1,200-lb) bomb load but by the end of the war and the coming of the SBD-5 model this had increased.

The UK obtained nine SBD-5 aircraft and named them Dauntless DB.Mk I. A machine which had been a top performer in 1940 was, by the time British test pilots flew it in 1944, regarded as underpowered and slow. British pilots also found the Dauntless fatiguing, noisy and draughty. There was never to be general agreement about the type's vulnerability to fighters, the Pacific war indicating that it was not unduly vulnerable, RAF test pilots being persuaded that it was. The British machines were evaluated extensively but it was too late for the Dauntless to have an operational career in British service.

Foreign users

In July 1943, No. 25 Squadron of the Royal New Zealand Air Force received 18 SBD-3s from US Marine Corps inventory. Later to receive 27 SBD-4s and 23 SBD-5s, the RNZAF squadron fought at Bougainville. Another foreign user of the Dauntless was France, which equipped two units of the Free French Navy, Flottille 3B and Flottille 4B, with A-24s and SBD-3s at Agadir, Morocco in the autumn of 1944. Dauntlesses went into operation in metropolitan France against retreating German forces and fought in dwindling numbers until VE-Day. Though production of the type ended on 22 July 1944, French SBDs were used at the fighter school at Meknes as aerobatic trainers until 1953.

In American service, where the A-24 was redesignated F-24 in 1947, an unpiloted QF-24A drone and its QF-24B controller aircraft (both rebuilds with 1948 serial numbers) kept the Dauntless type in service until 1950.

The pilot of an SBD-6 Dauntless found himself sitting high up front in a machine of all-metal construction with fabric-covered control surfaces. His cantilever, low-mounted wing had a rectangular centre section with outer panels tapering in chord and thickness to detachable wing tips. The 'Swiss cheese' pierced flaps and dive-brakes, above and below the trailing edge of the outer wings and below the trailing edge only of the centre section beneath the fuselage, together with the 'multi-cellular' construction of the wing itself, were hallmarks of the design's indebtedness to Jack Northrop. The oval

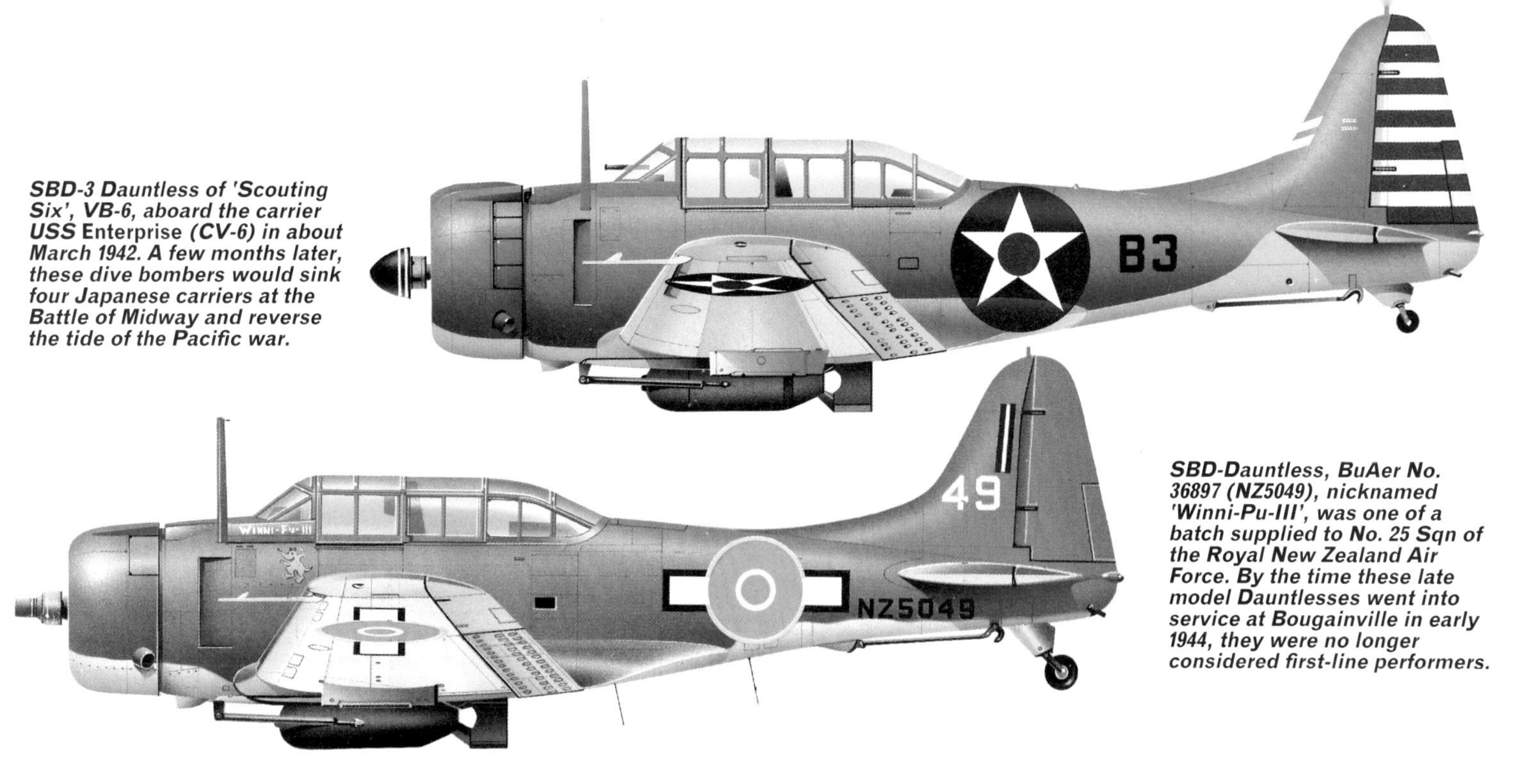

SBD-3 Dauntless of 'Scouting Six', VB-6, aboard the carrier USS* Enterprise *(CV-6) in about March 1942. A few months later, these dive bombers would sink four Japanese carriers at the Battle of Midway and reverse the tide of the Pacific war.

SBD-Dauntless, BuAer No. 36897 (NZ5049), nicknamed 'Winni-Pu-III', was one of a batch supplied to No. 25 Sqn of the Royal New Zealand Air Force. By the time these late model Dauntlesses went into service at Bougainville in early 1944, they were no longer considered first-line performers.

duralumin monocoque fuselage was built in four sections, and the crew was housed beneath a continuous transparent canopy with a bullet-proof windshield and armour plate. A swinging bomb cradle with a maximum capacity of 454 kg (1,000 lb) was centred beneath the fuselage and a bomb rack was mounted under each outer-wing section.

Flying the Dauntless, pilots found it a forgiving machine of few vices, although it had a troublesome tendency to stall in tight turns. On dive-bombing missions, the pilot approached his target at 4570 to 6095 m (15,000 to 20,000 ft), took position almost directly overhead, pulled up the nose, and deployed upper and lower dive flaps. He then 'rolled in', the Dauntless accelerating less rapidly than might be expected while plummetting at over 70°. Using the Mk VIII reflector sight which, from the SBD-5 model on, had replaced the earlier extended telescope, which had a tendency to fog over in a dive as a result of temperature changes, the pilot aimed his bomb load literally by pointing his aircraft at the target. His bomb release was a red button marked 'B' on the top of the stick and he could drop his ordnance singly or in salvo. US Navy legend has it that pilots were prone to 'target fascination', which could lull them into failing to pull out of the dive in time. With its bomb load gone, the Dauntless pulled out quite handily, with an easy motion on the stick. The machine generally handled well in normal flight and the pilot's visibility was excellent, both when level and when descending for a tricky landing on a carrier deck. Few aircraft were tougher or more reliable, the Dauntless often coming home with severe battle damage.

A few A-24B Dauntlesses found their way, post-war, into the hands of the Mexican air force, which was apparently the last user of this type, employing it until 1959. Today, a beautifully preserved Dauntless is in the US Marine Corps Museum at Quantico, Virginia, and the sole remaining flyable machine is with the Confederate Air Force at Harlingen, Texas.

Douglas SBD Dauntless variants

XSBD-1: conversion of Northrop XBT-2, Bureau of Aeronautics number (BuAer No.) 0627; total 1
SBD-1: initial production version, BuAer Nos 1596/1631 and 1735/1755; total 57
SBD-1P: eight conversions to reconnaissance role
SBD-2: improved armour, self-sealing tanks, BuAer Nos 2102/2188; total 87
SBD-2P: 14 conversions to reconnaissance role
SBD-3: improved production version; BuAer Nos 4518/4691, 03185/03384 and 06492/06701; total 584
SBD-3A: aircraft from US Navy contract diverted to USAAF as A-24
SBD-3P: 43 conversions to reconnaissance role and 24-V
SBD-4: production aircraft, improved propeller and electrical systems, BuAer Nos 06702/06991 and 10317/10806; total 780
SBD-5: production aircraft, R-1820-60 engine, BuAer Nos 10807/10956, 10957/11066, 28059/28829, 28831/29213, 35922/36421, 36433/36932 and 54050/54599; total 2,965
SBD-5A: aircraft from USAAF contract, originally intended for US Army as A-24B but delivered to US Navy, BuAer Nos 09693/09752; total 60
XSBD-6: prototype for SBD-6, BuAer No. 28830; total 1
SBD-6: final production version, R-1820-66, one converted from SBD-5 (BuAer No. 35950); other, BuAer Nos 54600/55049; total 450
A-24: originally designated SBD-3A, delivered to USAAF, serial numbers 41-15746/15823 and 42-6682/6771; total 168
A-24A: USAAF version of SBD-4, serials 42-6772/6831 and 42-60772/60881; total 170
A-24B: USAAF version of SBD-5, serials 42-54285/54899; total 615
RA-24A: redesignation after 1942, to indicate obsolescence
RA-24B: redesignation after 1942, to indicate obsolescence
F-24A: redesignation after 1947
F-24B: redesignation after 1947
QF-24A: rebuild as target drone, serial 48-44; total 1
QF-24B: rebuild as drone controller aircraft, serial 48-45; total 1

A formation of Douglas SBD-5s of VMS-3, US Marine Corps, high over the Atlantic. The dark grey and off-white colour scheme was adopted for Atlantic theatre operations in early 1944.

SBD-5 or Dauntless Mk I (JS997) of the Royal Navy at RAE Farnborough in about October 1944 for very belated flight tests comparing it with the Curtiss Helldiver and Vultee Vengeance. Why RAF and Royal Navy pilots were testing the Dauntless at this late stage in the war is unclear. They found it pleasant to fly but not breathtaking in performance, and it never saw combat wearing British roundels.

The Mighty Mustang

The greatness of the Mustang is beyond question: the British-inspired, American-built World War II fighter proved itself a potent and versatile weapon operating in roles as varied as long-range escort and close air support. It was a pilot's dream: handy, hard-hitting and very tough, with first-class performance under all combat conditions.

The North American P-51 Mustang was one of very, very few aircraft that fought in World War II to be designed after the conflict had begun. It was purely a private venture (not built to any official US specification), and was carried through with incredible speed for a foreign customer who doubted the company could build a good fighter at all. And when it was given a different engine and even greater fuel capacity, it flew missions far longer than any fighter had ever flown before.

Reichsmarschall Hermann Goering once claimed no enemy bomber would ever fly over Berlin. By 1944 he had got used to intrusions by the Allied bombers, but he was shattered when the US Army Air Force flew fighters all the way to Berlin, and even to Poland and Czechoslovakia. He is reported to have said, "When I saw those Mustangs over Berlin, I knew that the war was lost."

North American Aviation was one of the youngest of the major planemakers; it set up shop in 1934, with just 75 employees. A year later it flew the prototype of what became the world's No. 1 trainer, the AT-6 or Harvard, of which over 20,000 were eventually built. In 1938 this attracted the attention of the British, who placed big orders. Soon after the outbreak of war, in September 1939, the British Purchasing Commission asked NAA whether it could build an American fighter, the Curtiss P-40, for the RAF. The P-40 was a second-rate fighter, and NAA's immediate response was that it had long wanted to build a really first-class fighter and was eager to do so for the UK. The US Army had more new fighter prototypes than it wanted, and was quite uninterested.

In retrospect it seems obvious that the British should have signed a contract then and there, stipulating a US-made Rolls-Royce Merlin engine which was already being planned. Instead the Commission found every possible reason for not letting NAA go ahead. Finally, in late April 1940, it agreed, on the strict understanding that the company wasted $15,000 buying P-40 wind-tunnel data from Curtiss. NAA bought the information, but was far too busy designing the new fighter to waste time looking at it. The contract with Britain, for 320 N.A.73 fighters, was signed on 29 May.

NAA undertook to have the prototype ready in an incredible four months. It beat this target, rolling the N.A.73X out into the Los Angeles sunshine after 102 days. But Allison, suppliers of the 858-kW (1,150-hp) V-1710 engine, were 20 days late with delivery and test pilot Vance Breese finally flew the trim unpainted ship on 26 October.

The new American pursuit was a sleek all-metal stressed-skin machine like the Messerschmitt, but it was considerably larger – about the same size as the old fabric-covered Hurricane. Its aerodynamics were much newer than either. It had one of the new supposedly laminar flow wings with the thickest part much further back than usual. The liquid-cooled engine had its coolant radiator far back under the rear fuselage in the most efficient position, and it was installed in a long profiled duct with a variable-exit shutter so that, instead of causing drag, the heated air could behave like a jet-propulsion unit and help push the fighter along. This leaves the question of why the N.A.73X was so much larger than the Bf 109: it was so that it could carry more fuel, far more than in any European single-engined fighter.

More fuel means not only a bigger aircraft but more weight, and the N.A.73X could have been cumbersome and ineffective. In fact, as Breese soon discovered, it was an absolute winner. It reached 615 km/h (382 mph), much faster than any of the European fighters,

The first of the many: the trim N.A.73X prototype, photographed immediately the Allison engine had been installed and before any markings had been applied. It subsequently received military rudder stripes and civil registration NX19998.

A standard Mustang I (AG528) after arduous service at low level with RAF Army Co-operation Command in 1942-43. One of the 0.5-in (12.7-mm) guns can be seen projecting from the lower front of the cowling.

including even the smaller Supermarine Spitfire which carried less than half as much fuel. It had devastating armament: four heavy 12.7-mm (0.5-in) guns and four 7.62-mm (0.3-in) guns.

World beater

On the fifth flight Paul Balfour switched the fuel incorrectly, and the engine cut at a crucial moment: the aircraft arrived on the ground upside down and was wrecked, but that was of little consequence. The RAF order for 320 was soon followed by another 300, and the first Mustang I reached Liverpool on 24 october 1941.

With full military load the RAF found the Mustang still reached 603km/h (375mph), just 56km/h (35mph) faster than a Spitfire V. The Mustang's only shortcoming was that the Allison engine's power faded rapidly as the Mustang climbed, so that above 4572m (15,000ft) it was little better than an Allison-engined P-40. But low down it was a world-beater, and by 1942 it was serving with Army Co-operation Command and the Royal Canadian Air Force. It did well on low-level offensive sweeps over Nazi-held Europe, and in October 1942 some RAF Mustangs shot up targets on the Dortmund-Ems canal to become the first British single-engined aircraft to fly over Germany in World War II.

At the start of the N.A.73 programme NAA had been forced to agree to supply two early examples to the US Army at no cost, and Wright Field duly received the fourth and tenth off the line. The test team tried to to be unimpressed by this unwanted 'foreign' machine, but the results were so good that the new fighter was soon on US Army contracts. The first orders comprised 150 P-51s, with four 20-mm cannon; 500 A-36A dive-bombers with six 12.7-mm (0.5-in) guns and two 227-kg (500-lb) bombs (and delivered with dive-brakes which later were wired inoperative); and 310 P-51As with just the four 12.7-mm (0.5-in) wing guns. In 1943 the A-36A was wreaking havoc in the hands of the Army Air Force in Sicily and southern Italy. At first the name Apache was used, but this was soon changed to the British name. Some of the very first in the US Army service were examples of the cannon-armed P-51-1 (converted P-51) designated F-6A, for photo-reconnaissance.

New engine, new power

It seems strange that the idea of putting a high altitude Merlin into this superb airframe should not have occurred at the outset, and certainly as soon as the need had been shown by tests in Britain in 1941. Yet it as not until well into 1942 that Ron Harker, Rolls-Royce test pilot and an RAF flight lieutenant, did a work-out in a Mustang and immediately wrote a recommendation for the Merlin 61. The Rolls performance engineers calculated this would give a speed of 695km/h (432mph) at 7772m (25,500ft). Meanwhile Lt-Col. Tommy Hitchcock, US Air Attaché in London, had likewise suggested

The P-51 was swiftly moved to the war zones as soon as it was available. These 31st Fighter Group aircraft are seen over Italy, one of the many theatres in which the aircraft served. No enemy fighter could match its mix of altitude performance and speed.

North American P-51 Mustang cutaway key:

1 Plastic (Phenol fibre) rudder trim tab
2 Rudder frame (fabric covered)
3 Rudder balance
4 Fin front spar
5 Fin structure
6 Access panel
7 Rudder trim-tab actuating drum
8 Rudder trim-tab control link
9 Rear navigation light
10 Rudder metal bottom section
11 Elevator plywood trim tab
12 Starboard elevator frame
13 Elevator balance weight
14 Starboard tailplane structure
15 Reinforced bracket (rear steering stresses)
16 Rudder operating horn forging
17 Elevator operating horns
18 Tab control turnbuckles
19 Fin front spar/fuselage attachment
20 Port elevator tab
21 Fabric-covered elevator
22 Elevator balance weight
23 Port tailplane
24 Tab control drum
25 Fin root fairing
26 Elevator cables
27 Tab control access panels
28 Tailwheel steering mechanism
29 Tailwheel
30 Tailwheel leg assembly
31 Forward-retracting steerable tailwheel
32 Tailwheel doors
33 Lifting tube
34 Fuselage aft bulkhead/ break point
35 Fuselage break point
36 Control cable pulley brackets
37 Fuselage frames
38 Oxygen bottles
39 Cooling-air exit flap actuating mechanism
40 Rudder cables
41 Fuselage lower longeron
42 Rear tunnel
43 Cooling-air exit flap
44 Coolant radiator assembly
45 Radio and equipment shelf
46 Power supply pack
47 Fuselage upper longeron
48 Radio bay aft bulkhead (plywood)
49 Fuselage stringers
50 SCR-695 radio transmitter-receiver (on upper sliding shelf)
51 Whip aerial
52 Junction box
53 Cockpit aft glazing
54 Canopy track
55 SCR-552 radio transmitter-receiver
56 Battery installation
57 Radiator/supercharger coolant pipes
58 Radiator forward air duct
59 Coolant header tank/ radiator pipe
60 Coolant radiator ventral access cover
61 Oil-cooler air inlet door
62 Oil radiator
63 Oil pipes
64 Flap control linkage
65 Wing rear spar/fuselage attachment bracket
66 Crash pylon structure
67 Aileron control linkage
68 Hydraulic hand pump
69 Radio control boxes
70 Pilot's seat
71 Seat suspension frame
72 Pilot's head/back armour
73 Rearward-sliding clear-vision canopy
74 External rear-view mirror
75 Ring and bead gunsight
76 Bullet-proof windshield
77 Gyro gunsight
78 Engine controls
79 Signal-pistol discharge tube
80 Circuit-breaker panel
81 Oxygen regulator
82 Pilot's footrest and seat mounting bracket
83 Control linkage
84 Rudder pedal
85 Tailwheel lock control
86 Wing centre-section
87 Hydraulic reservoir
88 Port wing fuel tank filler point
89 Port Browning 0.5-in guns
90 Ammunition feed chutes
91 Gun-bay access door (raised)
92 Ammunition box troughs
93 Aileron control cables
94 Flap lower skin (Alclad)
95 Aileron profile (internal aerodynamic balance diaphragm)
96 Aileron control drum and mounting bracket
97 Aileron trim-tab control drum
98 Aileron plastic (Phenol fibre trim tab)
99 Port aileron assembly
100 Wing skinning
101 Outer section sub-assembly
102 Port navigation light
103 Port wingtip
104 Leading-edge skin
105 Landing lamp
106 Weapons/stores pylon
107 500 lb (227 kg) bomb
108 Gun ports
109 Gun barrels
110 Detachable cowling panels
111 Firewall/integral armour
112 Oil tank
113 Oil pipes
114 Upper longeron/engine mount attachment
115 Oil-tank metal retaining straps
116 Carburettor
117 Engine bearer assembly
118 Cowling panel frames
119 Engine aftercooler
120 Engine leads
121 1,520 hp Packard V-1650 (R-R Merlin) twelve-cylinder liquid-cooled engine
122 Exhaust fairing panel
123 Stub exhausts
124 Magneto
125 Coolant pipes
126 Cowling forward frame
127 Coolant header tank
128 Armour plate
129 Propeller hub
130 Spinner
131 Hamilton Standard Hydromatic propeller
132 Carburettor air intake, integral with (133)
133 Engine-mount front-frame assembly
134 Intake trunk
135 Engine-mount reinforcing tie
136 Hand-crank starter
137 Carburettor trunk vibration-absorbing connection
138 Wing centre-section front bulkhead
139 Wing centre-section end rib
140 Starboard mainwheel well
141 Wing front spar/fuselage attachment bracket
142 Ventral air intake (radiator and oil cooler)
143 Starboard wing fuel tank
144 Fuel filler point
145 Mainwheel leg mount/pivot
146 Mainwheel leg rib cut-outs
147 Main gear fairing doors
148 Auxiliary fuel tank (plastic/ pressed-paper composition, 90 gal/409 litres)
149 Auxiliary fuel tank (metal 62.5 gal/284 litres)
150 27-in smooth-contour mainwheel
151 Axle fork
152 Towing lugs
153 Landing-gear fairing
154 Main-gear shock strut
155 Blast tubes

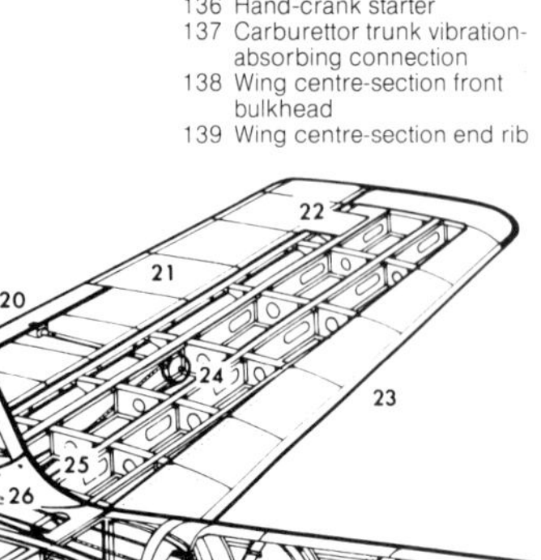

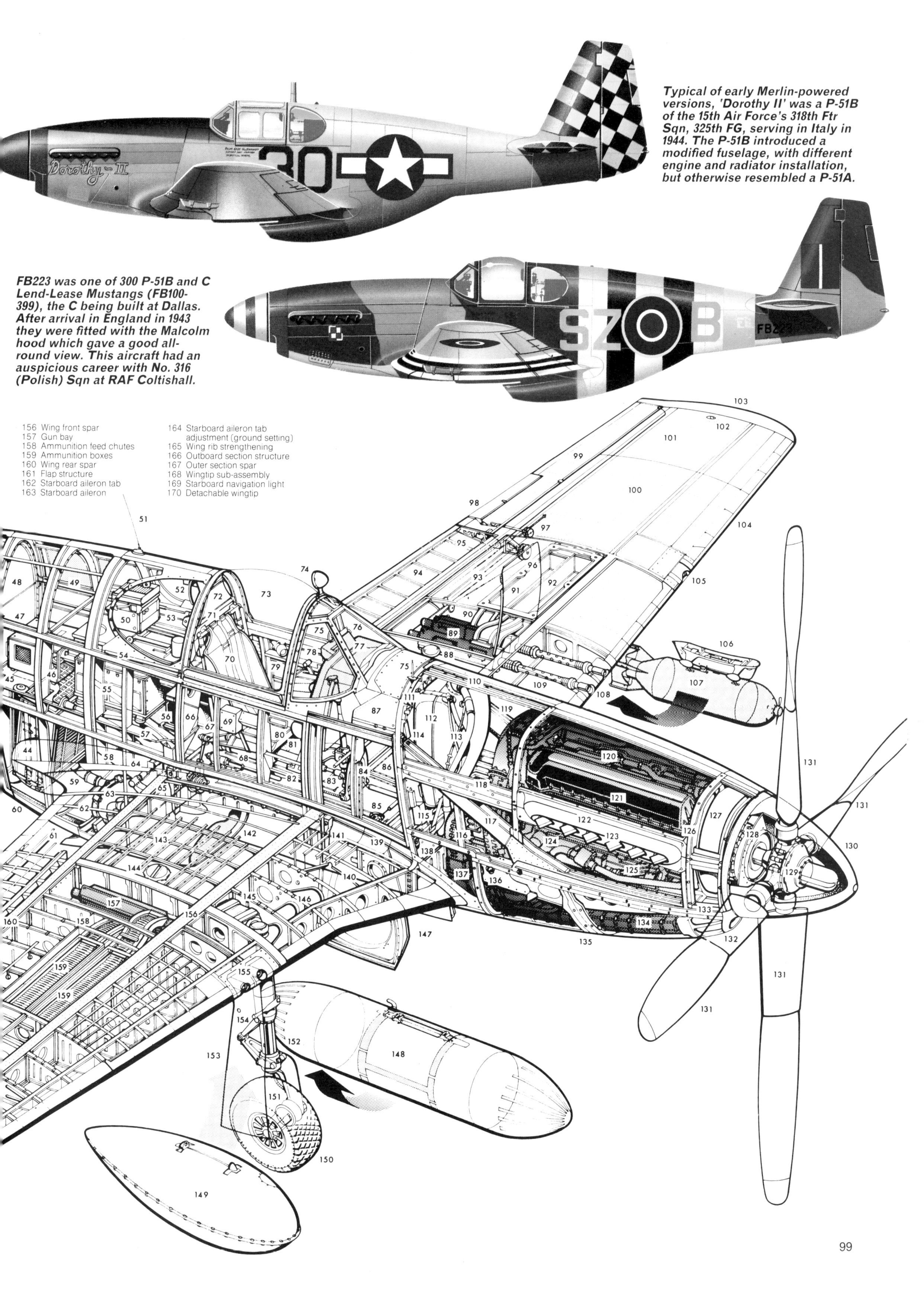

Typical of early Merlin-powered versions, 'Dorothy II' was a P-51B of the 15th Air Force's 318th Ftr Sqn, 325th FG, serving in Italy in 1944. The P-51B introduced a modified fuselage, with different engine and radiator installation, but otherwise resembled a P-51A.

FB223 was one of 300 P-51B and C Lend-Lease Mustangs (FB100-399), the C being built at Dallas. After arrival in England in 1943 they were fitted with the Malcolm hood which gave a good all-round view. This aircraft had an auspicious career with No. 316 (Polish) Sqn at RAF Coltishall.

156 Wing front spar
157 Gun bay
158 Ammunition feed chutes
159 Ammunition boxes
160 Wing rear spar
161 Flap structure
162 Starboard aileron tab
163 Starboard aileron
164 Starboard aileron tab adjustment (ground setting)
165 Wing rib strengthening
166 Outboard section structure
167 Outer section spar
168 Wingtip sub-assembly
169 Starboard navigation light
170 Detachable wingtip

Though it was in service only in the final 18 months of World War II, the P-51D and basically identical K (different propeller) have since hogged almost all the Mustang limelight and also accounted for most of the 15,586 of all models produced. This aircraft, USAAF 1944-13926, served with the 361st Fighter Group of the 8th Air Force, at Bottisham (England) and in late 1944 at St Dizier (France).

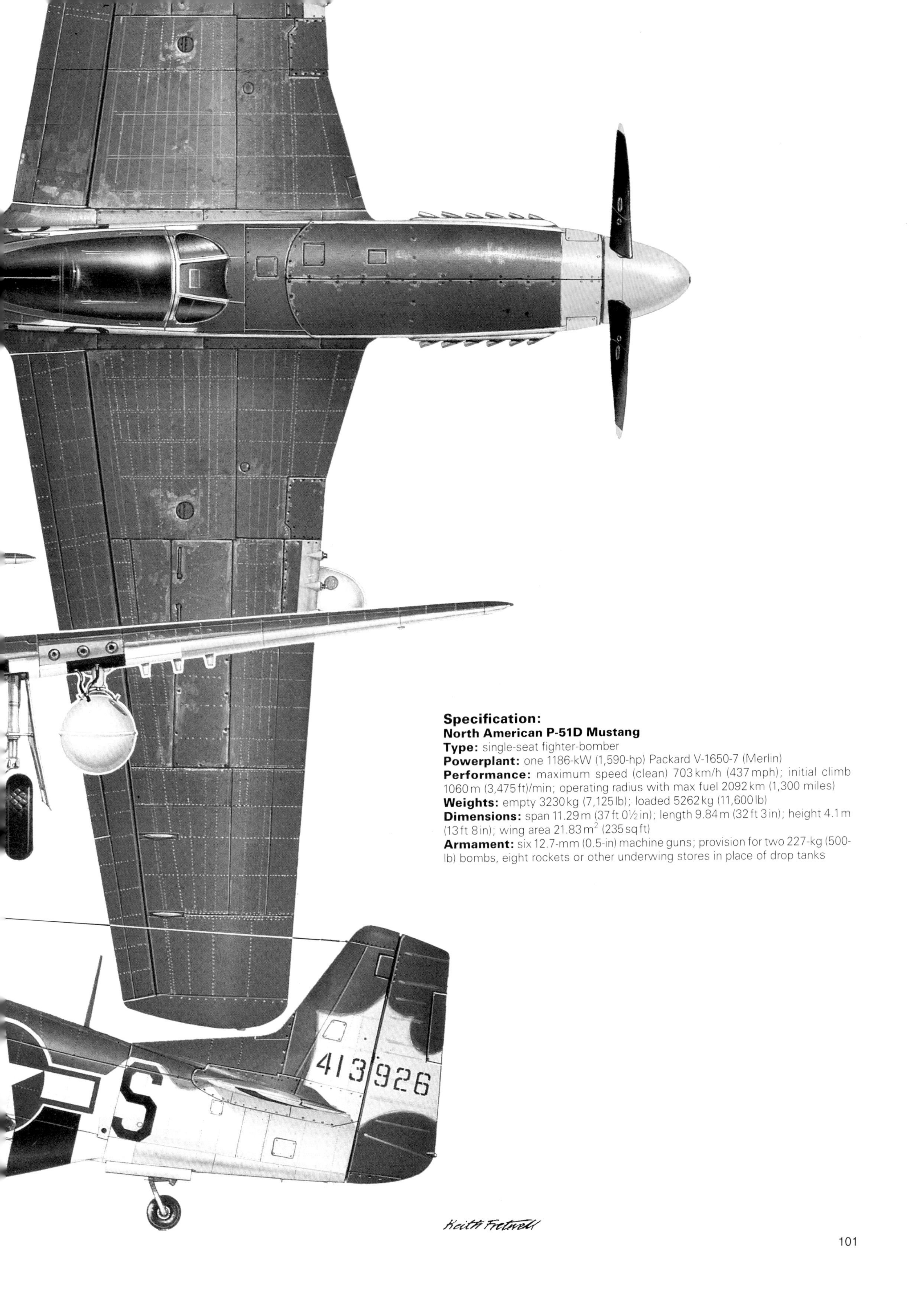

Specification:
North American P-51D Mustang
Type: single-seat fighter-bomber
Powerplant: one 1186-kW (1,590-hp) Packard V-1650-7 (Merlin)
Performance: maximum speed (clean) 703 km/h (437 mph); initial climb 1060 m (3,475 ft)/min; operating radius with max fuel 2092 km (1,300 miles)
Weights: empty 3230 kg (7,125 lb); loaded 5262 kg (11,600 lb)
Dimensions: span 11.29 m (37 ft 0½ in); length 9.84 m (32 ft 3 in); height 4.1 m (13 ft 8 in); wing area 21.83 m^2 (235 sq ft)
Armament: six 12.7-mm (0.5-in) machine guns; provision for two 227-kg (500-lb) bombs, eight rockets or other underwing stores in place of drop tanks

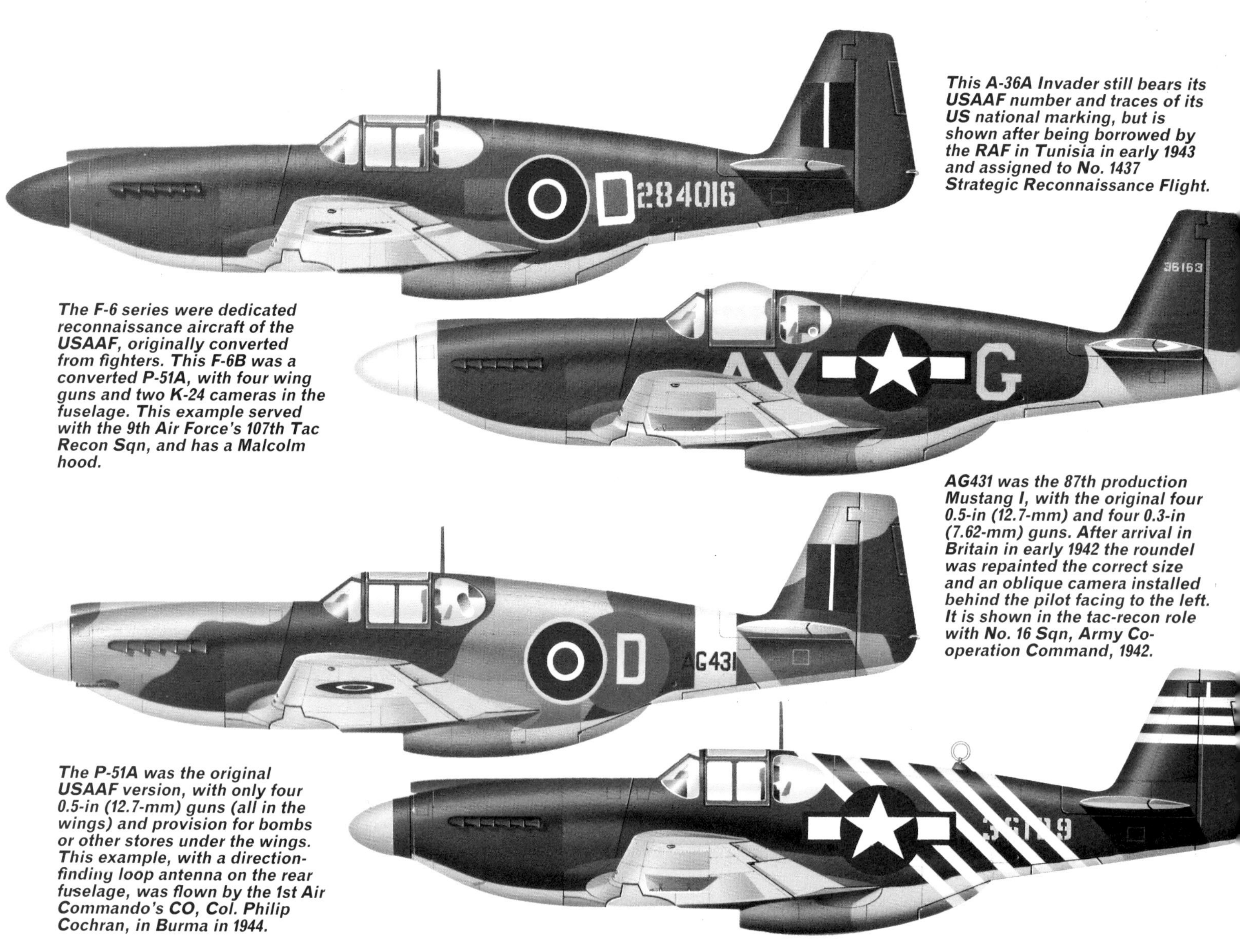

This A-36A Invader still bears its USAAF number and traces of its US national marking, but is shown after being borrowed by the RAF in Tunisia in early 1943 and assigned to No. 1437 Strategic Reconnaissance Flight.

The F-6 series were dedicated reconnaissance aircraft of the USAAF, originally converted from fighters. This F-6B was a converted P-51A, with four wing guns and two K-24 cameras in the fuselage. This example served with the 9th Air Force's 107th Tac Recon Sqn, and has a Malcolm hood.

AG431 was the 87th production Mustang I, with the original four 0.5-in (12.7-mm) and four 0.3-in (7.62-mm) guns. After arrival in Britain in early 1942 the roundel was repainted the correct size and an oblique camera installed behind the pilot facing to the left. It is shown in the tac-recon role with No. 16 Sqn, Army Co-operation Command, 1942.

The P-51A was the original USAAF version, with only four 0.5-in (12.7-mm) guns (all in the wings) and provision for bombs or other stores under the wings. This example, with a direction-finding loop antenna on the rear fuselage, was flown by the 1st Air Commando's CO, Col. Philip Cochran, in Burma in 1944.

installation of the Merlin, which by 1943 was in mass production at the Parkard company as the V-1650. Rolls got a Merlin conversion into the air on 13 October 1942, but NAA designed the P-51B as a largely new aircraft with an optimised V-1650-7 engine installation planned for mass production. The first XP-51B flew on 30 November 1942.

The new fighter had better lines, and a new propeller with four very broad blades to turn the power into thrust at high altitudes. The carburettor inlet above the engine had vanished, but reappeared in enlarged form on the underside. The radiator was deepened, and an intercooler added in the same duct. The whole aircraft, especially the fuselage, was strengthened. It turned in the remarkable speed of 710km/h (441mph) at 9083m (29,800ft).

On test the XP-51B behaved like a different animal. Whereas the original Mustangs, then at war all over Europe, were smooth and silky, the new model was more like a sports car. It needed a bit more attention, was noisier in the cockpit, and seemed to splutter and crackle. Such things were mere first impressions; what mattered was that at height it could outperform anything in the sky. The US Army, still looking on the P-51 basically as a tactical attack aircraft, ordered 2,200 of the new model before the first flight. By mid-1943 the new Mustangs were pouring from the Los Angeles plant and from another factory built at Dallas.

Fighter escort over Germany

For more than a year the embattled US 8th Air Force in England had been seeking a superior long-range escort fighter for its heavy bombers. It sent Col. Cass Hough to try the new P-51B; he said it was terrific, but directional stability was poor. NAA switched to the P-51C at Dallas with a sliding bulged hood and six guns, and then to the P-51D with a teardrop canopy and six guns. Soon after the start of P-51D production a dorsal fin was added to cure the directional problem. Already the Mustang was by far the world's best escort, with fuel consumption half that of the Lockheed P-38 or Republic P-47, and combat capability better than that of either (though the P-47 had eight guns). But back in the USA a massive new fighter, the Fisher XP-75, had been designed specifically to do the long-range escort job.

Col. (later General) Mark Bradley tested the XP-75 and was very worried. Something else had to be found, and quickly. He called

FX893 was a Mustang III retained for armament trials, and is seen here equipped with unusual rocket rails, each carrying a 60-lb (27-kg) RP (rocket projectile) above and below so that the single hardpoint on each wing could serve to launch two pairs of RPs. Like most RAF Mustang IIIs this aircraft was fitted with the Malcolm hood.

NAA's boss, 'Dutch' Kindelberger, the man who had finally convinced the British he could build the Mustang in the first place. Bradley asked for a big 322-litre (85-US gallon) tank to be installed behind the pilot's seat in a Merlin-Mustang, and filled. He knew this would make directional stability almost unacceptable, so that for the first hour or two the pilot would have to concentrate to keep flying the way the nose was pointing. After that time the extra tank would be empty, the pilot could switch to the usual 697 litres (184 US gallons) in the wings and forget about stability problems. With two 284-litre (75-US gallon) drop tanks under the wings, the Mustang could only just stagger into the sky, but with 1586 litres (419 US gallons), ought to go quite a distance. NAA quickly put in the extra tank, and Bradley did the testing. On the first trip he flew to Albuquerque, circled the city and flew back; he had just done the equivalent of England to Berlin!

This ability to put a first-class high-performance fighter anywhere in Europe was something that, a few months earlier, had seemed impossible. It really did mean, as Goering said, that Germany had lost the war. The build-up in P-51 strength was so rapid that over 9,000 reached combat units in 1944 – 1,377 of them being Dallas-built P-51Ks with a different propeller. Mustangs dominated the sky not only over north-west Europe and across to the advancing Russian armies, but also in northern Italy – where among many other exploits, Mustangs smashed the Pescara Dam – and in the Pacific theatre.

Pride of the Eighth

The only aircraft the Mustang could not catch were the new German jets, and even here the Mustang was far more successful than any other Allied fighter. On 7 October 1944 Lt Urban L. Drew of the 361st Fighter Group surprised two Messerschmitt Me 262s taking off and shot down both. On 25 February 1945 Mustangs of the 55th FG did the same to a whole Me 262 squadron and destroyed six. Audacious exploits by Mustangs came almost every day. On at least three occasions, twice by the US 8th AF and once by the famed CO of No. 315 (Polish) Sqn, RAF, Mustangs landed in enemy territory, picked up a shot-down comrade and flew back to base with one pilot sitting on the other.

By far the most numerous Mustangs were the P-51D and P-51K, and though they did not really get into action until 1944 the Merlin-powered models accounted for some 13,600 of the total production of all versions of 15,586. This impressive total includes 266 of the P-51D model built under licence by Commonwealth Aircraft of Melbourne.

By 1944 NAA's main development effort was on two fronts. While recognizing that it was mainly the excellence of the P-51 that stopped

The Mustang is the most widely used World War II aircraft for modern Open Class air racing. 'Miss Suzie Q' is typical of the breed, with its lines relatively unaltered, but the engine considerably modified to produce high power for a relatively short time. Modified racing Mustangs are capable of speeds up to 430 mph (692 km/h) around pylon-marked circuits, indicating straight speeds of 475 mph (764 km/h).

the development of America's shoal of unconventional fighter prototypes during World War II, there is never anything so good that it cannot be improved. The chief effort was concentrated on making the Mustang lighter, but a totally different development was the unusual N.A.-120, the Twin Mustang. First flown as the XP-82 in April 1945, the Twin Mustang comprised two lengthened Mustang fuselages joined together by a new rectangular wing centre section and tailplane. The propellers turned in opposite directions, and the main landing gears were new, there being just one under each fuselage retracting inwards. Production Twin Mustangs were post-war aircraft, designated F-82 after 1947. They included heavily-armed night fighters with SCR-720 or APS-4 radar in a large pod on the centreline. Twin Mustangs, which had Allison engines, served in Korea where their few victories – mainly at night – were among the very first to be credited to the US Air Force.

Post-war development

As for the lightweight Mustangs, these began with the XP-51F and XP-51G, moved on to the XP-51J with the Allison engine, and also yielded 555 of a planned 4,100 of the P-51H model, the fastest fighter of World War II (apart from German jets) with a speed of 784 km/h (487 mph). Though it had six 12.7-mm (0.5-in) guns, it had a structure more than 454 kg (1,000 lb) lighter than that of the P-51D, the P-51H's internal fuel capacity was actually greater. The P-51H just got into action in the Pacific in the summer of 1945.

Surprisingly, it was not the P-51H but the mass-produced P-51D

The Cavalier Mustang was derived from the P-51D in the mid-1960s, but was fitted with the taller fin associated with the P-51H, the V-1650-7 engine, and a strengthened wing able to carry two 1,000-lb (454-kg) bombs and six 5-in (12.7-cm) HVARs (High-Velocity Aircraft Rockets).

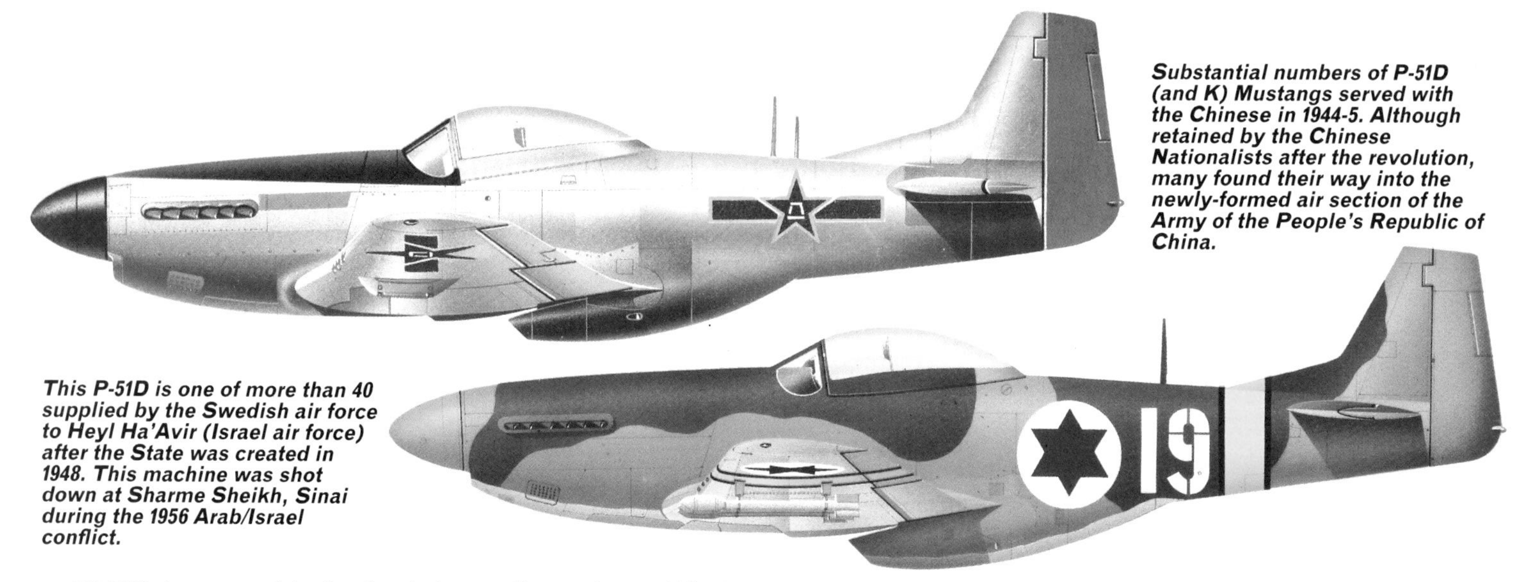

Substantial numbers of P-51D (and K) Mustangs served with the Chinese in 1944-5. Although retained by the Chinese Nationalists after the revolution, many found their way into the newly-formed air section of the Army of the People's Republic of China.

This P-51D is one of more than 40 supplied by the Swedish air force to Heyl Ha'Avir (Israel air force) after the State was created in 1948. This machine was shot down at Sharme Sheikh, Sinai during the 1956 Arab/Israel conflict.

and P-51K that were picked up by air forces all over the world in the immediate post-war era, until the Mustang was probably the world's most widely used combat aircraft. Instead of compiling a list of users, it would be simpler to make a list of the few countries which did not have at least one P-51D or P-51K squadron. Very large numbers saw action in Korea, and many were rebuilt by various companies as tandem two-seaters, either for special liaison or as dual trainers. Others emerged with various kinds of modifications as civilian racers, one of the fastest having its normal radiator replaced by long radiator pods on the wingtips. In a rather similar-looking conversion a USAF machine tested large ramjets on the wingtips, easily exceeding 805 km/h (500 mph).

In the 1950s Trans-Florida Aviation actually marketed a two-seat executive model, and this led to a long series of not only rebuilds but even completely new Mustangs in the 1960s by Cavalier Aircraft. As they were unarmed, most of the Cavaliers had even more fuel than wartime Mustangs, and in 1961 for $32,500 one could buy a variant with tandem seats, full airline avionics and 416-litre (110-US gal) tanks on the wingtips yet fully stressed for aerobatics. By the late 1960s the range of new Mustangs included several for counter-insurgent and Forward Air Control duties with the USAF, as well as lengthened Turbo Mustangs with a Rolls-Royce Dart turboprop. From the latter stemmed the Piper Enforcer of 1971, and anyone who thought that by this time the Mustang must surely have been obsolete should note, that in 1980 the Enforcer was again studied as a light attack machine for the USAF!

North American P-51 Mustang variants

N.A.73X Prototype: 1,100 hp Allison V-1710-39 engine. Provision for four 0.5 in and four 0.3 in guns but these not fitted. US civil registration NX19998 but flown with no markings except US Army style rudder insignia, 26 October 1940

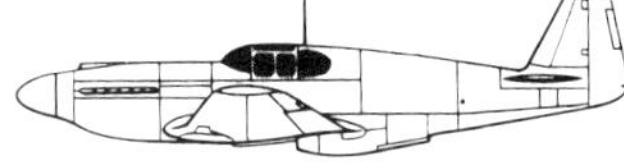

N.A.73X

N.A.73 Mustang I: first production batch of 320 aircraft, 1,150 hp V-1710-F3R (export designation of V-1710-39). Four 0.5 in and four 0.303 in guns; fitted in England with vertical and oblique cameras for tac-recon duties. First aircraft (RAF serial AG345) flown 1 May 1941
N.A.73 XP-51: aircraft Nos 4 and 10 off production line, US Army Air Corps numbers 41-038, -039
N.A.83 Mustang I: second batch of 300, minor changes. RAF serials AL958/AM257 and AP164/AP263. AL975/G became prototype Merlin-Mustang (Merlin 61) and AM121, 203 and 208 became Mustang X (Merlin 65); AM106/G fitted with two 40 mm Vickers S guns

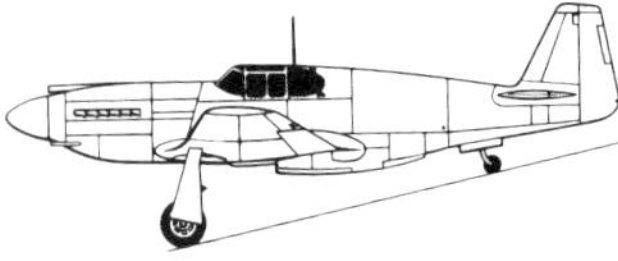

Mustang I

N.A.91 Mustang IA/P-51: lend-lease funds, 150 for RAF with four 20 mm guns; only 93 supplied (serials between FD438/509), rest retained for USAAF after Pearl Harbor with RAF camouflage (serials between FD418/567) and US insignia; 57 later converted to recon (F-6A, P-51-1)

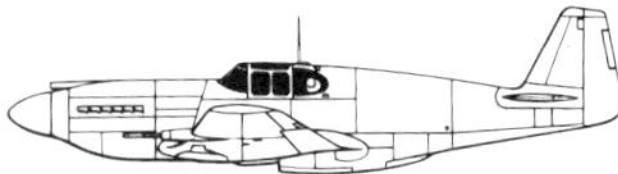

P-51/Mustang IA

N.A.97 A-36: dive bomber, 1,325 hp V-1719-87. Six 0.5 in guns, two 500 lb bombs; wing-mounted dive brakes (later made inoperative). First of 500 flown September 1942, USAAF numbers 42-83663/84162 (83685 to RAF as EW998)
N.A.99 P-51A: multi-role fighter/bomber, 1,200 hp V-1710-81 (export V-1710-F20R). Four 0.5 in guns all in wings (no guns under engine), two wing hardpoints for bombs up to 500 lb or drop tanks up to 125 Imp gal; no dive brakes. Batch of 310, USAAF 43-6003/6312, 50 being passed to RAF (FR890/939) to replace N.A.91s retained by USAAF for conversion to F-6A; 35 USAAF P-51A converted to recon as F-6B
N.A.101 XP-51B: NAA conversions to 1,450 hp V-1650-3, two aircraft (41-37352, 37421) from P-51 batch retained by USAAF. Guns removed

N.A.102 P-51B: productionized N.A.101 with V-1650-3, four 0.5 in wing guns; 400 built at Inglewood 1943 (USAAF from 42-106429)

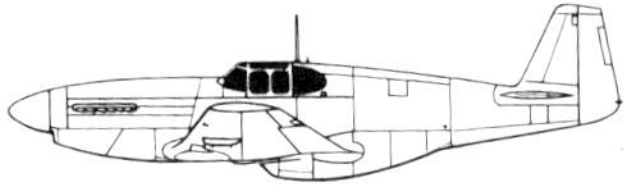

P-51B, C

N.A.103 P-51C: as N.A.102 but built at new Dallas plant as P-51C-1-NT and subsequent blocks eventually totalling 1,350
N.A.104 P-51B: with wing hardpoints rated at 1,000 lb, and from P-51B-7 onwards with 70.7 Imp gal fuselage tank; total 1,588 including 25 to RAF as Mustang III (FB100/124)
N.A.105: seven experimental aircraft with completely redesigned airframes to reduce weight and increase performance, built 1944. First five designed for V-1650-3, actually built with 1,695 hp V-1650-7, four guns; first three only to this standard (USAAF XP-51F, 43-43332/43334,

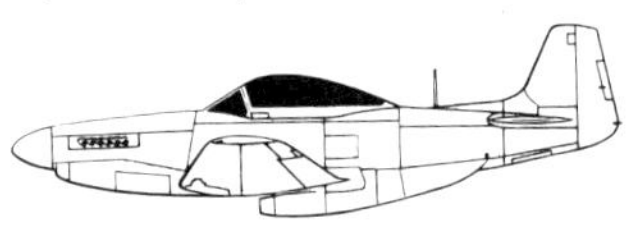

P-51F

one to RAF as FR409) final pair fitted with six guns, more fuel and 1,910 hp RR-built Merlin 145M and British five-blade propellers (USAAF XP-51G, 43-43335/43336, one to RAF as FR410); last two airframes completed with 1,720 hp Allison V-1710-119 as XP-51J (44-76027/76028)

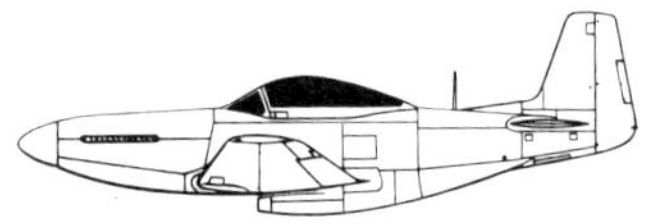

P-51J

N.A.106: first two prototypes of **P-51D** with six wing guns, cut-down rear fuselage and sliding teardrop canopy; taken from P-51B-10-NA (Inglewood) line (USAAF 42-106539/106540)
N.A.109: first production **P-51D** order, 2,500 aircraft with 1,695 hp V-1650-7, six guns, and from late in D-5 block with added dorsal fin. Some early aircraft retained folding canopy and Dash-3 engine, most later converted, and all with 70.7-gal rear fuselage tank

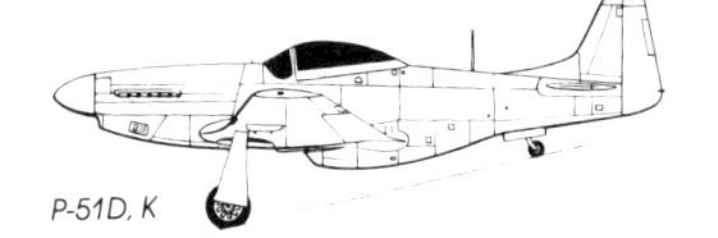

P-51D, K

N.A.110 P-51D: 100 shipped in kit form to CAC, Melbourne, for assembly with various Australian designations
N.A.111: covered three batches of P-51C, D and K, all from Dallas: 400 P-51C included 275 to RAF as Mustang III (RAF FB125/399) fitted on arrival with Malcolm sliding canopy; 600 P-51D; and 1,500 P-51K similar to D but with Aeroproducts propeller (594 to RAF as Mustang IVA, from KH671)
N.A.122 P-51D: blocks totalling 4,000 aircraft, from Inglewood
N.A.124 P-51D: blocks of 2,000 from Dallas, cut at war's end to 1,000, plus single P-51M (intended as first of large batch) with Dash-9A engine
N.A.126 P-51H: production derivative of N.A.105 lightweight family, six guns, V-1650-9A giving 1,380 hp for take-off and 2,218 hp with water injection for combat at best height; block of 2,400 from Inglewood but terminated at VJ-Day after completion of 555 (USAAF 44-64160/64714)
Note: RAF received 281 P-51D from various blocks as Mustang IV (RAF KH641 onwards); unarmed photo-recon conversions included **F-6B** (35 ex-P-51A), **F-6C** (71 ex-P-51B and 20 ex-P-51C), **F-6D** (146 ex-P-51D, Dallas) and **F-6K** (163 ex-P-51K)

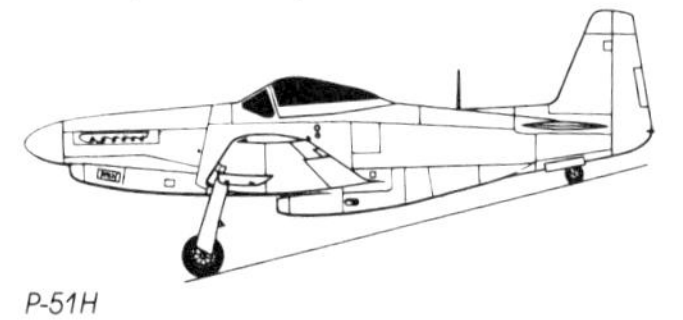

P-51H

Twin Mustangs
N.A.120 two prototypes with V-1650/23/25 (Merlin); USAAF XP-82 (44-83886/83887); No 3 completed as XP-82A with V-1710-119 engines
N.A.123: production version of N.A.120, 500 ordered as **P-82B** but 480 cancelled (20 delivered as 44-65160/65179); No 10 converted as **P-82C** night fighter with SCR-720 radar in external pod, No 11 converted as

F-82Gs of 347th F(AW) Group.

P-82D with APS-4 radar
N.A.144: first post-war procurement, 100 **P-82E** (later F-82E) escorts with attack capability; 1,600 hp V-1710-143/145 engines, bomb/rocket load 4,000 lb, no radar
N.A.149 P-82F: (F-82F) night fighter, 100 with APS-4 radar
N.A.150 P-82G: (F-82G) night fighter, 50 with SCR-720 radar. A total of 14 F-82F and G were given designation F-82H after winterization for Alaskan service
Post-war variants
F-51D, H and K: designations of surviving P-51D, H and K in 1951
RF-51D, RF-51K: post-1951 designations of F-6D, F-6K
TRF-51D: two-seat conversion of RF-51D (there were several wartime two-seat conversions, some effected by field units but including TP-51D series (ten aircraft) rebuilt by NAA
TP-51D: post-war designation for (a) P-51Ds rebuilt by Temco Aircraft as dual trainers, many having P-51H tall vertical tail, and (b) P-51D single-seaters used as trainers by ANG
Cavalier Mustang: in 1954 Trans-Florida Aviation purchased all rights to F-51 design and began marketing two-seat civil 'executive' and liaison rebuild of F-51D as Cavalier 2000; company changed name to Cavalier Aircraft and from 1961 offered range including Model 750, Model 1200 with extra 40 Imp gal in each wing, Model 1500 with extra 52.5 Imp gal in each wing, Model 2000 with 91.6 Imp gal tip tanks, and Model 2500 as 2000 with extra 50 Imp gal in each wing. Cavalier followed in 1967 with Mustang II family of military aircraft rebuilt from F-51D with civil Merlin 620, tip tanks and six or eight wing hardpoints. In addition the Cavalier F-51D was a remanufactured two-seater with F-51H vertical tail, Dash-7 engine, six guns and eight hardpoints for wide variety of loads (eg two 1,000 lb bombs and six HVAR). Rear seat normally for observer, but one, TF-51D, had dual control. Most supplied under MAP to S American air forces, but two stripped of armament and used by US Army at Ft Rucker as AH-56A chase aircraft

Civil Cavalier with Cavalier F-51D.

Cavalier Turbo Mustang III: single prototype with restressed airframe for increased airspeeds, longer fuselage with Rolls-Royce Dart 510 of 1,740 hp driving Rotol propeller. Civil registered N6167U

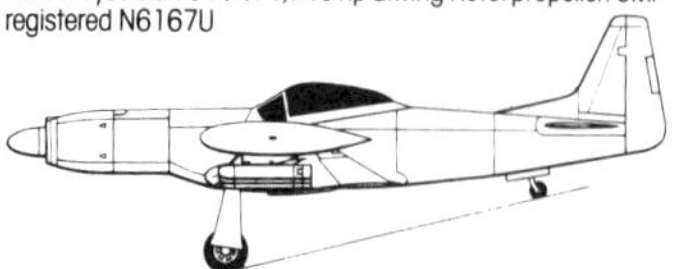

Turbo Mustang III

Piper Enforcer: second and third Turbo Mustang IIIs taken over by Piper Aircraft and completed to different standard with Lycoming T55-L-9 turboprop of 2,535 hp in shorter nose with exhaust stack on left side; two seats in second aircraft only, ten wing pylons, tip tanks and large rear ventral fin ahead of tailwheel. First crashed July 1971; second selected by USAF in Pave Coin evaluation for tactical Co-In aircraft

Piper Enforcer (single-seat).

F4F Wildcat

The Wildcat was the first of Grumman's great carrier fighters of World War II. Its potential was evident from an early age, and in the hands of US Navy pilots it was the F4F which stemmed the tide of the Japanese advance across the Pacific. In British hands, as the Martlet, it could claim equal success.

It was known universally as the Grumman Wildcat, although most were not built by Grumman and many were really named Martlet. It is best remembered in the hands of outnumbered American pilots pitted against the Mitsubishi Zero in 1942-43, yet a British naval pilot of No. 802 Squadron from HMS *Audacity* was flying one when he shot down a four-engine Focke-Wulf Fw 200 Condor near Gibraltar as early as 20 September 1941. It was the fighter used by Lieutenant Edward (Butch) O'Hare of squadron VF-42 from the USS *Lexington* who shot down five Mitsubishi G4M bombers in five minutes near Rabaul on 20 February 1942, becoming the US Navy's first ace of World War II and earning the Medal of Honor. Yet O'Hare, for all his achievement, was only the second man to win this medal while flying the Wildcat.

All things to all men, the Grumman Wildcat (7,815 of them built before VJ-Day, most by the Eastern Division of General Motors Corporation) has one principal claim to fame that no other American aircraft can make: it was the fighter flown by US Navy and US Marine airmen in the dark hours at Pearl Harbor, Coral Sea and Wake Island, and amid the glimmering at Guadalcanal when it first was hinted that the war might be turned against an until-then unbeaten Japanese enemy. The Wildcat never outperformed the Zero, but it won battle after battle nonetheless, and when those battles were over the war had turned in the direction of an Allied victory.

Like many great aircraft, the Wildcat was almost not built at all. A 1936 US Navy requirement for a new carrier-based fighter went not to Leroy Grumman's well-established Bethpage, Long Island, firm but to the forgettable Brewster Aeronautical Corporation for its XF2A-1 Buffalo. The F2A-1 thus became the US Navy's first operational monoplane fighter, but US Navy planners were so sceptical of its promise (wisely so) that they authorised one prototype of Grumman's competing biplane design, the XF4F-1. Later, the biplane proposal was shelved and on 28 July 1936 an order was placed for a prototype Grumman monoplane fighter, the XF4F-2.

First flown by company pilot Robert L. Hall on 2 September 1937 and almost immediately moved to NAS Anacostia, Washington, DC, for tests, the XF4F-2 was powered by a 783-kW (1,050-hp) Pratt & Whitney R-1830-66 Twin Wasp engine and was able to demonstrate a maximum speed of 467 km/h (290 mph). Of all-metal construction with a riveted monocoque fuselage, its cantilever monoplane wing set in mid-position on the fuselage and equipped with retractable tail-wheel landing gear, the XF4F-2 proved to be marginally faster than the Brewster prototype in a 1938 'fly-off' evaluation at Anacostia and Dahlgren, Virginia. It also outperformed the Seversky XFN-1, a derivative of the USAAC's P-35. But speed was the XF4F-2's only advantage over the Brewster product and the latter was ordered into production on 11 June 1938.

Clearly, the US Navy believed the XF4F-2 had hidden potential, for it was returned to Grumman in October 1938 together with a new contract for its further development. The company introduced major improvements and changed its own designation from G-18 to G-36 before this prototype flew again in February 1939 under the designation XF4F-3. Changes included the installation of a more powerful version of the Twin Wasp (the XR-1830-76 with a two-stage supercharger), increased wing span and area, redesigned tail

The final moments of preparation as six Grumman Martlet Mk IVs of the Fleet Air Arm await clearance to take off. Evident in the photograph are the portly fuselage contours and the comparatively narrow undercarriage track.

surfaces, and a modified machine-gun installation. When tested in this form the XF4F-3 was found to have considerably improved performance. A second prototype was completed and introduced into the test programme, this aircraft differing in having a redesigned tail unit in which the tailplane was moved higher up the fin, and the profile of the vertical tail was changed again. In this final form the XF4F-3 was found to have good handling characteristics and manoeuvrability, and a maximum speed of 539 km/h (335 mph) at 6490 m (21,300 ft). Faced with such performance, the US Navy had no hesitation in ordering 78 F4F-3 production aircraft on 8 August 1939.

British service debut

With war seemingly imminent in Europe, Grumman offered the G-36A design for export, receiving orders for 81 and 30 aircraft from the French and Greek governments respectively. The first of those intended for the French navy, powered by a 746-kW (1,000-hp) Wright R-1820 Cyclone radial engine, flew on 27 July 1940 but by then, of course, France had fallen. The British Purchasing Commission agreed to take these aircraft, increasing the order to 90, and the first began to reach the UK in July 1940 (after the first five off the line had been supplied to Canada), being designated Martlet Mk I. They first equipped No. 804 Squadron of the Fleet Air Arm, then based at Hatston in the Orkneys.

Two aircraft flown by No. 804 Squadron were the first American-built fighters in British service to destroy a German fighter during World War II. Later variants of the Grumman fighter served with Nos 802, 806, 881, 882, 888, 890, 892, 894, 893, 896 and 898 Squadrons, mostly on board small escort carriers, like the *Audacity,* in the Battle of the Atlantic.

Subsequent versions of the Martlet to serve with the Fleet Air Arm included the Twin Wasp-powered folding-wing Martlet Mk II; 10 F4F-4As and the Greek contract G-36A aircraft as Martlet Mk III; and Lend-Lease F4F-4Bs with Wright R-1820 Cyclone engines as Martlet Mk IV. In March 1944, all were redesignated Wildcats in a major policy decision to standardise names of US and British aircraft. All retained their distinguishing mark numbers.

The name Wildcat was in use in US service from 1 October 1941. The first F4F-3 Wildcat for the US Navy was flown on 20 August 1940, and at the beginning of December the type began to equip US Navy squadrons VF-7 and VF-41. Some 95 F4F-3A aircraft were ordered by the US Navy, these being powered by the R-1830-90 engine with single-stage supercharger, and deliveries began in 1941. An XF4F-4 prototype was flown in May 1941, this incorporating re-

The legacy of the Wildcat lives on, in this case as an FM-2, beautifully restored and maintained in the United States, where it continues to fly as one of a growing number of 'Warbirds' which regularly appear at air shows.

Grumman F4F-4 Wildcat cutaway drawing key

1 Starboard navigation light
2 Wingtip
3 Starboard formation light
4 Rear spar
5 Aileron construction
6 Fixed aileron tab
7 All riveted wing construction
8 Lateral stiffeners
9 Forward canted main spar
10 'Crimped' leading edge ribs
11 Solid web forward ribs
12 Starboard outer gun blast tube
13 Carburettor air duct
14 Intake
15 Curtiss three-blade constant-speed propeller
16 Propeller cuffs
17 Propeller hub
18 Engine front face
19 Pressure baffle
20 Forward cowling ring
21 Cooler intake
22 Cooler air duct
23 Pratt & Whitney R-1830-86 radial engine
24 Rear cowling ring/flap support
25 Controllable cowling flaps
26 Downdraft ram air duct
27 Engine mounting ring
28 Anti-detonant regulator unit
29 Cartridge starter
30 Generator
31 Intercooler
32 Engine accessories
33 Bearer assembly welded cluster joint
34 Main beam
35 Lower cowl flap
36 Exhaust stub

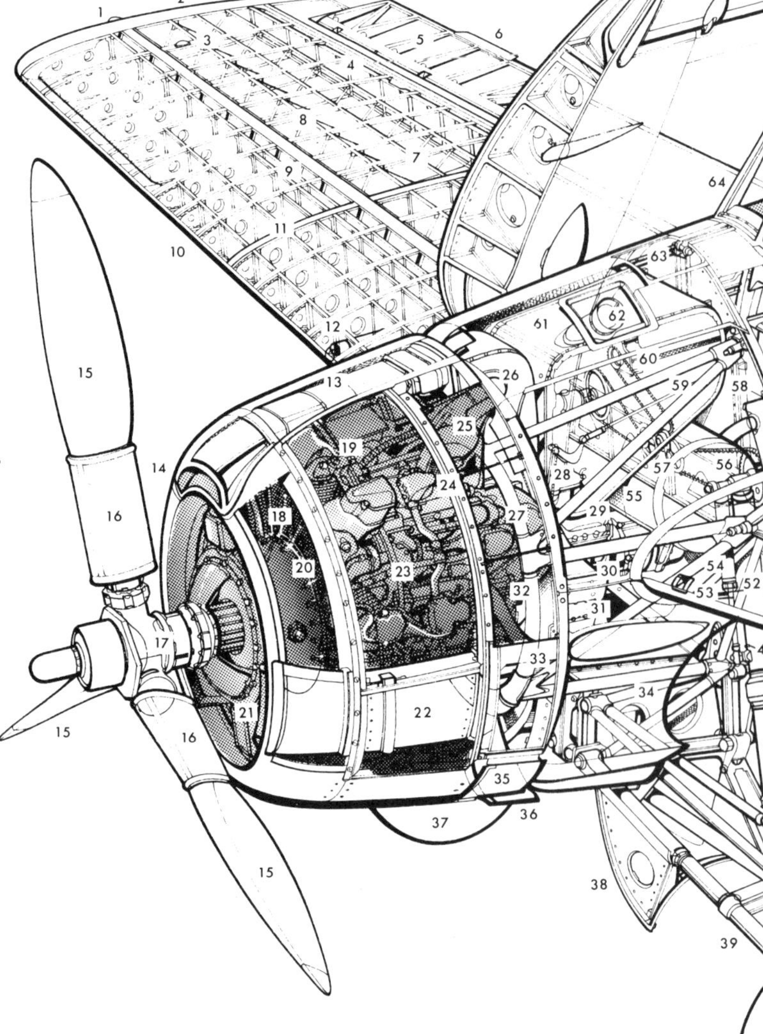

Grumman F4F Wildcat variants

XF4F-1: Grumman G-16 biplane proposal; not built
XF4F-2: Grumman G-18 monoplane prototype; first flew on 2 September 1937; one built
XF4F-3: Grumman G-36 prototype with XR-1830-76 radial; first flew on 12 February 1939; one conversion
F4F-3: first production version, with R-1830-76 radial; first flew in February 1940; 285 built
F4F-3A: developed production version, with R-1830-90 radial; 95 built
F4F-3P: conversions to reconnaissance role; few converted
F4F-3S: unofficial designation for two conversions to floatplane configuration with Edo floats; first flew on 28 February 1943
XF4F-4: prototype of improved model, with R-1830-86 radial and folding wings; first flew on 14 April 1941
F4F-4: principal Grumman-built production model, with folding wings; 1,169 built
F4F-4A: Lend-Lease designation of Martlet Mk III, with fixed wings
F4F-4B: Lend-Lease designation of Martlet Mk IV, with fixed wings
F4F-4P: designation of a few conversions to the reconnaissance role
XF4F-5: designation of two Grumman G-36A prototypes, with Wright R-1820-40 radials; first flew in June 1940
XF4F-6: single prototype for F4F-3A production series
F4F-6: initial designation of F4F-3A
F4F-7: designation of **Grumman G-52** reconnaissance variant with cameras and increased fuel; first flew on 30 December 1941; 21 built
XF4F-8: experimental prototypes with new flaps and cowlings; first flew on 8 November 1942; two built
FM-1: General Motors production version of the F4F-3; first flew on 31 August 1942; 1,151 built
FM-2: General Motors production version of the XF4F-8; 4,777 built
XF2M-1: proposed development by General Motors; none built
Martlet Mk I: British designation of **Grumman G-36A** fighters ordered by France; first flew on 11 May 1940; 181 built; later redesignated **Wildcat Mk I**
Martlet Mk II: British designation of **Grumman G-36B** fighters with folding wings; first flew in October 1940; 100 supplied; later redesignated **Wildcat Mk II**
Martlet Mk III: British designation of F4F-4A supplied to the Fleet Air Arm with fixed wings; 30 supplied; later redesignated **Wildcat Mk III**
Martlet Mk IV: British designation of Lend-Lease F4F-4B; 220 built; later redesignated **Wildcat Mk IV**
Martlet Mk V: British designation of Lend-Lease FM-2; 312 built; later redesignated **Wildcat Mk V**
Martlet Mk VI: British designation FM-2; 370 supplied

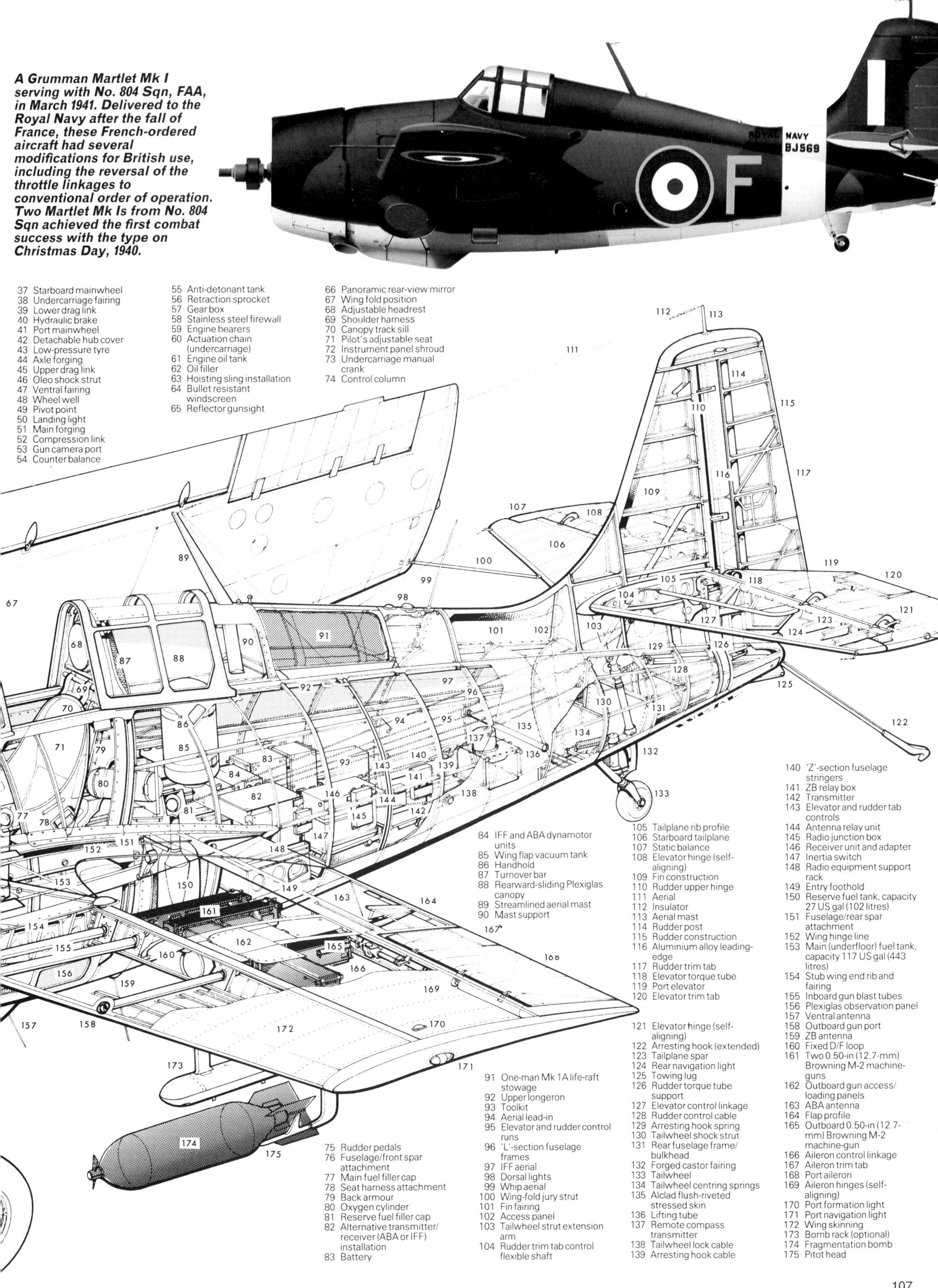

A Grumman Martlet Mk I serving with No. 804 Sqn, FAA, in March 1941. Delivered to the Royal Navy after the fall of France, these French-ordered aircraft had several modifications for British use, including the reversal of the throttle linkages to conventional order of operation. Two Martlet Mk Is from No. 804 Sqn achieved the first combat success with the type on Christmas Day, 1940.

37 Starboard mainwheel
38 Undercarriage fairing
39 Lower drag link
40 Hydraulic brake
41 Port mainwheel
42 Detachable hub cover
43 Low-pressure tyre
44 Axle forging
45 Upper drag link
46 Oleo shock strut
47 Ventral fairing
48 Wheel well
49 Pivot point
50 Landing light
51 Main forging
52 Compression link
53 Gun camera port
54 Counter balance
55 Anti-detonant tank
56 Retraction sprocket
57 Gear box
58 Stainless steel firewall
59 Engine bearers
60 Actuation chain (undercarriage)
61 Engine oil tank
62 Oil filler
63 Hoisting sling installation
64 Bullet resistant windscreen
65 Reflector gunsight
66 Panoramic rear-view mirror
67 Wing fold position
68 Adjustable headrest
69 Shoulder harness
70 Canopy track sill
71 Pilot's adjustable seat
72 Instrument panel shroud
73 Undercarriage manual crank
74 Control column
75 Rudder pedals
76 Fuselage/front spar attachment
77 Main fuel filler cap
78 Seat harness attachment
79 Back armour
80 Oxygen cylinder
81 Reserve fuel filler cap
82 Alternative transmitter/receiver (ABA or IFF) installation
83 Battery
84 IFF and ABA dynamotor units
85 Wing flap vacuum tank
86 Handhold
87 Turnover bar
88 Rearward-sliding Plexiglas canopy
89 Streamlined aerial mast
90 Mast support
91 One-man Mk 1A life-raft stowage
92 Upper longeron
93 Toolkit
94 Aerial lead-in
95 Elevator and rudder control runs
96 'L'-section fuselage frames
97 IFF aerial
98 Dorsal lights
99 Whip aerial
100 Wing-fold jury strut
101 Fin fairing
102 Access panel
103 Tailwheel strut extension arm
104 Rudder trim tab control flexible shaft
105 Tailplane rib profile
106 Starboard tailplane
107 Static balance
108 Elevator hinge (self-aligning)
109 Fin construction
110 Rudder upper hinge
111 Aerial
112 Insulator
113 Aerial mast
114 Rudder post
115 Rudder construction
116 Aluminium alloy leading-edge
117 Rudder trim tab
118 Elevator torque tube
119 Port elevator
120 Elevator trim tab
121 Elevator hinge (self-aligning)
122 Arresting hook (extended)
123 Tailplane spar
124 Rear navigation light
125 Towing lug
126 Rudder torque tube support
127 Elevator control linkage
128 Rudder control cable
129 Arresting hook spring
130 Tailwheel shock strut
131 Rear fuselage frame/bulkhead
132 Forged castor fairing
133 Tailwheel
134 Tailwheel centring springs
135 Alclad flush-riveted stressed skin
136 Lifting tube
137 Remote compass transmitter
138 Tailwheel lock cable
139 Arresting hook cable
140 'Z'-section fuselage stringers
141 ZB relay box
142 Transmitter
143 Elevator and rudder tab controls
144 Antenna relay unit
145 Radio junction box
146 Receiver unit and adapter
147 Inertia switch
148 Radio equipment support rack
149 Entry foothold
150 Reserve fuel tank, capacity 27 US gal (102 litres)
151 Fuselage/rear spar attachment
152 Wing hinge line
153 Main (underfloor) fuel tank, capacity 117 US gal (443 litres)
154 Stub wing end rib and fairing
155 Inboard gun blast tubes
156 Plexiglas observation panel
157 Ventral antenna
158 Outboard gun port
159 ZB antenna
160 Fixed D/F loop
161 Two 0.50-in (12.7-mm) Browning M-2 machine-guns
162 Outboard gun access/loading panels
163 ABA antenna
164 Flap profile
165 Outboard 0.50-in (12.7-mm) Browning M-2 machine-gun
166 Aileron control linkage
167 Aileron trim tab
168 Port aileron
169 Aileron hinges (self-aligning)
170 Port formation light
171 Port navigation light
172 Wing skinning
173 Bomb rack (optional)
174 Fragmentation bomb
175 Pitot head

The second US Navy fighter squadron to receive the Grumman Wildcat was VF-7, which accepted its complement of F4F-3s at NAS Norfolk, Virginia, in December 1940. This illustration shows the national insignia on the forward fuselage in accordance with a March 1940 directive covering types participating in the Neutrality Patrol. The red lower cowling indicates the third aircraft of the 1st Section of VF-7.

finements which resulted from Martlet combat experience in the UK including six-gun armament, armour, self-sealing tanks, and (above all) folding wings. Delivery of production F4F-4 Wildcat fighters began in November 1941, and by the time that the Japanese launched their attack on Pearl Harbor a number of US Navy and US Marine Corps squadrons had been equipped. As additional Wildcats entered service, they equipped squadrons aboard the carriers USS *Enterprise* (CV-6), USS *Hornet* (CV-12) and USS *Saratoga* (CV-3), being involved with conspicuous success in the battles of the Coral Sea and Midway, and the operations at Guadalcanal. They were at the centre of all significant actions in the Pacific until superseded by more advanced aircraft in 1943. They also saw action with the US Navy in North Africa during late 1942.

The XF4F-5 and XF4F-6 designations went to experimental variants of the Wildcat, and the F4F-6 designation was initially applied to the machine which became the F4F-3A.

The first Wildcat pilot to win the Medal of Honor belonged to US Marine squadron VMF-211, which lost nine F4F-3s on the ground during the 7 December 1941 attack on Pearl Harbor and seven more on the ground at Wake Island on the next day. The battered defenders of Wake fought on, and on 9 December two VMF-211 pilots teamed up to shoot down a Japanese bomber, the first American Wildcat 'kill'. Before Wake was overwhelmed, Captain Robert McElrod achieved a direct hit on a Japanese destroyer with a bomb dropped from his Wildcat, sinking the ship and losing his life, and winning the Medal of Honor posthumously.

Wildcat-Zero dogfights at Wake, Coral Sea and Midway are the stuff of legend. At Midway, Lieutenant Commander John S. Thach of squadron VF-3 on the *Yorktown* devised a criss-cross dogfighting tactic which compensated for the Wildcat's inferior manoeuvrability, and the 'Thach Weave' became part of Wildcat lore forever. O'Hare did more than win the Medal of Honor: he shook President Roosevelt's hand and got an airport in Chicago named after him. The carrier war was tough and brutal; merely landing the easily-stalled Wildcat on a pitching carrier deck amounted to a supreme achievement. But to many men, the Wildcat earned its spurs not aboard ship but in the heat, stench and muck at Henderson Field on Guadalcanal, where Americans mounted the first offensive action of the Pacific conflict.

Major John L. Smith's VMF-223, the 'Rainbow' Squadron, was launched from the escort carrier USS *Long Island* (CVE-1) on 20 August 1942 and landed at Henderson. On the next day, the squadron was strafing Japanese troops at the Tenaru river. On 24 August, accompanied by five USAAF Bell Airacobras, Smith's aircraft intercepted an enemy flight of 15 bombers and 12 fighters. VMF-223 pilots shot down 10 bombers and six fighters, Captain Marion Carl scoring three of the kills. Soon Carl had become the first US Marine ace of the war, Smith became the third Wildcat pilot to rate the Medal of Honor, and the men who flew from Henderson Field ('a bowl of black dust or a quagmire of mud' according to its official history) had learned to put the F4F-4 against its Mitsubishi nemesis.

Flying characteristics

Piloting the Wildcat was experience enough: its stalky landing gear gave it dubious ground-handling characteristics; it could be 'mushy' when manoeuvrability counted most; there was a violent draught if the cockpit hood was slid open in flight; there existed no provision at all for jettisoning the hood; and the pilot's seat was cramped and too low relative to the location of his head and his need for visibility. In short, the Wildcat could be tricky and unforgiving.

Fighting the Zero was something else. US Marine and US Navy men learned early in the war not to dogfight with the more manoeuvrable Zero any time that the situation could be resolved in some other way. Where possible, they sought instead to break through a screen of Mitsubishis and attack the enemy's big bombers directly. At times, a brace of Zeros could be lured into an overshoot, making it easier to break through to the bombers. At Guadalcanal, the bombers would approach 26 at a time in Vee formations, and the Wildcats could dive on the bombers and destroy some before the Zeros pounced them. These hit-and-run tactics forced the Japanese pilots to over-use precious fuel. Reliance on one's wingman was cru-

The Grumman XF4F-2 photographed in its original short-span configuration with rounded tail surfaces. Assigned BuAer No. 0383, the aircraft was powered by a Pratt & Whitney Twin Wasp 783-kW (1,050-hp) R-1830-66 engine. The belly windows were to facilitate the pilot's downward view.

Gathering speed as it races down the deck, a Grumman Martlet Mk IV of the Fleet Air Arm prepares to lift off. In the field of carrier launches and landings the Martlet introduced the tail-down take-off and the stinger-type arrester hook.

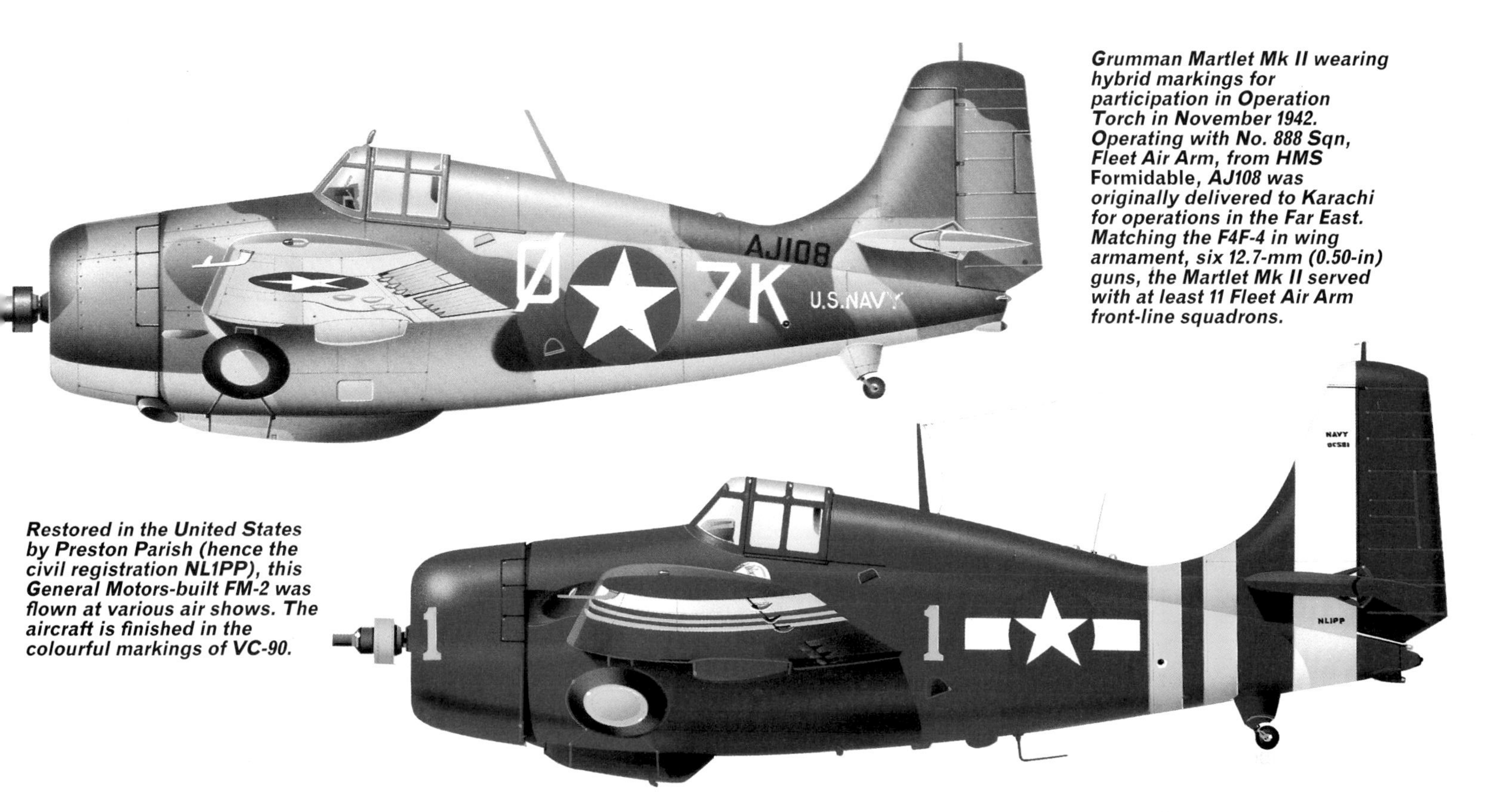

Grumman Martlet Mk II wearing hybrid markings for participation in Operation Torch in November 1942. Operating with No. 888 Sqn, Fleet Air Arm, from HMS Formidable, AJ108 was originally delivered to Karachi for operations in the Far East. Matching the F4F-4 in wing armament, six 12.7-mm (0.50-in) guns, the Martlet Mk II served with at least 11 Fleet Air Arm front-line squadrons.

Restored in the United States by Preston Parish (hence the civil registration NL1PP), this General Motors-built FM-2 was flown at various air shows. The aircraft is finished in the colourful markings of VC-90.

cial: once the dogfighting started a Wildcat pilot had to depend on his wingman to shoot the enemy off his tail. No 'lone wolf' survived very long, although some individual Wildcat pilots excelled. Major John L. Smith was credited with downing 19 Japanese aircraft, and Major Marion Carl with 18½.

One of the more intriguing tests involving the Wildcat was a 1942 effort in Philadelphia to evaluate the idea of fighters being towed by bombers, to serve as long-range escorts. The idea was one which recurred throughout the 1940s, although it was never tried in actual operations. The Wildcat was an ideal candidate because its three-bladed Curtiss Electric propeller could be easily feathered and the engine restarted in flight. A hook-on and break-off system was devised, which enabled the Wildcat to be towed from an attachment point beneath the wing, the Wildcat pilot being able to connect and disconnect at will. In May 1942, an F4F was towed by a Douglas BD-1 (the US Navy version of the A-20 Havoc) and later two Wildcats were towed by a Boeing B-17 over a 1930-km (1,200-mile) eight-hour course.

The system worked: the Wildcat pilot could remain idle while his aircraft flew effectively as a glider, its range thus being limited only by the endurance of the tow aircraft. But no practical application of the arrangement was ever made.

The final production variant built by Grumman was the long-range reconnaissance F4F-7 with increased fuel capacity, camera installations in the lower fuselage, and no armament. Only 21 were built, but Grumman also produced an additional 100 F4F-3s and two XF4F-8 prototypes. With an urgent need to concentrate on development and production of the more advanced F6F Hellcat, Grumman negotiated with General Motors to continue production of the F4F-4 Wildcat under the designation FM-1. Production by General Motors' Eastern Aircraft Division began after finalisation of a contract on 18 April 1942, and the first of this company's FM-1s was flown on 31 August 1942. Production totalled 1,151, of which 312 were supplied to the UK under the designation Martlet Mk V (later Wildcat Mk V).

At the same time, General Motors was working on the development of an improved version, designated FM-2, which was the production version of the two Grumman XF4F-8 prototypes. Its major change was the installation of a 1007-kW (1,350-hp) Wright R-1820-56 Cyclone 9 radial engine, but a larger vertical tail was introduced to maintain good directional stability with this more powerful engine, and airframe weight was reduced to the minimum. A total of 4,777 FM-2s was built, 370 of them supplied to the UK and designated Wildcat Mk IV from the outset, the only British machines never to bear the Martlet name.

Carrying an extra fuel tank under the starboard inner wing, a US Marine Corps Grumman F4F-4 Wildcat taxis on a rough-field airstrip on the island of Guadalcanal in late 1942. Marine units were in the forefront of the air battles over the island.

With good forward vision, a strong undercarriage and effective slow-speed handling characteristics, the Wildcat gave its pilots a better chance of a successful trap than some types. Here a Fleet Air Arm Wildcat Mk V raises smoke as it hits the deck.

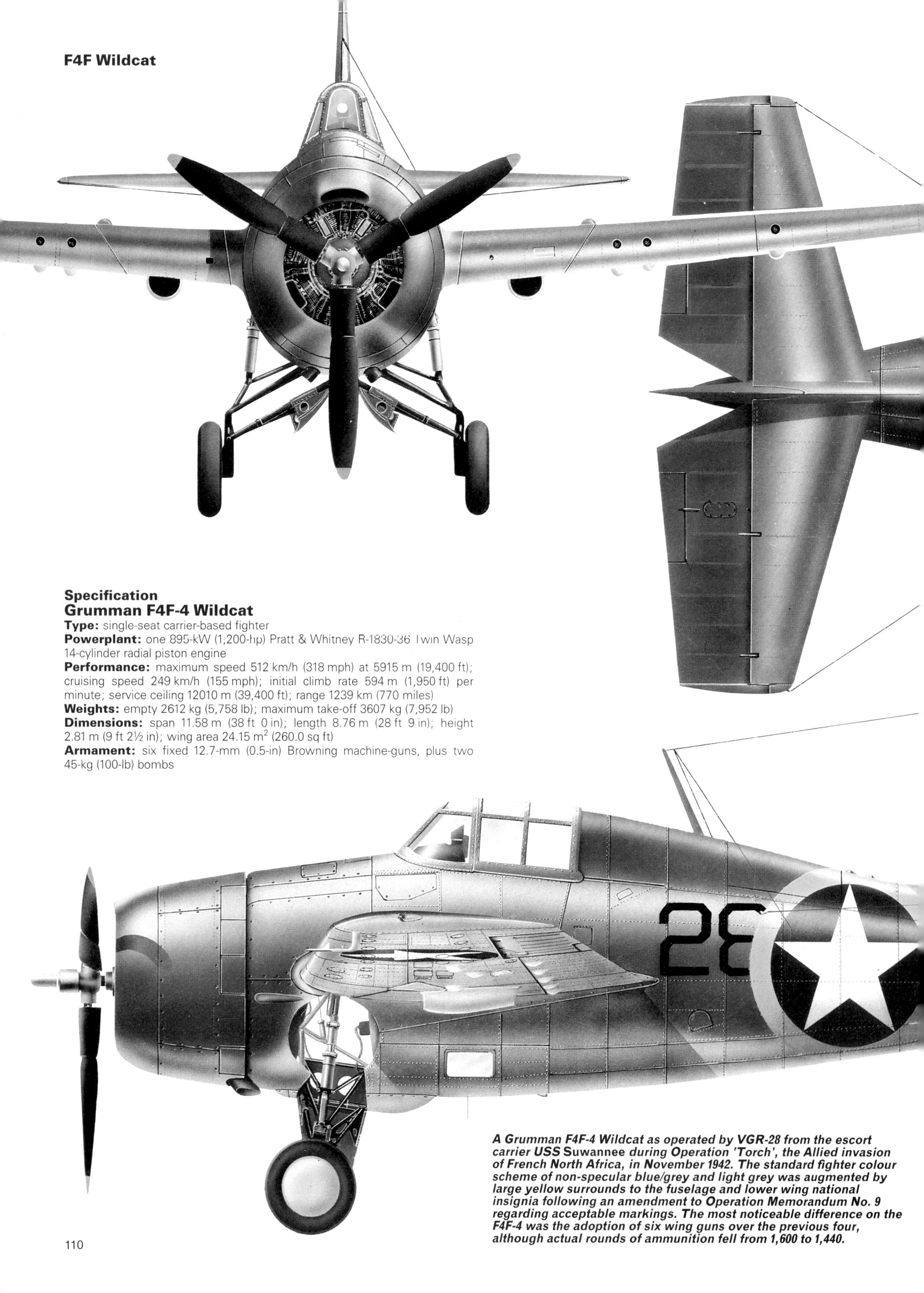

Specification
Grumman F4F-4 Wildcat

Type: single-seat carrier-based fighter
Powerplant: one 895-kW (1,200-hp) Pratt & Whitney R-1830-36 Twin Wasp 14-cylinder radial piston engine
Performance: maximum speed 512 km/h (318 mph) at 5915 m (19,400 ft); cruising speed 249 km/h (155 mph); initial climb rate 594 m (1,950 ft) per minute; service ceiling 12010 m (39,400 ft); range 1239 km (770 miles)
Weights: empty 2612 kg (5,758 lb); maximum take-off 3607 kg (7,952 lb)
Dimensions: span 11.58 m (38 ft 0 in); length 8.76 m (28 ft 9 in); height 2.81 m (9 ft 2½ in); wing area 24.15 m^2 (260.0 sq ft)
Armament: six fixed 12.7-mm (0.5-in) Browning machine-guns, plus two 45-kg (100-lb) bombs

A Grumman F4F-4 Wildcat as operated by VGR-28 from the escort carrier USS Suwannee during Operation 'Torch', the Allied invasion of French North Africa, in November 1942. The standard fighter colour scheme of non-specular blue/grey and light grey was augmented by large yellow surrounds to the fuselage and lower wing national insignia following an amendment to Operation Memorandum No. 9 regarding acceptable markings. The most noticeable difference on the F4F-4 was the adoption of six wing guns over the previous four, although actual rounds of ammunition fell from 1,600 to 1,440.

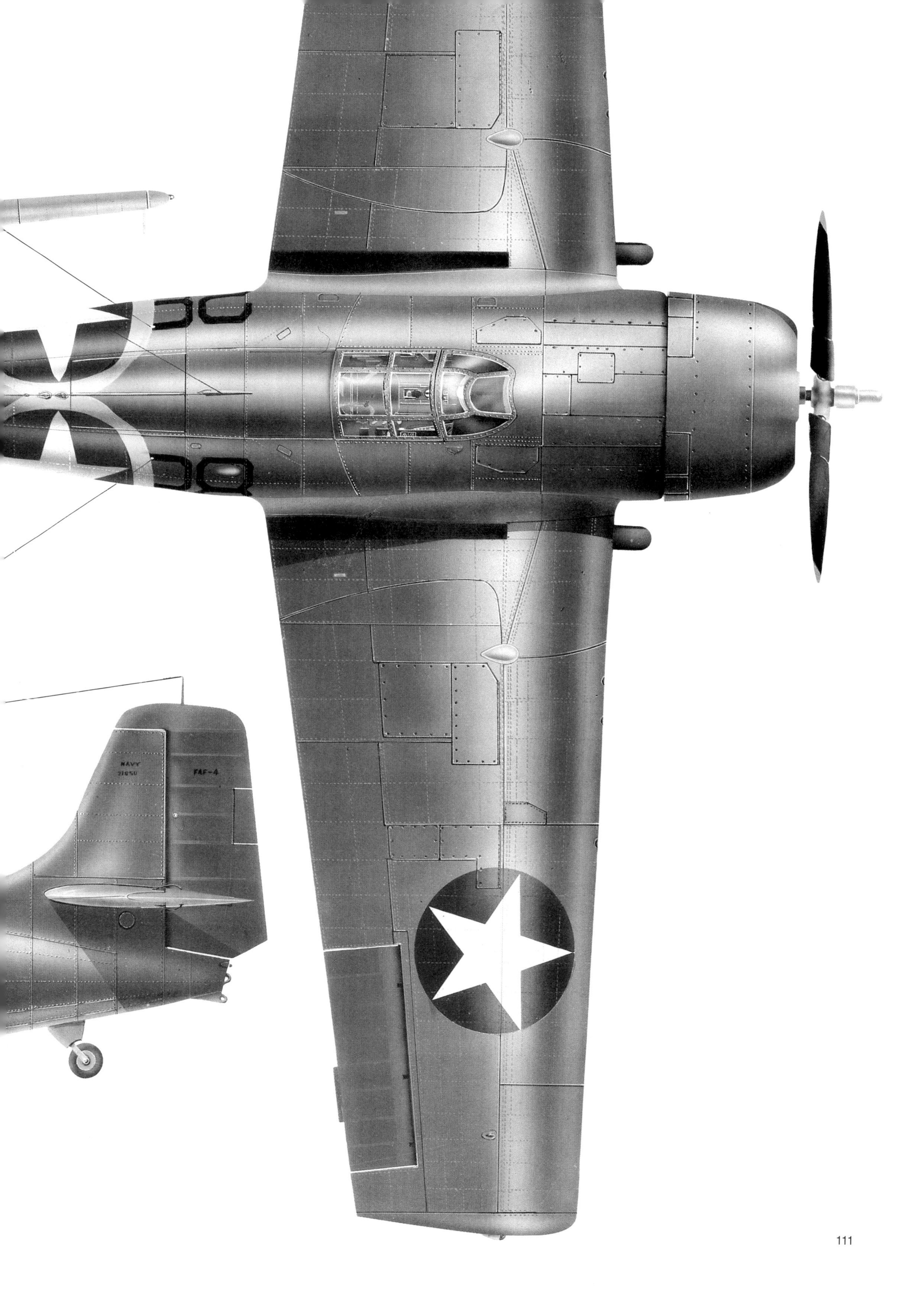
NAVY
F4F-4

INDEX

Page references in *italics* refer to photographs/figures or their captions.